SAY WHEN

To Lydia
Something we do
just because we can
love you.
NK
AKA
Sharyo L.

SAY WHEN

A COOKBOOK OF COGITATIONS IN LUST OF LIFE

THAT MAY DISTURB, INCITE, EXCITE, SHOCK,

INSULT AND INTRIGUE THE IDLE MIND

ELARNZO LEWIS

To order additional copies of this book, contact:
Xlibris Corporation
1-888-795-4274
www.Xlibris.com
Orders@Xlibris.com
56946

CONTENTS

I dedicate this effort to my family.

I dedicate this effort to my ancestors.

I dedicate this effort to the woman who once asked me,
"How is your mind?"
To which I responded, "Getting better, I hope."
I have gotten better.

I dedicate this effort to anyone in the world
who feels they have something of value to add
to our world of being. Express yourselves.

And finally,
this is for my son, NID. It is my responsibility
to pass the world to you
in better condition than I received it.

Preface

When I turned eighteen years old, I received a gift from a neighbor. The gift was a journal, and the giver, the mother of a good friend. At that time, I thought it was the dumbest present I had ever received. It turned out to be the most inspirational. I have not stopped writing since.

The thoughts and confessions I wrote in that journal were the beginning of my feeling comfortable expressing my self to myself. It seemed those expressions were the key to some basic level of personal discovery. I became willing to expose sensitive areas of my person that I once guarded. In writing about my experiences and the moments that composed them, I was better able to regulate the emotional component that I attached to being. Once I discontinued allowing emotion more than its fair share of influence on my thinking, I was able to be honest to my self about myself and the world around me. The fair share of emotion is that which motivates compassion.

Eventually poems began to emerge. It would be more accurate to say they fell out of my mind like water being launched from a thunder-clapping sky. My mind's sky was mostly clear and black and dotted with stars that shone like the twinkle in a child's eyes after having discovered something new and exciting. The scene is completed by a bright, full, rude moon and a single small gray cloud that stalked my self-image.

The poems naturally turned into raps and remained so for the next several years. Like many of the young adults living in New York City during the eighties, I wanted to be like one of the pioneers of the rap industry. I realized in time I was no rapper. I was neither that fun guy that brought the party with him nor that tough guy that females sought and males admired. Fortunately, I did not have to be. I only had to be me. I certainly am not complaining about the results of that lifelong assignment.

The raps eventually turned to short essays as the need to become more detailed with my voice began to evolve. At that time, I was enrolled at the College of Staten Island (CSI). I took a class in basic writing with Professor Edward Hack. The class was a requirement in my pursuit of that scholar's parchment, and he came with the class. He was an easygoing guy whose passion for the craft seemed genuine. He was invested in education. His interest in the written word was guarded by a thug of a red pen. That red pen of his bullied me into developing an acceptable level of discipline in expressing my position with the English word. It was a challenging time.

This is where I think the reason for this effort gained motivation. When that professor was able to get an unfocused mind like mine to care about how literary expression took form, it was an awakening. I realized the various stories within me had already developed five of the necessary components of tale-telling. The stories had who, what, when, where, and how the tale developed or would develop. I, though, lacked the mechanical ability to show why the story should unfold.

I practiced. I did not practice with the intention of becoming the next literary giant whose prose ignited great emotion in the reader. I practiced to become proficient at expressing me.

That is why I made this effort. This is an expression of self-control. I believe the development of a person's self-control is the point of education. I believe any instructor whose efforts to guide a student to such self-enlightenment, even if the fruit of that labor takes many years, has performed the most necessary of actions. They have assisted in creating an adult.

It is not merely that the student is familiar and comfortable with the level of discipline necessary to the defining of being and environment, but that the student becomes an adult who accepts responsibility for continuing that education of their self.

This life, like those stories this mind conjured, lacked the discipline of control. Now there is more control, and the education continues.

In good compliance with being, I write this because I can. This is one way to effect control over being. This is a willful articulation of me. This is some of what can be done with a focused will, and that is my point. What more can the person achieve with a disciplined and focused will? I may develop the technology to found a civilization, or I may develop into a human whose contribution to the world is not contributing to the pain and suffering of its inhabitants.

However I proceed with the remains of this life, I will continue to pay great attention to those other minds around me, but especially mine. I have learned that inspiration can come from anywhere, and shall. That is probably the point of life, that we need each other because none of us can say with surety what experiences the next moment shall bring. Therefore, it is probably a better idea to take charge of one's will and develop the discipline to accept ourselves en route to accepting each other.

Now there's a story I would like to write, what would society be if people actually loved?

Introduction

I am a professional. I am trained in the arts and sciences of being and that education is continuous. I have practiced within the dynamics of being for thirty-eight years. I have determined this life has occurred in neatly prepared chapters whose content, words, and ideas are bound to disturb, shock, insult, excite, and intrigue the idol mind.

This life has occurred beautifully, although the specifics of it have forced me to ask these questions: Who am I? What am I? Why am I here? And as long as I am asking, who are you? I have discovered I am a collective of motives, ideas, thoughts, words, and behaviors that have been passed to me through my ancestry and society. I am the good and the better, and I am the bad and the worse. Which I am is a matter of perspective, mine and yours, though ultimately mine.

In any case, these expressions are mine. I believe in God. I believe in me. I believe in you. I believe that you are the many expressions and judgments of myself; and I am the single expression and judgment of your self. It remains, though, a matter of perspective.

We engage in the same activities—education, politics, war, government, economy, belief, and sex. The seeming few differences may be in how and why we do these things. Despite whatever differences may exist in the hows and whys of our expressions, there is one thing that is eternally unchanging, and that is our impulse to discovery. It is my hope that along the path of discovery, I may find my answers. I hope you find yours. I hope you will one day feel compelled to share with me your contemplations on the path to personal discovery.

I am a professional and so are you. This life has occurred beautifully and so has yours. There has been joy and lament, feast and famine, moments that have caused pause in self-definition, and moments where we have clearly defined ourselves. Speak on it.

Your life is a reflection of the greatest experience you have had. I am certain you were present as it occurred. The question is, were you paying attention?

Our ancestors transferred wisdom through story and song. The information they passed along was used to guide the lives of the younger members of their collective. That information contained a history of a people that included such things as ideas of God, moral code, laws, social order, and male or female relations, to name a few. I am certain they were motivated.

There was probably no greater hell than watching helplessly as children suffered a fall into disrepute because of lack of counsel.

We have maintained that tradition. We do all have a song inside of us. We do all have an opinion, a poem, or a story inside of us. Thankfully, we all do not have to be musicians or people of many letters to articulate that divine wisdom that is the blessing of life. We are all professionals in the field of living, and we have practiced every day since birth. But were you paying attention?

What follows are some of my contemplations. They are expressed in poem, essay, song, and short story. The collective composes a short history of who I have been. I had been directly involved in some parts of these accounts, some I had observed, some I had been informed of, and some are the product of creativity. I will not be concerned about how they are received. I will not be bothered that I may not be well trained at English writing, and so the punctuation and grammar may be in err. I will not hesitate to offer an honest expression. At end, if in reading my mind you discover some part of yourself that is too much to take, then just say when and close the book.

Blood, Sweat, and Tears

I remember that time I came running in the house
with blood streaming from my brow.
That red on my brown and the tears
made the scene appear sincere.

I remember that time my brother came home
really late for the first time.
He wore worried eyes, and the funk of street life
hung around him like a thug.

I remember that time my sister had a crisis.
It had something to do with girlfriends, boyfriends, and life.
She cried like it was the end of the world, again.

Your stance seemed hard, seemed unconcerned,
seemed unforgiving and unable to relate to
those tragedies children are drawn to.
We are a wino to that ambrosia, man.
Like moths who can get burned in the flame and not return;
on the other hand, that flame is home to that spirit.
So there were more bloody parts, late nights,
and hurt feelings.

All the time, though, you seemed more angry with us
than the circumstances that assaulted us.
Nevertheless, we grew, and you grew.
We grew because of you,
because if not for you, then not us, and I like us,
so I'm digging you.

All that time you did not seem to blink
or hesitate to correct us, to console us,
and to defend and encourage us in your way.

I think, though,
you did worry about us during those wonder years,
that blood, that sweat, and those tears.
I think you felt every bit of it, those growing pains.
We went through childhood together,
and mostly because you missed yours.
But it made us stronger.

My Mother's Work

As she lay, only night falls softer.
And I wanted to be angry at you
because you put her there,
indirectly or not.
But I could not summon the strength
to take my mind off her.
Then the music started playing
at the nurses' station. It was an oldie,
something from the fifties, when she was new.
It transported her mind and spirit
to a time of hopscotch and penny candy.
Her lips moved, narrating a playground tale
from a hospital bed.
She was every bit at that playground, though,
enjoying childhood.
And when she said it was time to go in the house,
I knew it was God calling and not my grandmother.
I was prepared to hate you
for the rest of my life.
As my siblings and I walked from that hospital,
I saw how they held on to hope.
I did not tell them I saw the heavenly shade
drawn in her eyes
because we need hope,
and we certainly need each other.
And I was prepared to hate you for the rest of my life
when my sister passed me the word.
The wisdom of life. God's message.
That word that can only be experienced through living in truth.
The word reminded me of things
like love and love.

Like love of the things that pass our fancy,
and the love of the things that are eternal.
She chose love and all of its potential
however unsophisticated, however childish,
however you;
And you chose like love
because you saw love take your mother away from you too soon,
and you probably vowed to never let love kill you.
That made your love bitter.
That made us bitter because we lived through you.
So we lived in bitter love like a ramshackle house
that was the most comfortable you laid your head in.
We grew like you.
We grew against you
because my mother's work
was to make us stronger than our circumstances.
And just when I thought
she should have washed her hands of the whole damned thing
and left your ass, she stayed.
She remained despite unknowing children
and a husband.
She remained despite the haunting sweet taste of those cotton candy
dreams she thought had died—
those that God lent her in that playground.
She thought she had
lost the power to dream.
In those last moments, though, she found herself and us.
And at that moment when we could have washed our hands
of the whole damned situation
and allowed our history to consume us
like the number of our ancestors who forgot God and how to dream,
that divine love grew within us
—the fruit of her lifetime's work—
and she became the dream for us
because she knew we would forget how.
She knew you forgot how,

but she knew you wanted to remember.
So my mother's work soothed your savage breast.
And my mother's work guided her lost souls.
And my mother's work took the hate from me
and turned it into a profound appreciation for life.
Now I am a father,
and my mother's work is not done.

When I Can't Think

When I can't think,
there's always a reason
without a rhyme,
and a place
without time.
Nothing relevant to good life
seeks my attention.
Only bits of media trivia
plague me. They haunt me.

When I can't think,
I find it hard to be fair,
but still more rational
than the average.
There is no beauty.
There is no love.
In this state,
I can barely find the words
to express such things.

I think about me
at times like this.
I think about me
and how I relate to you.
Although, I really could not care.

At times like this,
I am all that matters
because at times like this,
it's hard to think clear.

The Fallen

It's a sad thing, the fallen.

God's souls pepper the earth
like too-soon courageous chicks
lain among the tall grass.
No worse
because life is life.

They sing a song of remorse.
Can you hear them angels crying?
They forgot God
and lost that most powerful
part of themselves
that loves.

The Traveler

Do you know what peace is?
It is the journey of a single ripple
among an ocean of possibilities
aware of only itself.

It is the story of evolution
a rock could tell,
but is wise in allowing things
their destiny in their time.

It is being a traveler
whose beginning and end
was set in motion by a word,
and in the journey
has been everything in time.

What I Want to Be

I remember watching my father preparing himself for work. He wore long johns (thermal underwear), thick wool socks, another thick undershirt, jeans, boots, and finally a thick sweater or flannel shirt. He would grab his bag. It was a dusty brown thing stained by some number of unknown liquids and torn in various places. He would carry it with him across the room to fetch some other item, which was sometimes a thermos or brown paper bag. And I don't know how much of this is real and how much are the imaginings of a child in awe of his father, but it feels real.

Sometimes he would carry me downstairs, and other times, I would lead while he carried one of my other siblings. He and my mother spoke in some tongue I did not understand, or I was indifferent to whatever it was they were muttering as I was a child fully engrossed in a child's world. We climbed into the car, a station wagon, I think. I mean, I know we had one at some point in my youth. But then we had several vehicles during the course of years from my first recollection of a vehicle when my age was single digit through high school. The early days, however, where cars are concerned, are dominated by images of a big yellow station wagon.

I don't know what more I could have done in the rear of that car. That is in addition to the common distractions children occupy themselves with—for example, counting cars, making faces at the other travelers, and interacting with my siblings. Whatever I did, though, it passed the distance from home to my father's job in a blur. I remember pulling off our block, then, just as suddenly, pulling into that parking lot area where we dropped my father off.

As for that in-between time, perhaps it has gone to that ethereal place where children's thoughts and adult minds go when not carefully attended to. It is that misty dream place between here and there, like that space between your face and that nearest light in the sky; indeed, that dominating blackness must be made of children's stray thoughts and adult's lost dreams.

My father would exit the car after some words with my mother and some more to us children. He would walk across the lot to an opening crowded with others dressed like him. They filtered into the entrance of a crowded dark box. The box then sank into the ground. That was the last I would see of my father until the next time I saw my father. And I don't know how much of this is real and how much are the romantic fabrications of a thirty-four-year-old reflecting on the life moments of a four- or five-year-old, but it feels real.

What is it about ourselves or our parents that makes us children want to walk in their shoes? My father's did not fit me particularly well. They did have personality, though, and as I was engaged in the development of my personality, especially subconsciously, I would borrow and take suggestion from whatever source available. The shoes were always available. He could only wear one pair at a time after all, so the others lay helpless to my inquiries: Why do they make that noise when he walks? Will I ever get big enough to fit these? What is that odor? When he or my mother saw me trotting about in his shoes, usually his dress shoes, they would laugh softly or issue a warning: be careful! Sometimes they would become annoyed and remove me from the shoes. They would always try to redirect my attention to some other item, or just the hell away from the shoes. I would comply, mostly—my childlike attention being temporarily diverted—but I would be back.

He had several pairs of mostly dress shoes to match his suits and casual wear. Then there were those dusty boots he wore to work. He did not own a pair of sneakers or tennis shoes as I have heard them referred to by someone my parents' age. I do not believe any of the men in my father's generation wore tennis shoes at all or on a regular basis, unless of course, they played tennis.

My father's shoes were dark and shiny, and they made a loud noise when clapped together. You could slide your arms into them and race them against each other. Their hard leather soles made a very agreeable noise when slid across a wood floor. When the black ones became boring, there were white ones and multicolored ones. Each pair made a different sound and had a different design, which naturally made for different characters: Speed Racer, Racer X, or Richard Petty.

They all smelled the same, though, and they all were deformed in the same place. My father had a bad case of bunions, so every pair of his shoes formed a knot on the inside next to the big toe. Not a curiosity then. However, as I became older, and my big toe began to turn into its neighbors, my mother became more and more interested in finding some way to discourage its rudeness. I began to pay attention to other feet whose big toes were not as intrusive. Before this, I had no reason to question the normalcy of my father's or my feet as they were all just something one covered with some type of shoe. And shoes were what was important.

So my father's deformed feet and mine that were maturing into some deformity were of no social detriment. They could not keep me from getting a job. My mother, though, said his feet were "jacked up!" But he works. He does what he does. So if all I turn out to be is a big chip off a bigger block, then that will be fine with me. I will at least be able to rise and shine, shit, shave, bathe, and dress. I will then disappear through the opening of some gate and into a box that disappears into the ground, only reappear some following day to the smiling faces of my children who are just glad that daddy is home.

So I play walked in my father's deformed shoes, not realizing that one day I would play at walking in my form of shoes. My shoes that logically could not be my father's, as time and space are prohibitive. Shoes, though, that were so curiously similar in personality, which is to indicate thought and behavior, that my mother spent a great deal of time and spirit trying to keep my feet from becoming bent like my father's; and certainly, that would ruin what could be a great pair of shoes. I knew none of this then. I knew only that he put on one pair with this type of clothing and another pair for a different type of clothing.

27

Then there were those dusty brown boots. I can only imagine that it was those boots and what he wore with those boots that affected me so profoundly. It was what he did when he wore that uniform. It was how he behaved toward the world. Mostly, though, it was how he held himself to himself that made such an impression on me that I now prefer that uniform. It allows me a level of comfort that if forced to name, I would call fatherly.

However, I must say again that I knew none of this then. I knew only that when he put that uniform on, he put those boots on. He rambled about gathering things until we finally walked down the stairs and into the car. We drove through some undefined time and space to a place where he said his words and walked across a dusty, rocky gray lot to a gate. He passed through the gate and into a box where he and others dressed like him disappeared into the ground. I knew only that I wanted to do what he did. I did not know what he did, although I did know he put on that uniform to do it, and it all mostly agreed with me—those many uniforms he had and the work attached to them, the shoes that carried him to that work, the way he held himself to himself, the way others reacted to him. It all mostly agreed with me.

I did not know then the range of work he did in those other uniforms, but when he wore that uniform, he carried things in that dusty brown bag that he used in his work. Neither he nor my mother appreciated any of us children tampering with that bag. Their concern was misplaced in me. I had no interest in what was in that bag. In fact, I had little interest in what the items in that bag stood for. My father often removed a number of those items when he was repairing, installing, removing, tightening, loosening, cutting, measuring, marking, and banging things around our home.

Apparently, my father was good at what he did with those items. Plumbing and lights would not work, then they would. Tables would not stand and windows would not hold back the cold and wind, then they would. A portion of the house burned down twice—once because of my older brother and I—nonetheless, we could not live there, then we could. It seemed my father was good at his work.

However, I had no interest in that work. Even when I would sit and watch him work and, at times, in the capacity of an assistant handing him simple items upon request. I still had no interest in those things or the things he did with those things, except to the extent that it made him shine. He would shine when he did what he did with those things out of that dusty brown bag. He would shine, not always in the face, which was oftentimes as dusty and bent from wear as those boots. Likewise, his voice would sometimes be as hard as the soles of those boots. Nonetheless, I could see through that tanned to leather mask he wore when he was agitated that he was proud of his work. That work that was as many and varied as the uniforms he performed it in.

He was proud of most of it in any case. He was proud despite the critics whose cosmopolitan tastes on aesthetics did not agree with his Mississippi roots. He was proud despite the engineers whose expert opinions on form and function was made a slave to his eye and instincts. He was basic—round peg, round hole—and it always fit. So I watched the way he worked and what he worked in. I passed him his simple tools and stayed out of his way. This worked for me because it was a very unsettling thing to try to walk, talk, and bend my posture to the demands that other personalities made upon my young person.

He and my mother would occasionally find me mimicking his ways. My father would smile, and my mother would frown. I was so confused. My father encouraged me when I exhibited behavior my mother would punish me for, and I was confused for a while about which way to go. There seemed to be two choices being forced on me when essentially, ultimately, there was only one. I was my mother's child; at the same time, I was my father's child. My mother created me in my father's image. Mother/father is the symbol of God to all children; therefore, my mother/father-God became my model.

It was a long road, though, as involvement with the tutelage of children is. There were times where the road was made more difficult for my mother and her children by the seemingly unnecessary work my father's bent-ass feet frequently found a path to. He seemed to have a knack for walking those other paths at just the right times to cause great disruption of us, the family: mother/father-God, God/children. However, he never seemed to do enough to stop her wisdom, her compassion, or her love. He could never do anything to dull her sense of humor. She loved to laugh. She loved him.

I have since found that love is why anyone does anything substantial. Material profit is a weak motivation in the face of a great challenge. When life is broken down to the will or won't of it, it is not a few dollars more, a few more inches, or a shade or two either way that will be the catalyst for any person's devotion to you. God is proof of this because God has granted favor to people, or so say the people, and this for some time. Yet the world grows more and more infected with disobedience.

So I chose what I wanted to be, although I did not know it. I battled with everything my fathers/mothers were and everything I had become. With every small step I took, I made a point to be open to the wisdom that created the road so as to be informed of what the next step should be and in what direction. I do not want to find myself taking small steps in the wrong direction. So much as I could intuit right from wrong. I chose to be what my mothers were and what my fathers were. I chose to be what my fathers could be and what my mothers could be. I chose God's way because that is the wisdom that created the road, and who would know better than the engineer/builder where the road goes? Who would know as well as my mothers/fathers who have already walked that road and can serve as guides? I chose my ancestors and God because, otherwise, I am just another fool walking a dark road guided by a multitude of fools who think they know what they want to be. But their shoes are misguided.

Maybe
(not-so-stray thoughts)

Maybe there is a good reason too many black women refuse to look me in the eyes and acknowledge my hello, good afternoon, or good evening, but white women do.

Maybe there is a good reason why too many Afro women brush me off with some half glance and an annoyed face. And that is if they recognize me at all.

Maybe there is a good reason why some black males in Philadelphia have boys, dogs, niggers, peeps, shorties, young'ns, bitches, and hos, but no friends or lovers.

Maybe there is a good reason why some of our females are turning to each other for companionship.

Maybe there is a good reason why some Afro females no longer view the Afro male as the tribesman, lover, and protector they once did.

Maybe there is a good reason why there is such a high level of tension and animosity between the Afro female and Afro male, the Afro male and the Afro male, and the Afro male and the Caucasian male.

Maybe there is a good reason why some percentage of Afro females no longer feel their genetic attributes are desirable and attractive.

Maybe there is a good reason why I have never seen a white woman wearing a kinky hair weave, but maybe there is a good reason why they tan.

Maybe there is a good reason why Philadelphians seemed more concerned with gathering funds to build a new stadium for a sports franchise that

31

has never won a championship and whose stadium was only thirty-plus years old than they were, and still are, concerned with rebuilding four or five of their grossly outdated high schools, and some of those are at least fifty years old, and some of their students are setting records in academics, music and arts, and sports.

Maybe there is a good reason why I abhorred and never used the word *nigger*, but since I've lived around and worked in Philadelphia, I have been compelled to use it.

Maybe there is a good reason why children and the childlike all over the country no longer see the family unit as the source of love, guidance, and protection, and are turning to gangs.

Maybe there is a good reason why our children are growing bigger, more violent, and less intellectually capable.
　　—Maybe they have something in common with the livestock used for food in this country.

Maybe there is a good reason why our ancestors of antiquity maintained a vegetarian or near-vegetarian diet.

Maybe there is a good reason why the FDA and medical association support certain foods and drugs as safe and/or healthy, though the population suffers from mass addictions, and homes, hospitals, and cemeteries are full of the slow dying or dead whose lives were proof to the contrary.

Maybe there is a good reason why in Genesis 1:29, woman and man are instructed to have the fruit of the trees and herb-bearing seed for their meat.
　　—Maybe there is a good reason why pesticides and genetic altering are being used on those.

Maybe there is a good reason why it takes more than the passing of a date on a calendar to create a man or woman, but a male and female can be born.

Maybe there is a good reason why my ancestors recognized woman and man as the embodiment of God on earth, and symbolized it with the Ankh.

Maybe there is a good reason why a mind and spirit that is developed into adulthood and at peace is required to establish and maintain a civilization.

Maybe there is a good reason why a great deal of the American population is so gullible and permissive of abuses from elected officials.

Maybe there is a good reason why news programs show as many nonwhite faces involved in incidents of crime as they can get away with.

Maybe there is a good reason why the American justice system is so blatantly bigoted against nonwhite males, and has never been brought to justice because of its crimes against citizens.

Maybe there is a good reason why our government requires a large portion of the children of the common population to be deprived of proper education, food, and opportunity.

Maybe there is a good reason why government takes money from education to build prisons and other tools of war.

Maybe there is a good reason why a population would continue to support a system with their economic and personal efforts after having been betrayed repeatedly by its government.

Maybe there is a good reason why there is no democracy in our democratic system.

Maybe there is a good reason why 911 is just the most recent governmental insult and injury the American populace has felt compelled to excuse.
　　—And then even to this spectacular point of absurdity.

Maybe there is a good reason why Americans need to believe and support such an obvious lie.

Maybe there is a good reason why a president accused of sexual misconduct can be put on trial for impeachment, while a governor can lie and cheat to steal an election, then murder American citizens and lie about it so he can steal American tax dollars to fund a personal business venture, then send Americans to die to protect his lies and the business venture, and no one has so much as whispered the word *treason*.

Maybe there is a good reason why Bush's administration could mobilize U.S. resources, which included tax dollars, goods, and people to support his business venture in Irak, and that in less than a week, but American taxpayers (refugees?) who are suffering in Louisiana and Mississippi have to depend on the compassion of other taxpayers to find relief from tragedy within their first week.

Maybe there is a good reason why the American people have allowed its government to allow the banking system, as regulated by the Federal Reserve System, to become the new plantation master that holds a vastly larger portion of the nation's population, which is larger than the population of slaves before emancipation, in economic slavery.

Maybe there is a good reason why the horrors Africans face daily have not been and are not now an issue for the majority of American politicians and government as a whole.
   —Maybe their land is worth more than their lives.

Maybe there is a good reason why American society is the way it is.

Maybe there is a good reason why the separation of church and state no longer exists.
   —Perhaps it never did.

Maybe there is a good reason why no major religious organization in the United States has voiced an opinion in strong opposition to the ill actions of government, but stood in support of the evil done in the guise of a righteous war, proudly poised for photo opportunities with elected officials, and received grant money for their support in an election.

Maybe there is a good reason why a person can spend a lifetime dedicated to some religious system: Christian, Islam, Hebrew, Catholic, etc., and still be the most ignorant and ungodly piece of shit you have ever met.

Maybe there is a good reason why churches take more money out of some communities than neighborhood grocery, liquor, foreign foods, and check-cashing stores, and proportionately put back even less into those communities, yet remain above criticism.

Maybe there is a good reason why most people do not know themselves half as well as they should, then marry someone who they don't know half as well as they should.

Maybe there is a good reason why the divorce rate is as high as it is.

Maybe there is a good reason why I think the way I do.

Maybe these opinions are only valuable to me.
　　—Maybe I should shut the fuck up.

Maybe there is a good reason why the people of the world suffer these moments.
　　—Maybe we have not yet learned from our history.

Fear of Tomorrow

My mind:
it is that part of me
that clings to the reality of now.
This moment and this body.
It religiously denies
the pleasure of aspirations.

It is like a cage around my spirit
that is God's.

Tomorrow's an extended today.
My mind regulates my lifemares
as destiny rolls through me
with a pulse.
The power of a delinquent's choice
pushes it back in moments,
rushing, further,
and away.

My mind will not allow
what has already happened
to become.

Living for the City (Immortality)

I feel
surrounded, trapped, and caged
inside of a polluted host
called home.

Diseased minds
are trying to infect me.
They seek to poison my mind
and cripple my body
with that diabolical energy
that has perished so many persons.
They are trying to bring me down slowly
to a level of disgrace.

Pressure.
Man the pressure.
I am barely holding on.
And I want to die;
I'm just looking for a clean spot.

She

She wears it well,
the rays of faint blue television light.
They ply her hue with promises of elegance,
but ebony needs no compliment.

She wears it well;
the cloak of slumber
that descends on her like soft kisses
punishes her being in bliss.

She wears it well.
Her cover. Her thoughts are sometimes as dark.
Her mask tries to hide her heart.
To conceal. To protect.
To not feel pain.

She wears it well.
That smile. It is the hope of a promise.
It is the source of her humility
and the fuel of her expectations.

Human, Being
(essay)

The point of this writing is to tell my opinion on free will. If I am successful, I will have articulated a manner in which a person's will can determine their quality of existence.

I thought I would use the popular, but not very seriously discussed, topic of marital disposition to illustrate my point. I am not speaking of the obvious question of married or single, but that more sensitive issue of monogamy vs. polygamy. However, as these are simply titles used to describe this or that activity that people willfully engage in, the subject need not be anchored to it.

Both monogamy and polygamy, as well as titles of other social activities that can be articulated, are only what they are made to be. We the people of the world control what we reflect through our thought and action. That means that as easily as an idea can germinate into a thought and then a word, that action we will reflects either our higher or lower potential as a being. I believe for now that reflection can only be that of a human or not human.

To be aware of the difference between human and not human, I think at the very least one must be informed about the choices to the extreme of human. I will use two, animal and God: the animal being supposedly below the rank of human and God being above. The *Living Webster Encyclopedic Dictionary of the English Language* defines animal as

> a living being characterized by having sensation and voluntary motion; an inferior or irrational being, in contradistinction to man; also, often popularly used to signify a quadruped.

And God:

Creator and ruler of the universe; eternal, infinite Spirit; the Supreme Being, almighty and omniscient, worshiped by men; a person, spirit, or object worshiped and adored, to whom supernatural powers are attributed; a deity in mythology; an idol; a person possessing extreme authority, etc.

An animal exists in animalism: "the state of being actuated by sensual appetites only" (p. 41). This state refers to behavior and not appearance. Animality is the state of being animal by having the physical traits of an animal.

It is possible to appear as an animal yet not exhibit the behavior that would animalize one's being. I believe this is the current condition of people. Conversely, I think it would be impossible to show those behaviors requisite of an animal, despite one's appearance, and not be convincing as an animal.

So what is an animal? I think the individual must decide for themselves. However, whatever a person ultimately decides an animal is, they will then be aware of what a human must be—not animal.

We are not God as the legitimizing attribute of omniscience is wanting, and whatever claims on the universe could be made, I suspect would be highly disputed. There are those, though, who have believed that their particular bloodline contained some distinguishing trait that set them apart from the common person and made them like gods on earth; and let us not forget how some are treated as though they are godlike because of some skill they possess in arts, entertainment, sports, religion, politics, etc.; but none of these are the same as being a god, which is a universe apart from being human, which is in turn a school apart from being animal.

Some of us are certainly not fully animal in behavior, although physically we are all still very much animal. We seem slaves to those animal impulses and what they suggest of our intellectual and physical needs: the drive for procreation, to eat and sleep, and especially that range of emotions that is always in the company of our wants; additionally, we appear to be helpless against the growth of hair, nails, and teeth. And despite the attributes of reason, will, and logic, we are still closer to being animal than being human.

The world's population of people consider ourselves human. I think the assigning of the title is premature. In our descriptions of ourselves in any context, there is a marked lack of recognition of any of those animal conditions, thoughts, and behaviors that we engage in and maintain daily. This may be because we as a group or as individuals feel we are so independent of that animal component that it is beneath us. If it is beneath us, then it is an unworthy and unwanted influence on our being. I am certain that we all believe this.

If that is true, though, then why have people handed God such a raw deal? We allow ourselves the luxury of not being associated by behavior with what some would like to consider a lower life-form, animals. Naturally, this is done by smoke and mirrors and with an agreement to agree on the illusion. At the same time, though, we impose on God, our creator—the Supreme Being—every cruel idea, base thought, and animal behavior that can be believed.

I offer for your consideration the content of whoever's holy book you care to examine. That god is frequently described through that god's words and actions by those parties that have since been deified because of their defining that god. The words themselves just sit on the paper; indeed, it is how those words are accepted that has led to the authors being revered as apart from the common person, and the god figure solidly deified. Through those words, I feel God has been reduced to an immortal who is susceptible to all those animal passions of a person.

I believe there are examples of both this bad and some good in the texts of every major religious system. There are two reasons for this: One, I believe the good of all beliefs that create religious systems is linked not only at their divine core, but also in their mutual origins; and two, the bad of these religious systems is in the fact that they were expressed by people who maintained fear as a motivation for being, and thus those expressions of the divine and the divine order of things are replete with thinking and behavior that I consider anti-God.

A good example of the bad is found in the Christian/Catholic/Jewish text called the King James Version Holy Bible. I am not picking on these groups; I did grow up Christian though, so it is what I am most familiar with.

I will begin and end in Exodus 32. Although there are many points I could make about the Bible and its many books, I will concentrate on that book and chapter and will direct attention to verses 7-14. In short, God became angry at the people taken out of Egypt by Moses because they corrupted themselves at the foothills of Mt. Sinai. God wanted to destroy them all. Moses then interceded for the people and stayed God's hand by shaming God. Moses told God that it would look bad to free the people from the Egyptians, only to murder them in the mountains. Moses also reminded God of the oath sworn to Abraham, Isaac, and Israel—that their seed shall multiply as the stars in heaven. Moses then asked God to turn from wrath and repent of that evil against the people. God complied and repented of the evil.

If that god is the Supreme Being, whose attributes are omniscience, omnipotence, and omnipresence, then why is there space to suffer an injury from people? Not only are we animal based and not currently divine—the difference I would like to describe as an infant to an adult person—but we are said to be the creation of this being. The very idea that people could through thought or action offend or injure that god disturbs me. It means that either those people felt themselves in a comparative class to that god, or that god was not the Supreme Being. I do not agree that a person could offend or injure a supreme being and not be a supreme being.

A superior being, though, is a being that is presently more capable than the common person is. Being more capable at a particular thing does not eliminate the tendency to err from one's being. Because there is fallibility in a superior being, there is space for injury.

How is it that the idea of God behaving like us was not found as unreasonable and/or illogical as the idea of us (people) behaving as a wild pack of animals? How has every major belief system been able to get away with this heinous abuse of we the people of the world and of our ideas of God?

I believe these evils and more have been possible because we the people of the world have abused by neglect our powers of will. Furthermore, I think if any of us are ever going to realize being human, a good start may be to take control of our will.

There may be consequences. To be in control of one's will may lead to more responsible thoughts and actions. I believe this is true because no matter what those thoughts and actions, the participants will no longer be allowed to use the idea of other influence as a crutch retarding their responsibility. Either you are or you are not, being human.

I recall a phrase, "To err is human." Perhaps, but to commit to the same lapse or lack of wisdom repeatedly over the course of one's life cannot be reflective of what it is to be human, and neither is it animal. An even less flattering fact is that people willfully engage in these behaviors to the detriment of the quality of their own life and/or another. To be human is to not be less than human.

I think most animal species learn from costly errors in judgment in short time. This may be because the quality of their life, if not in fact their life, will be lost for lack of wisdom. In any case, they seem to learn to not repeat those decisions that tend to lead to a diminished quality of life.

People, however, will commit to a lifetime of injurious thoughts and actions. The injury can be to themselves or to others. Where an animal will learn from its mistakes within the context of its natural environment, a person seems to not learn from similar examples within its environment.

A person will in fact seek to create a lifestyle of damaging thoughts and actions. A person will reason why these thoughts and actions are legitimate. A person will die comfortably in the familiar embrace of the very thoughts and actions that they claim are contrary to their beliefs and being.

A human will commit an offense but a single time. A human is not an animal and not a person. A human is a being whose goal is to become divine. Since the goal is to become divine, a human takes full responsibility for its will, its thoughts, and its actions. A human strives for ever-decreasing incidents of lapses in wisdom (judgment). The goal is human perfection and then divine perfection. A person certainly cannot graduate to the divine until they first graduate to that state of being that precedes divinity, the human.

I think that if we make the pursuit of the divine the goal of our existence, then our existence can only experience greater levels of freedom from the limitations of our physical (animal) component. It is we people who have been produced by the fusion of divine and animal components.

Inherit to people is emotion. Emotion is the mind's tool for learning how to cope with the seeming differences between the spirit world and the material world. Unfortunately, people have been corrupted by emotion. I believe this is because we are no longer trained by our elders on the dynamics of our being, and then especially our capacity for emotion. Emotion is a beautiful tool. I can see that in the earliest stages of our evolution, it was key to our survival. However, I believe we were meant to move beyond the need for it.

The person chooses a life replete with errs because the person chooses to try to avoid pain and pursue pleasure. This is a decision motivated by emotion. The constant and lifelong repetition of these poor decisions becomes the blinders about the perceptive powers of the person. This lack of vision disallows a person from receiving and/or perceiving divine guidance from the all-knowing source (God).

Lack of vision means a lack of divine guidance. Lack of divine guidance means a lack of love, for God is love. Lack of love means that the chief governing influence to the person is fear. Fear is a product of undisciplined emotion, and emotion is the out-of-control and obsolete tool of the animal that is the whole half component of the origin of people.

I think love would make a better guide for the will than fear. I think fear is what has gotten the world's people in such a sad state of being as we are currently enjoying. I mean, enjoying as a state of satisfaction. If we came to the present by vehicle of fear and are dissatisfied, then why do we not abandon that damned transport and ride that love machine until we realize our goal? The goal is to be human.

It is not the fool who will not change their circumstances when faced with great discomfort. A fool tends to make poor decisions, but they are not stupid. It is the fearful that will convince themselves that the pot of water they are sitting in is not getting hotter. The fearful have more than enough reasons why neither they nor you should seek change. I would not believe any of those reasons would be logical, and the great majority of them would likely be unreasonable. But when a person is oppressed by fear, they work well as a crutch.

The fearful is an otherwise healthy person. They can be physically sound. Your mind is your body because you cannot do what you cannot imagine. There are those whose bodies are not physically sound, yet they are able to find a way to achieve because their mind is sound.

People have satisfied ourselves with limping about our reality with the aid of a whatever psychological crutch we have imagined we need or have been convinced we need. Those crutches are for the sole purpose of not having to be burdened with one day being expected to walk straight with those legs, to one day run with those legs, or ultimately, to leap and soar beyond whatever limits on reality have been insisted were the truth.

I can imagine an entire town, country, and world full of people who have learned to cripple their own potential of being: body, mind, and spirit, by so simple and removable a device as fear; and I can see the very same town, country, and world having evolved so far beyond the influence of their animal component that death has been put on pause.

Both love and fear are only words used to describe an intellectual and physical reaction we persons have to some stimuli. Neither has any influence but what we choose to accept and reflect. Love becomes divine when its components are willfully accepted and reflected. Fear becomes diabolical when its components are willfully accepted and reflected. Every person is in the process of living. It is those decisions made with the influence of either love or fear that have gotten we the people of the world to this point. What will we do now?

I think, for me, it would be best to will being human.

The Biggest Lie
(A nice rant)

A sobering slap in the face is when a person realizes that their open and honest relationship has fallen woefully short of both open and honest.

I think it would be more accurate to describe adult relationships as conditional. A person is usually willing to entertain another's openness and honesty as long as they do not have to feel encumbered by it. In this instance, *encumbered* most relatively means that a person does not want to feel any sense of alarm through loss of confidence in their mate or especially in themselves. To this end, what *open* and *honest* comes to mean for the individual is only to tell what you think I would want to know, and if that is still too caustic, then tell a plausible lie. I believe this is true. I have observed it and been contributory to it enough times to understand its details have been integrated into common interaction and codified by society as part of the way of things.

So what is it about open and honest that is so frightening that most avoid it with great energy? I think a part of it would have to be some insecurity. I am a witness to how insecurity can destroy a person's potential at being. A person's insecurities have become the default crutch used to guide thinking when common sense, logic, and/or reason are too taxing a burden to bear.

What can make a person feel as though they are unworthy as a mate? I say unworthy because I feel this would have to comprise at least a part of the motivational force behind a person insisting on being another's "one and only" love. "One and only" is a condition I have witnessed being imposed on/by myself and others through some action.

"One and only" indicates the exclusion of others. To exclude others means that you are denying your mate and those others their right to love freely. This is oppression, and oppression is prejudice in action. Prejudice is a product of one's fears concerning one's being; accordingly, when applied to your mate in an environment of others, your fears provoke an emotional response recognized as insecurity. This insecurity insists upon your conscious mind the feeling of being unworthy compared to those others, or perhaps compared to that part of one's being that does know right from wrong, the conscience. So to quiet that unworthy noise, the one insists an oppressive condition upon the other.

Allow me to describe love as the divine manifest. The divine is an energy that when mixed with other material energies helps to comprise the fabric of life. Love is confidence, nurturing, and munificence. It is the greatest product of what I believe God is that we people are capable of expressing. It is not sex. Sex is when two or more interact for intellectual gratification through physical means. Lust is not love or sex. Lust is being intellectually stimulated by some idea that creates a fantastic goal.

You were not your mate's first love. I certainly was not my mate's first love. Do you find yourself troubled by your mate's sexual history? If not, and you are aware that they have loved others before you and hopefully since you, then why impose such a harsh condition as "one and only" on the relationship? You had nothing to do with their decisions in the past, the direction of their attention, and why. Still now these things are outside of your influence or control.

There have been many occasions where a person has realized their mate in a relationship, and then a sexual relationship with some other. If there was any pain at the point of realization, what hurt worse, the feeling of betrayal at being mislead or lied to by your mate? Or was it that barrage of emotion shot at you from your insecure place? A great shot from this place is, what is wrong with me that I was not enough for them? It is possible the answer is nothing other than your holding on to childish ideas of yourself and others.

There could be a third source of your intellectual pain. It could be that your realization of your mate with another insulted you on a more social-economic level. That emotional response may be the result of feelings of physical loss, like that of property. Many people claim that they love their people, and some may go further to say that love is unconditional. I will not challenge that at this point, however, for love to be valid, it must contain and show the attributes and behavior of love. I have established that love is confident, nurturing, and munificent as are inherit of its divine origins. It is also compassionate, forgiving and, most of all, free and all through divine inheritance. Love promotes freedom because freedom is the compliment of divine being. Without freedom, one has no choice; without choice, one does not have love, but obligations. According to a variety of opinions, God has not obligated people to obedience to the divine will, although all are subject to divine order, but has left us free to choose our path. That is love.

When some say they love another, I believe they mean they love to possess that other as if they were property. For them, possession is the key point of attachment. The attachment is the same as when you were a child and had your favorite thing—a toy, a book, a blanket; certainly, it was something that lent some level of security to you outside the knowledge and thus the influence of any other person. When you are a child, it is forgiven when you make an emotional slave of things and people as both become devices used to safeguard your emotions. I think it is expected of children to guard their emotions with devices because they are too inexperienced to know how to grow intellectually beyond the need to be a slave to their emotions and thus things. An adult, though, should have lived long enough to have had the requisite experiences to know the potential for damage to the person, both within and without, by maintaining a child's perspective of self and environment. If an adult has not yet come to adequate enlightenment of the difference between a child's and adult's realities, then they will continue to suffer those same emotional traumas a child does. When that adult realizes that their right to sole possession of this person has been challenged or defeated, that will be the prompt for the intellectual imposition that will trigger the insecurities that will render that adult helpless to those chaotic emotions. And they will become like a child once more.

The one who loves, though, understands love. To love, one must first have gained that experience that would qualify as an adult's. What one felt before this was an emotional dependency otherwise know as affection. That adult experience becomes the difference between being dependent and independent, slave and free.

The one who loves understands that the objects loved are transient, but love is a psychic energy and thus eternal. The brain is not the intellect or our psychic potential. The brain is a conduit for that energy called intelligence that is ever present. If true, then that energy that is ourselves, which can perceive yet not be perceived, is eternal. I believe once love has been focused, it cannot be unfocused by the removing of the object that was recognized. The object is material and so because it is the product of two immaterial energies, will and energy:

> Energy: inherent power; the power of operating, whether exerted or not; power vigorously exerted; strength of expression; *physl.* The actual or potential ability to do work.
> Will: the faculty or power of conscious and esp. of deliberate action; the act, experience, or process of exercising this power or faculty; choice; wish; desire; process of determination.

Both of these work within a reality where things are to be recognized and acted on. The primary thing to be recognized and acted on is the self. The one who loves feels love of self, and they express this through their person. And we are the thing, and thus not merely some material invention that can be made and unmade without regard. We are conscious, and that conscious is divine; and it seeks the answer to the question of its being.

So if there were another who soothed your mate's soul the way you do or more, and your mate did not inform you of this, would that make it easier to bear? That other person is there whether their form continues or not. Your mate loves them and possibly as much as they love you, and also possibly in the same way. Or theirs could be a relationship based upon the pursuit of their mutual lusts. In any case, does your not knowing make it all a mute point?

I have observed how a person moves on in a relationship, secure that they are the one and only interest to their mate but knowing of the mate's other relationship. I have observed that most do know of that other concern and choose not to address the issue with their mates beyond that point where a major life-changing decision would have to be made.

This act creates the basis of dishonesty for both you and your mate. You, because you would rather be lied to or have your ideas of self compromised than face your mate's reality. The difference between your reality and theirs can be tortuous. Your mate, because they now suffer the illusion of being imposed upon to continue to disgrace themselves with dishonesty in order to preserve your confidence in them and you.

Let me repeat, I am not saying that your mate has had sex with another. I will get to that later. I am saying that your mate has greater than commonly friendly feelings toward another. For the purposes of this scenario, this person reciprocates every bit of that intellectual energy toward your mate.

Why is this such a bitter pill to swallow? Someone besides you loves your mate. People are created to be the intellectual/physical reflection of the divine spirit, which is love, but are punished by society, their mates, and ultimately and most cruelly by themselves for loving. We punish ourselves for choosing to reflect the nature of God.

Society punishes by creating a societal standard that can make the individual or group feel weak and incompetent for anything but an animalistic and barbaric misrepresentation of that beautiful condition of being called love. This barbarism is best exemplified by the media industry. Those reenactments of life scenarios and those necessary character portrayals one might view in any media form are more reflective of a great lack of understanding of adult, love, and God. They are an example of the reality the spiritually lacking suffers.

Nonetheless, those ill images do represent a growing and accurate reality among all people. There is a punishment/reward system within society represented by phrases such as "good people finish last" and "love hurts." Good people usually finish last because they are observing the stated rules, and love hurts because you were never taught how to not have a child's understanding of it.

Your mate punishes by imposing on you emotional sanctions should you share your intellectual/physical self with anyone else. One method of punishment is to create some level of guilt of betrayal in one's mate. A most popular method for this is to create such a stress-and tension-filled environment between you and your mate that it becomes most beneficial for them to deny themselves that joy of free expression.

Finally, you will punish yourself by first denying yourself the enjoyment of the single greatest form of expression a person is capable of, love. A person then becomes a slave to the childish insecurities and anti-God sentiments imposed upon a person by society and one's mate.

Please allow me to define two things: open—to be receptive to a variety of categorized inputs; and honest—an uncensored expression of one's perspective.

These definitions are accurate enough to reflect my intent. For a relationship to be open or honest, or both, it would have to contain whatever elements are necessary to support the dynamic of each category. Each person would have to be receptive to the uncensored expression of the other and do it without prejudice.

I believe this is possible. Furthermore, I feel we as a world population of free peoples are being slowly converted into a population of slaves. I believe we persons of divine origins are systematically being converted into slaves to our animal emotions, specifically our insecurities or, more accurately, our fears.

If I may make a light suggestion, I would say let that shit go and be free. I have heard this phrase repeated by slavers and the minions of slavers, "What is the price of freedom?" My answer is whatever time must be spent to rid oneself of those internal or internalized ideas that are conducive to slavery.

Chief among these ideas for the individual is that we need anyone to defend freedom. Freedom is but a choice away because it is love. So choose love and let those Satanists figure out how to exist without our individual contributions to that evil they thrive on—those acts in contradiction to divine being.

Secondary among these ideas is incompetence. As individuals comprise couples and larger groups, I believe this would be a good place to start. When the individual is open and honest of themselves, it relieves their persons of the necessity of subscribing to those ideas that will transform their thoughts into the various poisons that will do intellectual harm to their persons; in fact, more intellectual harm to their persons and any who are influenced by their persons.

The poison first affects the mind in the simple manner of causing pause or great doubt within the individual of their ability to affect their reality. This lack of confidence, which began in the mind, begins to affect the body. Where the mind goes, the body follows, and the person becomes susceptible to a host of maladies, including depression and addictions such as food and drugs, alcohol, tobacco, firearms, and war to name a few. These things are used as a crutch to excuse their persons ability not to do. Or more accurately, they become the justification for their not being able to will a loving (godly) reality despite whatever resistance.

We persons accept, maintain, and nurture this invalid mentality. We carry it with us into every inter/intrapersonal encounter. When someone accepts us with our illnesses, we impose on them to become another form of crutch. Each person becomes a crutch that is used not only to excuse our inability to do in the divine manner, but to protect that fragile corner of the intellect where poison thoughts are created by malicious ideas. The one then comes to feel as though they cannot take another apparent betrayal of their confidence. The other (friend/mate) then becomes the crutch against their persons insecurities and impending emotional collapse. The insecurities are fueled by feelings of incompetence. Feelings of incompetence are a product of one's fears concerning the validity of one's being. The friend/mate then becomes a slave in this sick codependent relationship. And as long as that environment and those conditions are allowed to persist by either or both parties, neither will ever know freedom because neither will know love.

Finally, at the end of it, the biggest lie is the idea of "open and honest" in what qualifies as an adult relationship in America. The biggest lie is that we need anyone or anything other than our self and the *god* consciousness that is the origin of divine love both within and without our being to affect our realities.

Mirrors Make Me Silly

Most mornings
as I jump from my bed,
I can't help
but to see my reflection as I pass.
I stop to flex,
and every limb's just where I left them.
I assume some expressions of
humor and seriousness just to waken my all-day face.
Then I laugh
and continue my preday pace.

As I bathe, dress, and continue on
with some routine casualness,
I try hard to pretend
not to notice it as I pass.
It can see me though,
and it records my action.
My thoughts, "Then why resist."
I then burst to life
with eighties dance movements
and laugh.

The Place Where I Shall Pass

Who are these voices calling to me?
I recognize them; my spirit recognizes them.
My ears, though, are unfamiliar with the sound.
My mind is unaccustomed to the melody the river of my blood makes
flowing through eternity.

They whisper to me,
"What is your name?"
I can hear it. "Child, what is your name?"
My spirit speaks, "Gye Nyame," but my lips will not move.
My mind will not move them.
It has learned to fear.

The unknown will represent no confidence.
Confidence in the known has evaporated.
It is a version of death that eludes responsibility.
The mind fears.

This dark veil is not enough.
This coarse cloud of wisdom is not enough.
This ladder that extends to the beginning of things is not enough.
These will remain weak proof of my lineage.
They are transient.

I will stretch this dark form of things and no things through creation
until peace.
I will stretch until still.
I shall stretch until I am back to null.
I will speak my name there and be reborn again.

Road Hazards

This driver is not new.
I've been on this road before.

There are sharp curves ahead,
so proceed slowly.
Hill; slower traffic to the right.
Slippery when wet
—love is.

CAUTION:
Merge with the flow of traffic
at your own risk and
have suspicion for a stop sign.

Tension. Road rage. Regret.
People who move too fast
in the slow lane.
People who move too slow
in the fast lane.
Drunken, spiteful, hateful drivers.

I've got to make it home this time.
I don't want to be on this road again.

.

Good Question

Why am I not compared to
the best of things, both real and imagined,
rather than those lifemares
the dead conjure
while hoping through life
with their mind's eye wide shut?

Rude Moon

As I lie upon my back and prey
upon thoughts like helpless things,
this orb of light jumps before my eye
and demands my attention.

How dare this moon disturb me.
It interrupts me without so much as a "May I?"
But I would say nothing.
I simply shut my eye to its rudeness
and continue to ponder things that matter.

As I lie upon my back
and dwell on orbs of light and shiny things,
a voice sings to me.
Its rhythm is like the flow of Gaia,
and my spirit is drawn away.

So I drift on willingly.
I don't resist or question where or why.
As I rose, this bright thing caught my eye
and dragged me back to this world.
How dare this moon disturb me.

Death Dream

Wake up, wake up!
It's time for your death dream.

It is no accident
that you recall so much.
Those visions from your past and future.
They are moments from your lives
and certain ones you relive constantly.

I hope you have made amends by now,
or I hope you will do it soon.
Be the truth, or we will perish
without consideration.
It is only the dying
whose life is in review.

Wake up, wake up!

Why hide those ugly things
in the bleached recesses of your mind?
Go deep and release them all
so our self will be as light as the feather.
Then finally, we can live.

If you trifle along the way,
we may find ourselves here again
among the dead.

My God, My Self
(contemplations)

What if the greatest gift God has passed on to people is the potential to be gods?

It would make sense, existentially speaking. A man and woman, each of whom represents a whole half of the life dynamic, join together to create the conditions necessary to produce another whole half. This whole half then combines with another, and the circle of life is continued.

A child born through this fusion of whole halves should possess attributes from the two spheres of control inherent of its being. The most tangible are those passed on by the science of its physical (biological) design. These I call natural. The most intangible are those passed on by the science of its nonphysical (spiritual) design. These I call supernatural.

The physical component of our being provides us a vehicle that has an unlimited potential to do within the physical realm. Our current capacity to do is regulated by moment-to-moment enlightenment. Our ability to accept greater levels of enlightenment is conditional to our merging and evolving our natural and supernatural components.

The spirit must evolve from its animal stage of perception as our mind must evolve from its infant stage of development. Necessary to the natural process of learning and growth within the natural sphere, and specially conducive to the graduation of potential, is the seeming differentiation of our being both internally and externally.

Internal differentiation can be represented by the apparent separation of mind and spirit. The mind that processes thought is tangible, yet thought generated by the spirit is intangible. The mind is but a device whose function aids the processing of information realized during the process of decoding divine knowledge channeled through the spirit. Divine knowledge is what I call all energy that manifests itself as anything. This intangible energy eventually becomes things, such as images drawn in charcoal on stone, the spoken word, or they can remain in an intangible form as ideas are represented by laws.

In fact, I believe the intent of a person's behavior can be determined by discovering what picture was painted in the mind before proceeding into action. Indeed, that picture (idea) created the thought that motivated the behaviors that not only define your person but that are also an indication of what source a person takes guidance from.

In the differentiated person, there are two sources that can govern one's being. One is divine because it is lawful. The other is diabolical because it is chaotic. The point of separation is a person who comprehends their being as a whole unit connected to the source of all things and *no*things (God = Amen, Jah) and a person who does not.

The mind governs the body, though, and that relationship cannot be interrupted or severed without consequence. The spirit governs the mind, and though the mind possesses the ability to choose to devise other ideas and methods of coping with its reality, which is other than divine guidance, there are again repercussions for noncompliance.

> External differentiation is represented by the seeming difference between my body (person) and yours. Because of the delicate link between mind and body, one's person is the mind and body working in concert. More specifically, your person is your body and those intellectual activities and behaviors that have become typically associated with it from this moment to that. The activities and behaviors our minds guides us to range from the basic function of our person to those that are necessary to our continued social existence.

Whatever the activity and the function it serves toward the persistence of people to exist, it can be simplified to its root external expression. There are no two people who are exactly alike. However, the more mundane the description becomes, the more the vast variety of us becomes generalized into a single entity. This single entity is iconically represented by woman and man/we. We live.

I believe the learning is in realizing that each of us is undifferentiated at the core of our total being. Physically this means that the same material that lends us people form is the same material that lends all transient things form. Spiritually this means that the same intangible energy that allows us consciousness, and thus life, is the same energy that allows all conscious beings life. Once realized, I believe it is the practice of the discipline required to evolve as a single unit (me) that will lead to the discipline to evolve as a single unit (we). This is the growth in perception that may lead to the evolution of the being. We are the physical representation of the dual nature of a single life unit that is itself a whole half component to existence. In other words, each of us is seemingly a separate unit from our parents in form, but one unit biologically, intellectually, and spiritually.

God spoke the words and from a vast ocean of no-things came into being every-thing. We were formed through the intent of the word that was made material by speaking it. God breathed into us, giving us the spirit of God that animates this flesh; and finally, God gave us a brain with the potential of an imperceptible capacity to perceive and translate the divine will.

The brain is not the source of will but its conduit. The will is a facet of the divine consciousness being expressed through us. Therefore, in body, mind, and spirit, we are a perfect reflection of God's divine science. We are omnipresent because the spirit that is in one is in all, and all come from the one that is everything. We are omnipotent because God gave us a form that is perfectly suited to perform any conceivable task. Finally, we are omniscient because God gave us a brain that can perceive the imperceptible, and when divinely disciplined, it can become the imperceptible.

This is the natural process. We are born infants then grow to children, young adults, adults, and then elders. The cycle continues as we recycle ourselves through the ecology (physical body) of our source parent, Earth. These are terms that I am using in a very general way, those being *child*, *adult*, and *elder*. The important idea to remember, though, is that we move from a stage of development to another until that particular section of the spiral is completed.

If physically we go through this process, and that by the science of our animal (physical) form, then mentally and spiritually we should proceed through a similar process. That process should graduate us from the relative level of a child to that of an adult. The body, though, is tangible; and thus, it is its own best evidence that at a point, it did not exist.

The intellect and spirit, though, cannot be observed in such a way. First, it is an energy and, therefore, is as timeless as energy is. As an energy, it exists with or without our brains to channel through. The idea of two plus two existed before *I*, the oldest person on the planet, or the first person on the planet. Therefore, when we go through our life experiences, are we learning, or are we simply opening our minds to a vast wealth of divine knowing or intuitive knowledge that has existed before God spoke the word? Because God would have had to had access to such information before knowing that to speak the words would bring everything into existence. Thought before action; motive before thought; and awareness before motive.

By embracing our experiences in every detail, we can learn divine wisdom. There could not possibly be an action that will affect you that is not created by the divine will and governed by the divine consciousness. Whatever occurs is necessary for the development of one's intellectual sphere so that the person may realize it's self, and the self may unite the person with the in/out-dwelling god that is the source of all things. God (we) then finds itself made perfect by the person (I). The circle of life.

If the thing that is us—that which can perceive yet not be perceived, that thing that is not any one of your parts, but governs the mechanism that animates those parts—is eternal, then we are eternal.

If a person lost any of those parts, would they cease to exist? We firmly know that a person can exist even in some extremely diminished physical states. Vital organs such as eyes, lungs, and brain are only organic devices that assist in translating information into a form necessary in maintaining the physical person. The physical person is only a collection of devices and not a consciousness or a will. The person is inanimate without that animating component that can be referred to as the breath of God—the soul.

When the soul is introduced into our corporeal forms, it accommodates itself to the environment. It is no longer one and at perfect peace and stillness, but several and at a constant state of agitation. The soul separated into its working parts is the spirit. The spirit works in complement of our being, body, and mind.

If we are what our parents were, and their parents down the line of ancestry to the beginning—and if at that beginning there were two, because no thing can exist without its complement being in existence at the very same instant, then the very existence of things supports the equilibrium of the dual nature of being that is the foundation of the divine consciousness.

Imagine modern flowers and bees and if one came into existence before the other. The flowers, if first, would not exist today because there were no bees to tap them and spread their genetic material, allowing them to prosper. The same extinction-level event would occur for the bees which, if first, would have starved to death for not having the nectar from flowers to consume. Naturally both of these life-forms developed according to factors aside from the existence of the one or the other; however, within the system of their creation, they share a complementary existence that cannot be severed but for severe consequence.

Because of this, I find it highly unreasonable and illogical that anyone would discount such a blessing as the duality of things. No thing would exist without it. To claim that man came before woman, I believe, is as erroneous as the idea of God being a singular entity.

I find the idea that man existed before woman absurd. We are a complement of each other from being physical entities to being subatomic energies. Many of our wise and ancient ancestors represented the power of wo/man with symbols such as yin and yang, and the ankh. Both represent the complementary relationship of woman to man and wo/man:God, and neither can exist without the other being a perfect complement for the one.

As I have already shown, we are a product of our creator. Our parents were the conduits to the creation of our physical form, and it was designed by God to be the perfect vessel for the divine consciousness and will (energy). If we were not perfectly suited to this, we would not exist. Perfection cannot be channeled through an imperfect conduit. The conduit, whatever it is, will be destroyed in the effort. Perfection can only manifest itself through a perfect vessel.

Necessity is the mother of invention, or so I have heard it said. I say that God created us for a reason, and that reason was the necessary complement of its own existence. This would support the main reason for people procreating, in complement of our existence. And though our form is less subtle and more finite, we possess every attribute that God does, though in diminished quantity.

The potential of the single attribute of intelligence is proof for me that I was not only not created to worship blindly and without question, but that I am in fact a creation. Questions are the natural product of interaction. Interaction is preceded by contemplation. Contemplation is my mind organizing the perceptive, imaginative, reasoning, and logic inputs of my spirit's channeling of divine knowing. Unless my intellect and awareness is at a moment working on the level of the source that created the thing I contemplate, then I am bound to have questions concerning this thing. By asking questions, I open my mind to more divine input. Slowly and inevitably enlightenment is achieved.

Because I have questions about every thing, including my self, I then do not possess the level of intelligence and awareness that created these things and my self. I did not create my self or person, yet I am being. In being is the opportunity to come to some level of enlightenment of my being. That knowing requires contemplation. Contemplation creates questions such as, who am I? What am I? Why am I here?

Ultimately knowing requires that I be rightfully disciplined so as to be ready to accept what knowledge I may intuit. Because of the divine order I have observed in the natural order of life contained within our source parent, Earth, I believe every aspect of being (I) is a direct reflection of our (all life) divine parent. It is on earth as it is in heaven.

The greatest illumination I have experienced was in realizing God and I are the perfect complement of each other. I = Wo/Man. Therefore, if we were not the perfect vessel to complement God, then we would not exist because the necessity would not support it. However, we do exist, and in as whole a manner as we do as the perfect body for the divine spirit.

I hope I have made my point well enough, and that is if it is on earth as it is in heaven, then we are all a perfect reflection of our creator/s (mother/father; God). We are a complete, though differentiated, replica in body, mind, and spirit of the one god through our parents, and thus, potentially gods on earth. We need but choose to reflect that divine potential.

On Being Married and Relationships in General (opinion)

I think it is a beautiful thing when two people discover each other, make a commitment to each other, and honor it. I think the only thing that can spoil it is dishonesty.

I think being dishonest as an adult is a natural result of not having matured from that intellectual state of being a child. Children make decisions that are motivated by their emotions. What abilities at logic and reasoning they have guide them to avoid pain and pursue pleasure. Accordingly, a child's decisions are made from an uninformed position. I have lately endeavored to not make any decisions without enough good and reliable information about myself so as to be certain about my part.

I believe a part of the problem is most of us do not know who we are when we commit ourselves to this or that relationship. I was at such a state of immaturity when I committed myself to some past relationship that it had to end in disappointment on someone's part.

You don't know where to start, once you start. You are new, and being new, you are unaware of the rules. So you learn the rules as you go along. You learn from your spheres of influence, which might include your partner, your friends and family, and those movies and periodicals that infest your world. In fact, you learn from any source that you can respect as knowledgeable in the field. We are so afflicted because we tend to follow the poor examples of behavior our predecessors laid. Unfortunately, most or all of these were instructed by the deaf, dumb, and blind of other spheres.

I mean no insult. I do, however, mean to clearly define my point. That is, if your search for truth does not begin and end with you knowing yourself, then there is no truth that you can experience sensually that will be a fit vessel to reach whatever goals you have envisioned. It will fail, or you will hurt, yourself and others attempting to make an inadequate vessel meet your lofty goals.

It is better, I think, to develop I (self/person). It is better to develop I than to develop lusts for my wants. It is better to develop I than to develop a laundry list of dirty habits created by my pursuit of my lusts. It is better to develop I than to develop a relationship based on lies created by my dependence on those dirty habits. Naturally, it takes at least two to form a partnership/joint venture, but I can only be responsible for my part, as she can only be responsible for her part. I intend to become a more responsible partner.

For my part, if I come into the relationship underdeveloped but proceed as if I am fully developed, then I have committed an error. I can choose to learn from my mistake, providing I am perceptive of it, and correct it. Or I can let it lie and ignore it when it begs my attention. The result will be that a two-dollar problem I recognized but ignored at the beginning of the relationship has ballooned to a two-thousand-dollar problem only a few years later. I had two dollars to fix a problem back then. I still do not have two thousand dollars for any cause at this moment.

The point of my suggestion, that of constant and honest introspective and self-analysis, is to create the framework for a proper vessel so I can achieve any conceivable goal. For this moment, the goal is to articulate my thoughts on marriage and other relationships. However, as I am not a fully developed person, and I cannot say that I am acquainted with any, I will speak on that which I am acquainted.

All relationships have rules. All rules should be discussed, edited, and agreed on before any commitment is made. The rules themselves are an amalgam of our lusts and goals. They are a representation of our expectations of self and the other. You should discuss with your partner your lusts. Are there any physical addictions: gambling, alcohol, or tobacco, other drugs, sex, etc.? or intellectual addictions: gaming, reading, writing, sex, etc.? Once you discuss your lusts with that potential mate, they should have some questions that require answers. Are you a slave to these lusts? Do I need to be involved with you in your pursuit of these lusts? If I choose not to be involved, will you remain involved with others? And still if I protest? And if I cannot develop enough interest in your lusts to become proficient enough to satisfy you, then am I willing to allow you that outlet? Even knowing that it may often include others who share your interest and are proficient at it? Or will I have to walk away?

The mature person will admit when another's demands have gone outside the parameters of what is currently acceptable for them, and make the appropriate decision. The immature person will ignore that two-dollar warning. They will rationalize every part of the situation they need to in order to convince themselves that it will work out. It will never work out. Anytime a person compromises who they are by childish reasoning, it will not work out. It may pass, but the damage will be done. Until then, though, they will suffer, and they will continue to suffer until they assume strength enough to make the proper decision. Of course, for the average person, like me, by the time they recognize the need for a decision, that two-dollar warning has ballooned to a two-thousand-dollar problem. At that point, they, like I, will be at a shortage of the resources necessary to easily solve the problem.

There is always that difficult decision though. I call it difficult because given the circumstances of a particular situation, figuratively, you may have to jump off a cliff and into oblivion in order to save who you are. Such a decision is a most difficult thing to commit to once you're invested for at least 2k: time and resources, and all of your insecurities begin to whisper sour somethings in your head. The fear follows, and it is a monster in the figure of your worst enemy, you, and it is unrelenting. It is here that most will show their immaturity by choosing the path of slavery rather than freedom. Is it really easier to be an uncomfortable slave than a free person of any condition?

Fear runs a plantation that always has room for one more. There are no house niggers on that plantation. Everybody works the fields twenty-four hours a day, seven days a week, three hundred and sixty-five days a year, in whatever elements, until you die! Or until you assume the strength to make the proper decision.

I find it unreasonable and illogical to submerse oneself in a hell of a relationship for any reason. For love? Once you have love, it is with you no matter where you are in relation to the object loved. It is not necessary to be in possession of the object loved. Fear of loneliness? I find it absurd considering the number and type of outlets, both external and internal, that we all have access to. I find it most absurd, though, because loneliness is a state of mind that has to be created and maintained internally. We do it to ourselves despite interacting with at least a good number of people every day. We torture ourselves despite having most or all of the popular distractions—such as books, technology, physical activity—at our disposal, and in spite of that internal subconscious voice (self) that has been trying to have a heart-to-heart conversation with the conscious mind (person).

The person, though, is so consumed by its being and the fog of fear that has settled about its being that it cannot hear nor see nor speak the truth. The truth is you are beautiful all by yourself. The truth is you are a perfect and complete person all by yourself. The truth is that you have driven yourself to madness because you have convinced yourself that you need a particular thing from a particular person; and indeed, this is true. The person is you. You have never validated yourself, and this is why you seek validation through the other person. The other person represents those things that you both accept and deny about yourself. So you validate your love of self by projecting on the other all that love you cannot give yourself. Conversely, you validate your hate of self by projecting all that angst on the other that you cannot upon yourself.

I spent many years becoming aware of this psychological pitfall. I spent many years in suspicion of my other than tried and proven abilities. It was not until I began to remove any and every perceivable thing—both physical and intellectual, that stood between me and my self, my God—that I began to feel free.

If whatever you believe cannot teach you how to be a complete and perfect physical reflection of God and conduit for the divine spirit, both in and of yourself, then perhaps it is your continued subscription to those ideals that limit your being and retard your abilities by attaching your potential to Satanic conditions that are and will remain outside of your ability to affect, that are the chains that bind you. Purge them. Rid yourself of them. You have suffered someone else's version of your life long enough. Abandon it and everything else that anchors you to self-negating ideology, and live.

Once this is done, or something like it done, I think that a person may be qualified to engage in any type of relationship and enjoy great success at it.

When the rules have been observed by a woman and man who are whole and aware, then I think the success of that interpersonal relationship is as sure as its failure to succeed if they are not whole and aware, or working toward that goal.

In closing, I will speak briefly on the topic of marital sex. I am certain in theory we all approve of it. It is the practice of it, however, or the lack of practiced skill, I believe, that has been the secondary cause of marital distress.

Let me begin by reminding us all that honesty is fundamental of all successful intra/extrapersonal relationships. The purpose of honesty is to facilitate freedom. Freedom cannot be had or enjoyed when a person tries to establish their being upon a bed of lies. The most powerful reasoning against it being that unless a person finds the strength to make right the wrong, then they must continue to fabricate new lies to support the original falsity. This becomes a tiresome routine and one that will ultimately levy some tariff upon the teller of these fibs.

My point is that total, or at least sufficient, knowledge of self will lead to honest intra/extra-expression. You will be satisfied with your person because you will have been enlightened by your self. You will be free, and freedom precludes the urge to embellishment or mendacity in a person's expression. When you are articulating the details of your lusts, desires, and goals, you can trust your word. The other person can trust your word. Now mutually beneficial decisions can be made.

No one ever needs to change. No person should ever have to become something other than what they will. No person should change for the purpose of attracting and securing another. It is a lie that will not stand up after the years have passed. It is better to be who you are. It is better that the other person be who they are. Hopefully, you two will be a natural complement, and walking life's path together a joy.

In the event, though, that you two are not a natural complement, not full and whole people and have committed to a relationship, you can have that joy. However, it will take much more work. Two who are on vibe seem to intuit each other's needs and wants and rise to meet or exceed whatever mind and skills are required to satisfy those with great energy; conversely, two who are not on vibe may not only have to learn the other's needs and wants, but also learn to accept them en route to having to accept having to satisfy them.

In other words, a woman and man should not have to struggle to accept and sate each other's pleasures. If we are right for each other, any intimate interaction will be as natural as breathing. When two are in love, s/he is as necessary to being as oxygen. I will allow my mate a great many pleasures with very few exceptions if she felt the need to pursue them. Because she and I have made a commitment to each other does not make either of us the other's master. However, mastering the self will be the solution to mastering your mate's needs and wants.

We are free. Being committed to a person should not be oppressive. You should not feel your abilities at expression stifled by another's insecurities. You are man and woman, husband and wife, and you should be secure in that. You are not merely girlfriend and boyfriend who may have a valid reason for maintaining some dignity by not entertaining all of the other's lusts. If you are married and have been for three or more years and are still denying your mate some pleasure they crave because it unsettles you, then you may have to recognize that you may have made a poor choice in mates. I assure you, if this person was the embodiment of the divine person that you have kept in your mind since the age when fantasies were still to be believed in, you would have no difficulty in becoming the king/ queen of whore to sate them. But the one you are with falls short to some measure and in some vital category, and this gives you pause. It is not that you cannot do. We are all capable of doing anything we can imagine. However, s/he cannot imagine doing that service for you, and there is the pause. Just as one cannot see beyond a choice they cannot understand, they are likewise helpless to do what they cannot imagine.

If your mate does not dominate your fantasies of every type of intimate/ sexual intercourse that a person can conceive, or as much as a person can take—and if after all these years you still have great pause if not deliberate avoidance of acts that you feel compromise the integrity of your person—then perhaps you have made a poor choice in a mate.

You should have chosen the person with whom you could be open and free with impunity from judgment, and then especially your judgment. You should have chosen the person who makes you want to live forever. You should have chosen the person whom you could not live without. When you find that person, I guarantee you that the discomfort that others regularly experience within their relationships will not visit you.

You will not have to suffer the indignity of learning your spouse has shared with another those intimate things you thought were reserved exclusively for you. You and your spouse will believe that there is not another on the face of the planet that can satisfy the way s/he can. Another will not be able to slip between you and your spouse of many years, and in the span of only a few months, draw your spouse's attentions from you using only those sensual delights that you would not do, or not do well enough.

Although it is not spoken of, it is entirely likely that your spouse may cross paths with another who is as sensually good to them as you are. If your spouse can love you for the reasons that they do, then it is only reasonable that they can love another for the same or other reasons. You were not your mate's first love, and if your mate is progressive, you won't be the last. Do not make your spouse a slave to your fears. Do not cause them to shut off the most beautiful attribute God has passed on to us—love—because you fear where their body might go in misunderstanding its purpose.

So my final words, be free.

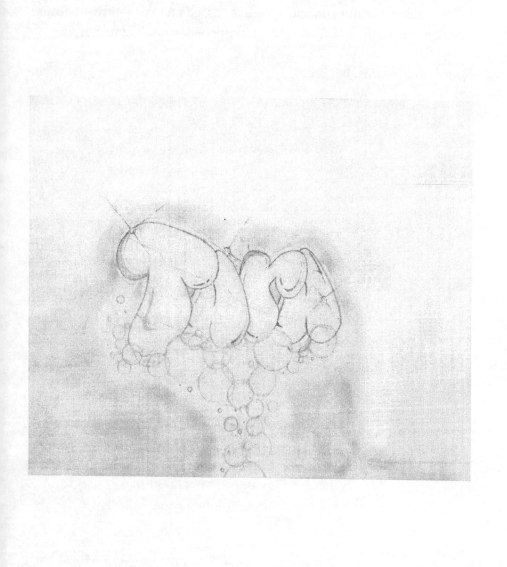

I Like

A kiss in the morning.
A whisper.
I like me and you.
Sun showers, sunflowers,
a hug, and the morning dew.
I like me and you.

Strolling hand and foot,
we turn and smile,
and everything's love.
Being here but not,
and all of everything stops
when she says a word.
Whether I perceive or not
is of no consequence,
I'll do her bidding anyway.
To please my queen is all important,
and what matters now is
I like you.

Flowers in bloom.
The color purple.
When you enter the room
I seem to smile.
The song of the birds.
A lover's moan.
Dancing naked in the dark.
Being nasty on the phone.

If I were to call,
what I would say is,
"Would you be with me
on the next rainy day?"
We could play
hide and go seek
and strip solitaire;
the last one to undress is it.

Does that seem a little silly?
I'll bet not as much as
if we are apart
when we wish to be together.
Well then,
this time is not to think.
I would rather
have you in my arms
and drink of your passion.

I like peace within me
and others within my sphere.
The music of the earth
soothes minds that don't know fear.
I like people of all kinds
and the ignorant of none.
Bright full moon in a sea of black,
after an orange sky,
resisting a setting sun.

Devotion

To feel her tight puckered eye
spread slowly.
Persistent gentle pressure
from my wet warm probing
orifice.

Strong desperate hands
and soft whispered words
of advice disguised as moans,
spread gloriously thick ass
just above my nose.
It rocks to and fro, teasingly,
out of tongue's reach.

My moral intentions
drip from her creamy smile.
Her hand holds tight
the pleasure end
of my long black leash.
Her anal collar
is around my servile neck.

Teach me devotion
and mine
would be a better service
to serve you
than to breathe.

Something I Love

I love nature.
I love my nature.
I love my auto-erotic nature.

I love pleasure.
It's always my pleasure.
I love the pleasure
from my auto-erotic nature.

My Dominatrix

Please believe me when I say,
I had no intention of being her slave,
but the will of this queen
cannot be denied.
She wants me.

Have me. Take me.
Make me yours.
Take me through the doors in your mind.
You want me on my knees and begging?
Darling, you don't understand,
I'm not the type.
But I might if you make me.
Treat me like a rodeo bull
and break me.
Girl, I hope you can,
but if you cannot,
I will not submit.

My dominatrix is my water,
my substance, and my life.
My master doesn't fuck around.

Tie me up, tie me down.
Whip me, beat me.
Lay me on your bed
and abuse me, ooh!
Who says pain isn't good.
I wouldn't change if I could.
I'll beg like a good man should.

I'm on my knees and behind you, mmm!
Keep me in check
with a riding crop.
Please bend over,
be my lollipop.
Mistress, please!
Tease me until I beg for your touch,
then touch me until I beg you to stop.
We'll assume the position
with you on top.
Only when you say so
I'll give the French tongue.
There, that's one; sixty-eight to go.

Please believe me when I say,
I have every intention on being her man,
because the will of this queen
is in motion.
She knows exactly what I need.
I submit.

Darkskin

I can't stand to hear a woman say
all men are about nothing but shit!

Skip all the crap
because I ain't the dirty Mac.
Don't you know I am
a handsome brown-eyed man?
And if you want,
we can swing your groove thang
through the night.
We'll do the freaks' delight,
or we might dance the tango.

I'm bugging, but I hope you gets my drift.
I ain't about the slanging and slinging
or bringing the noise
with those satanic toys.
I would rather wine and dine you.
We'll catch a jazz set,
then maybe shake a leg
and some other body parts
as the mood starts to hit me.
Is you with me?
This is an adventure to, lets say,
a prerequisite to some healthy foreplay.
Be it as it is,
I want to sweep you out of your shoes,
like Billy did Diana in "Lady Sings the Blues."
And all I have to do is try.
But I can't get up the nerve
to say hi, you are my darkskin.

Your darkskin has me like,
"Could I please have your number
so we could maybe chitchat.
Ya' know, just a little chitchat."
But I'm afraid you would be like,
"Scat you bat, hit the road, and the rest."
So I'm content to leave some leagues between us
and prefer to worship you from afar.
You are my star. Your darkskin.

Oooh . . .
What will I do when my darkness comes?
Probably lick it up, then begin again.
Am I your lover or your brother?
Don't confuse me with that talk
when I step to the dark
with the pep in my walk,
then slide in a seat with a grin on my face
and politely ask, "May I have a taste
of your nature?"
I mean the mind and soul if you please.
Knowledge me
about your needs and desires,
then we can do what comes with ease.
If you want to.
I want to make you my kin.
You are my earth, my moon, and my stars.
You are my darkskin.

Your darkskin has me like,
"Could I have your number
so we could touch souls?"
But I'm just not that bold.
So I'll leave the mad space
and worship you from afar.
You are my star. Your darkskin.

The Kiss
(an invitation)

What makes the kiss work? I think it is divine inspiration.

The kiss is the beginning of conversation between minds embattled in discovery. The uncharted territories that remain the mystery of people are the areas to be studied. The most mysterious thing about people is, why we do any of the things we do? Most specifically, why do we seek the kiss?

The kiss is the defining action of the hows and whys that are contained in some pair of eyes across a room. Sometimes the eyes are familiar and near to us, but most times they are not. Sometimes the lips have been kissed before, but most times they have not. Whatever the attitudes, the lips remain ripe with some mystery that must be pressed, nibbled, and licked until enlightenment is achieved.

The kiss begins as a desire. It is a desire to get beyond the kiss and do more; in fact, to do more while you kiss. In the kiss is the searching for that energy that binds minds and bodies. When we find what we were looking for, I think I will call it reason, our mind is again set in motion. It seeks to define the connection.

A portion of the kiss defined is the promise: I won't betray you. It is too often not honored.

The kiss is a fantasy. We often find the wanting of those visions the kiss conjures in our minds more desirable than the obtaining of those dreams.

The kiss is control. There is something to be said for a well-executed kiss and run. You go! After all, what could be more satisfying than to usurp a person's better judgments with so pleasant and nonlethal a tool as a kiss. When well-timed, it can leave them so desperately wanting as to put them at your disposal. It's always the simple pleasures, isn't it?

The kiss is not the beginning or end of passion, but it is among its strongest efforts at expression. It begins as subtly as love at first sight. Love at first sight is either a ridiculous excuse for the carnal lusts of people who want to fuck, or it is a term that describes how two spirits can recognize each other through the veil of being. In any case, people want to connect with each other despite those other considerations: societal standards and social mores, religious ideals, government sanctions, and marital status to name a few.

The kiss should never be subject to the rules that regulate your person. Your person is your mind and body. That action would reduce the kiss to a physical need and an intellectual desire. This is where the perversion takes place. Your body has needs that are crucial to its survival. Your mind maintains ideas that create the desires, which motivate your urge to fulfill those needs. It is an animal system because it is so committed to achieving physical comfort or avoiding physical discomfort.

The kiss though, while an animal action, is not motivated by the body for that is dead, but for the animating components of intellect and spirit. The kiss is not intellectual because it logically is not necessary to the perpetuity of the species. It is a spiritual action. In fact, it is as much a spiritual action as the variety of behavior people engage in that seeks to bring the person closer to divinity.

For example, one can desire that product of a kiss, a connection through reason. That reason, though, will never be pleasure for pleasure's sake. However, because of our misinterpretations of the desire for connection, animal pleasure has often been the result of the kiss. The effort then becomes as warped as the sapling when forced to grow in an inimical environment. It is bent away from the source of light and warmth. The kiss then becomes a means to a dishonorable end.

Then begins the effort to justify that end. We disguise our foul intentions in colorful costumes called *something like love*. These disguises are not designed to fool all of those external judgments, but to sate their expectations of the disgrace that love has become through passion. What a waste. The most authoritative of judgments is always that of our self, and that critic cannot easily be stifled. The others, however, will accept your lie. It makes for good drama.

The kiss should never be used as the means to an end. It is a powerful movement that is reflective of the spirit of love that motivates it. Love not only has no end, but is useless as a means because it demands nothing of the conscious mind. A means by its structure is the prelude to a demand (action) because something must always be done in order to affect some other thing. Love is eternal despite it being recognized or not. It is not a means because its existence is not conditional to affecting an action by any other thing. It is a part of the cornerstone of all life. It is the melody that all life plays. It is like the vowels of our language: *a, e, i, o, u*, and it makes all expression of being possible. It makes life worth living. It is a very humble usher of an eternity of possibilities. One needs only to check those maladjusted deliberations at the door and read the lips.

The want of the kiss and all of its fruit, though, never fails as motivation. Those who have known the better efforts will be hard-pressed to determine whether this is a good or bad thing. It is good when good self-analysis and sound judgment are used before, during, and after the kiss. It is bad when they are not.

The kiss is possibly our oldest and dearest nonparental physical acquaintance with affection. It is six years old in the bushes in front of the house. It is the wrinkled face of a twelve-year-old who feigns displeasure at having received a peck on the cheek from a love concern in front of everyone. It is that clumsy first embrace and press of lips you encountered in high school. It was your first serious attempt, and you were eager, but you did not know why. Now it is older. Though, it still attempts to disguise itself behind shields such as displeasure or indifference. In fact, to many, it is still a mystery.

The kiss is proof that we are still capable of expression from the divine perspective. The longing for the press of lips against our own is evidence of our intention to be recognized by some other spirit. Some dream about that embrace all day long.

Stranger after stranger pair of lips catch my gaze. Stranger after stranger pair leave their American brown imprint on my mind. I want more. I often want more than to fantasize about our encounters. As my imagination is especially strong, I have conjured images as tasty as Cinnabon Glaze-coated fingers. However, I never go too far with the dream for two reasons. Two, to imagine too much would ruin the fantastic possibilities of a real encounter with that person in ways that only those who fantasy would understand. One, because the kiss is pure, and it is my goal to discover all of its potential by word of mouth. A person's kiss can tell you all you need to know. Therefore, you owe it to yourself to take it in slowly and in small parts. Taste those lips and feel what they are talking about.

The kiss is on supple lips that form a wide Kool-Aid smile from the suggestions a kiss is famous for. The kiss is on sensitive parts that tingle horribly when touched in that way. The kiss is between soft thighs. Its preference is for the delight of its kind. Again, you do not know why, but you've got to. Humbly, you bow, whispering a language that only lips would understand. Lips know what lips like.

There is no greater aspiration for the kiss than to know its efforts at recognition effective. There is no greater joy than to recognize another.

Devotion is the key. Within the kiss, males and females everywhere seek to feel and connect with themselves, but through the perceptions of the other. The one is as much an expression of the many as the many is the one. With that kiss we seek to find the kind of unconditional validation of self that is inherent of love. With that kiss we try to become a version of the model that motivated us, our parents. Hopefully, there was a loving parental example. Loving or not, though, we tend to become some reflection of what created us. And despite whatever was wanting in our rearing, we still seek love. The anticipation is in discovering if we are ready to be everything our parents were and were not. That kiss begins that journey.

The kiss is passionate because it is a reflection of how we view ourselves. The kiss has transcended age, gender, and culture. It is powerful as even close relatives have fallen to the force of its movement. And while it is not the beginning nor end of being, it is its preferred means of expression. Kiss me!

About 110 Days
(friendly suggestions)

These are some of the activities I have imagined a husband and wife could practice together. These suggestions of alternative interactions are conceived for a man and woman who are dedicated to the practice of celebrating adulthood. They are slow and fast, passive and aggressive, submissive and dominant, and all shades of gray between. There is only one condition—that is that each person be sufficiently free of mind as to allow themselves and their mate an open and honest expression of themselves while on this road of discovery. Curiously, as free of mind as a child before it learns ignorance. Hopefully, neither party is a slave of those patterns of thinking, behaving, and interacting that as staples of some tradition have maliciously represented people. Be free to enjoy being.

Day 1: Creation

They have been trapped at work all day. They reach out to each other with their minds. He fantasizes about her. He imagines how soft her skin is. He remembers how it falls on him as easily as the night does earth and covers him in divine blessing. Her lips are built to be the conduit for the divine word. They are as thick and strong as the love sounds that pass through them. Her eyes are as deep as one's gaze to the farthest light in the night sky, and he has become lost traveling that space. Her nose inhales God's exhale, regenerating the circle, and her body is replenished once more. Her hair is like a thick mist of ancient memories. Each strand is the contribution of an ancestor, and every one is made of a lifetime of thought. They are the essence of order as each follows its certain path. Those paths cross and weave along their twisted journey, creating a divine purpose that becomes locked. The cumulative effort of her divine ancestry hangs about her head, patiently waiting for her contribution, though it has seen it already.

He believes she can fanta-see him from whatever place she may be at the moment. He believes she can feel his warmth and see his face in her mind the same as he experiences hers in his. He continues to work as they continue to recollect each other in those intimate ways that make the time pass quickly. Each wears only a sly smirk as proof of some fantastic goings-on behind their eyes.

Finally, quittin' time arrives, and they rush home to meet each other. He sees her, she sees him, and they meet at the front door. They already had their shirts unbuttoned and belts loosened, and they both fumbled with keys in their haste. They unlock the door, step into their home, and their shoes are flipped into the near wherever. They embrace.

Every time they get together, it is like the first time they got together. Every time is like that first time when she realized that it was he and he that it was she, and they that it was God in all of creation. And not a thing else in the world moved but them.

They pass the next bit of eternity whispering to each other the secrets of life that God reveals to his children when they embrace love like this.

Day 2: The Antidrug
All day long, her mouth has been wet for his dick. It is fetish worthy, the size and shape of it. It is beauteous. The taste of it, especially that "been hangin' around all day long" taste, wets her mouth. When that prize has been locked away all day is when the scent is strong. She can follow its trail from the front door clear to whatever room she finds him in. Being a companion oral addict, he understands her condition. So she will always find him with the object of her daily desire ready for her devotion. This is the kind of understanding and cooperation that they hold for each other.

It is comfortable in her mind where she stores all familiar things both loved and lusted. It is as comfortable in her hands and mouth as her fingers and tongue. Like those parts, she can't imagine trying to articulate her appreciation of life without it. For that reason, she adores him every day that she can.

He knows that she needs him to do nothing more than lie back, relax, and let her get him high. She will occupy herself at retrieving his sperm. It is her One a Day. In the interim, though, she will pass the time training that beautiful dick and her parts to some point of mutual arousal and gratification.

Oral sex, it is her antidrug.

Day 3:
He needs to celebrate her.

He first prepares the stages. The bedroom he sets with a variety of flowers placed in seven vases and arranged in a circle on the floor around the bed. Behind the flowers are three candles on three-foot-high stands. The stands form the points of a triangle around the circle. The bed is covered by a thick gold comforter and six large pillows.

The bathroom he sets with a peppermint-scented candle placed on a corner shelf. The room is freckled with red rose petals on the floor, in the sink and toilet, and in the hot bath he prepared. Finally, he sets a wineglass and a chilled bottle of wine on a tray next to the tub.

He bathes her with terry cloth mitts in soy-scented bath soap. He takes care to cover every inch. He pays careful attention to those inches found in those hard-to-reach nooks and crannies. His hands are slow and purposeful. She can feel the soft fibers of the mitt gliding over her brown. Those fibers move as if they were her very body hairs being moved by his warm breath. The stroke of his hands reminds her of the first time they met. Then his soft brown eyes washed over her body, caressing and warming her. His touch made her feel like fertile earth then, and it still does.

After the bath, he lightly towel dries her. He escorts her to the bedroom and places her on the bed like a precious thing. He begins a light touch massage using only his fingertips. They dance like warm raindrops along her body until they graduate to a full shower of touch aided by warm vitamin E oil. He continues this method until every inch of her has been soothed.

His kiss has a conscious, a mind, and a voice. He incorporates his lips into service, and they start at her feet where his fingers left off. His lips interact with her body like an entity apart from him, but governed by him. They both seek to drive her out of body.

Out of body—that level of sensual/intellectual high where the past, present, and future become one moment, peace.

Day 4: Duty

He knows her lusts. It is his job to know her lusts.

He forgoes his usual workout at the gym to perform a routine at home. It is a half-hour warm-up that includes stretching on the floor mat and running on the treadmill. His workout is push-ups, pull-ups, and jumping jacks; also bench presses, incline dumbbell presses, and shoulder presses; next, it is crunches, leg raises, and squat thrusts; and finally, it is all done while wearing God's favorite color: naked, and to some nice jazz music.

She sets up a beach lounge chair covered with a large white towel. She gathers her snack. It is some mixed dried fruits and a warm cup of ginseng tea—no sweetener—and lies naked and positioned in the chair to enjoy the show.

Day 5: The Slave Mind

He submits to her. There is something in him that wants to as there is something in her that wants him to. They both occasionally feel inspired to tyranny, and at times, these instances can only be articulated through acts of debauchery. Today, he is her property. He wants to feel the kind of fulfillment that can only be had through self-discipline, as governed by her ruthless application of principles of gender dominance.

He wants to be her dog on a leash. He wants to beg for the pleasure of being in her presence. He wants to be degraded in exchange for the delight of tasting her. He wants to lick her bare feet and toes after she has walked barefoot about their home. He wants her to demand he use his mouth to make squeaky clean her twitching anus, and that after a particularly steamy shit.

He needs to assume a positive slave-itude. It is an intellectual perspective that can open the door to insights on the joys of his being and her being; in addition, being whole and part, or master and slave; and finally, the difference between being slave or free, and animal or human.

Day 6:
They just want to fuck.

They both understand that this is not for the sake of the other, but for self. It is a selfish act that feeds that never-evolving beast within. That animal within is void of everything reasonable except the instinct to copulate.

There is no high contemplation, no creativity, and no accountability. That is what fucking is, sex without romance, passion, or responsibility. Fucking is sex without the benefit of the satisfaction of knowing and meeting your partner's higher needs.

Their needs now, though, are to honor no other obligation than the impulse to orgasm. So this is a safe fuck. It is an intense fuck. It is an aggressive five-minute missionary fuck that ends in panting, perspiration, and passing off to slumber.

Day 7: A Day of Rest
They take a long walk in a park. They walk hand in hand. They giggle and laugh like adults who can still remember the joy of youth, but who have successfully transformed that chaotic energy into a disciplined joy of life. They sit in an embrace at the foot of a great tree and cry joyfully at the beauty of the sun setting on the horizon. It reminds them of the potential of things.

Day 8:
He is oppressive today. He binds her to the bed with black nylon four-point restraints. He then begins an evening long torture of her frame with a feather and a coffee straw.

The goal is simple. He aims to teach her the joys of being helpless and in the care of he who adores her. He aims to teach her to enjoy her physical person, in part and in whole. Finally, he aims to demonstrate the joys that even the simplest tools can help to produce when animated by someone who is devoted to your pleasure.

He likes to work with the long dark feather of a raven. He works that dark quill spitefully over her parts. He pauses frequently to soothe the tingling trail the feather made with soft kisses. He trains each part: foot, lower leg, upper leg, hip and waist, abdomen and breast, shoulder and upper arm, forearm and hand, and neck. He moves methodically in that order until finally, her face lies in expectation of that torturous pleasure that has her entire left side alive with ghostly bolts of stimulation.

He starts at her ears. He brushes along them softly until she says when. *When* is a sound he has grown accustomed to. It can be a shriek, a sigh, a moan, or some other indication she has reached her current peak of tolerance. The sound she makes tells him she has been filled to capacity and needs a moment of release. He gives her that moment with the kiss.

He knows not to overfill her because of the danger of ruining the experience for them both. So he continues slowly up her hairline to her forehead, and then a kiss. He brushes away from the center of her face, and then the kiss. He strokes gently along her nose and over her eye, and again the kiss.

Finally, he comes to his lust, her lips—they're juicy. He fills them with the energy that the soft stroke of the feather is famous for. He fills them until he can see they are ready to burst. He then soothes them with his. He comforts them with his. He mingles the energy of his devotion with hers, and they explode with creative passion in a language that only devoted lips can speak.

It is then, when he is on top of her and they are face-to-face, that the urge to continue beyond the kiss dominates him. He stops, gathers himself, and begins the second half of the treatment.

He discards the feather and produces a shortened coffee straw. He begins the routine at her lips and traces the exact path he took with the feather. Now, though, he is on her right side and traveling south.

He is sure to be as careful, as attentive, and as devoted to her for the length of her body. He is sure to build in his desire to want to show his devotion for his lust. Those things she knows he lusts because all of her lips need kissing. He will build until he is full of devotional energy and he has no other recourse but to share the whole of it with her lips.

She finds his selflessness leaves her speechless.

Day 9:
She begins her tour of astrology starting with Aquarius, Pisces, and Aries.

She intends to guide him carefully along the route she laid in her mind. She put her mind to the work of creating a magnificent reproduction based on the graphic generality of a black light poster. This poster featured African American males and females demonstrating the sexual positions associated with astrological signs. She will show him how to fashion a reality out of her fantasies. He will submit to her every necessary control because he is her tool. He trusts her practiced hands.

She is careful to keep control over them both. She works not to lose control of either and spoil the session by turning it into a fuck—that action that lacks selfless purpose.

She moves him easily into the first position and holds it. She walks it slowly through creation until she has nurtured it long enough and must let it go. She eagerly replaces it with the next position, also nurturing it, and then finally the last.

She uses her mind and their bodies to develop each position to its fullest potential of the moment. She explores the subtleties of her mind and their bodies. She makes detailed mental notes of the movement of each, hers and his, how they move together, and the mind and body wetting energy that they can produce when in harmony.

She is disciplined in following her dream to the moment because harmony is her goal. She mimics every movement and sound she visioned until she embraces the goal—that goal being the harmony of wife and husband. His goal is being that willing man to help it happen. And it happens exactly as she saw it in her mind.

Day 10: Toys
They view the exhibit of West African art at the art museum. They swing by an Indian restaurant on Sansom Street for lunch. They take a well-planned moment to browse the selection at the adult-shop area.

They find that shopping together is as much fun as people say, but especially when you share a common interest. Today they are interested in preparing for what experiments in pleasure may come at some special future date.

So they shop. They not only shop for accessories for those acts they already know they like but also to accommodate for those acts that have yet to be experienced.

Day 11: The Fetish
She subdues him with the two most intuitive hands ever to caress a member. She is convinced that with the proper motivation, she can get him to blow a load at least four feet high. Her practice today is concerned with that and that alone.

First she lays him on their bed naked and on his back. She then produces four pieces of hosiery. She stretches then tightly twists the first piece until it resembled a rope. She then binds his hands together and above his head and lashes them to the headboard. She folds a hand towel and places it under his right knee. She then wraps the second piece of twisted hosiery around the knee, ties it, and pulls his knee to his side and binds it to the headboard. She repeats this process for the left leg. She then props his head up with some pillows; after all, she understands that visual stimulation is an important tool on this job. Finally, she removes her cotton panties and stuffs them into his mouth. She secures them by tying the fourth piece of hosiery over his mouth. Now that the subject is prepared, she can begin.

She starts slowly kissing and caressing his thighs and legs. She allows her mouth to glide down to his ass. She purposely avoids his divine U and moves her mouth and hands up to his abdomen, then to his chest. When he shows ready, which is always proved by the rate of his panting and the degree of intoxication on his face, she graduates her touch to a more aggressive kiss with lots of gentle gnawing and licking. Her hands instinctively become more occupied with his divine U, that line starting from the top of the crack of the ass down and up to the navel. She is practiced in his pleasure, so she cuts her method's intensity back to soft to allow him an exhale. When she builds him up again, she will gradually add another floor or two. Each floor represents a method and intensity of pleasuring her man. The techniques are the variation on her method. For example, anybody can suck on some balls, but a methodical technician (spouse) develops ways to suck those balls that force the man to seek that attention habitually. It is the process of mastering one's mate, and it is the least they can do for each other so they can both get high.

She builds her oral skills on him slowly so she can hear him testify with that deep man's moan. It happened when her hands replaced her mouth on his dick and balls and her mouth dropped to his anus. She kissed it, licked it, sucked it, tongue-fucked it; and all the while, her hand never missed a stroke. She continues with this until he again showed ready to ejaculate, then she pauses to find the beads.

The beads. It is a nylon string with a pyramid of five pearly spheres. The largest is about the size of a ping-pong ball. She uses only spit and pressure to push each bead into his ass. She soothes each insertion with her tongue, which naturally lubricates his anus for the next insertion. She continues with this until he has taken the entire string. She uses the pause to segue to the next phase.

The hands. They begin on him softly and slowly. It is as if she has an eternity to fondle that beautiful thing of a male principle. She trains it to full erection and maintains it with a steady graduation of her technique from simple to practiced. She makes certain that with each shift, she leaves him at the brink of orgasm.

The mouth chimes in lending assistance to her hands with his genital package. She tortures him in this manner for what seems to him like three days, but was no longer than thirty minutes. She allows him to come to the edge of orgasm many times before allowing him a short period for exhale. He had never appreciated how many seconds were in a pause until being subjected to this treatment.

Then she is back at him. Her hands and mouth work vigorously on his dick, balls, and asshole. She is riding his joy, he is riding her devotion, and they take each other still higher. She feels him nearing his peak. Soon she will not be able to discourage the conclusion of this beautiful session.

She begins on the beads, tugging at them gently, and this coaxes his anus open from the inside. The energy of her devotion grows as she hears his approval at birthing his first bead, the smallest. She steps up the action of her hands and mouth with the slow extraction of each bead, except for the last and largest. Each extraction made him sing his approval ever louder and more desperately than the previous. Then she felt him at his peak, so it was time.

Her one hand massages his stiffness with the stroke she knew could master him. Her mouth houses his scrotum and tugs at it softly so as to stretch his sack as her tongue washes and massages his balls. The finger of her other hand pulls on the ring that pulled the string that pulled that final bead; as a result, it exits to a chorus of his moans of pleasure at the greatest ejaculation he had ever felt. She realizes her dream as she watches stream after stream of his cream rise into the air to its apex several feet high and falls in a cloudy shower sprinkling his body and the sheets until his exhaustion.

She licks up all evidence of any goings-on that dotted his body. Then her mouth and hands engulfs his penis and makes damn well certain that every drop of the vitamins have been extracted. He made a hearty but futile attempt to escape her oral method on his still-oversensitive member. So he submits to it and lets his muffled cries and moans of pleasure dissolve into indifference. She then kisses him with the passion that a wife has for a husband. Then she unties him.

Day 12: The Thing

He has always had great adoration for every part of her. She is his fetish in part and in whole. It is that ass, though, that brings him to his knees. He becomes as pious as any true believer of anything that has ever been worshiped when in its presence. It is that ass that demands from him a particular devotion. It is particular because of the intensity of the energy he puts into his adoration, and accordingly because that ass stands out as one of three areas he worships with great zeal, and the other two are her sets of lips.

He watches her. She knows it wets his mind. Perhaps it is inherently a dynamic that neither of them have the words to describe or control. It is that ass that she has nurtured all these years, though incidentally, and she has still not tapped into its greater potential. She has only allowed it to be their muse, and as a result, they have tapped into much pleasurable, creative inspiration because of it.

She dresses it for him. She may go through four or five outfits that day in the process of inciting him to worship. It is not as if he is resisting. He wants to bow to her and probably more than she wants him to bow to her. There are days, though, when he is a more difficult nut to crack. At those times, she needs to find the proper combination of elements to put him in a more compliant frame of mind.

An all-day fashion show should do it. She will start the day in painted-on jeans. He has often stated through his variety of responses what the sight of that denim being strained to its limits by the force of her thickness does to him. She may then move into a sundress with its very feminine allure, and this especially when it clings to her form. Then perhaps, she may squeeze into some daisy dukes, bicycle shorts, way-too-small cutoff sweat shorts, or anything shiny like PVC, leather, and those metallic fabrics. As the night approaches, she may try on something in a thong or something silky and crotchless. Although he has always been weak for plain old white cotton. Finally, in the latest moments of the night, she allows him an unencumbered view of *the thing*. He refers to it as if it is apart from her. He says the very air and space about it seems to caress it like a knowing lover. He truly adores that big brown thing.

He will spend the day hugging it, kissing it, rubbing his face in it, and then especially in the crack; after all, that is were salvation is. He will wash it, oil it, and massage it. He will adorn it in fresh flower petals and unconditional submission. He will enjoy this part because it is her part, and she is delighted by his adoration.

Day 13: Animal Instinct
She uses black liquid latex and some bristles from an old brush to disguise him as her favorite animal, a black panther. He uses gold latex and her old strawberry blonde wig to disguise her as his, a lioness.

They stalk each other through their home. He lost her momentarily because he stopped to set the appropriate mood music: Kool and the Gang's "Jungle Boogie." He picks her scent up around the dining room, but she is gone when he arrives. He follows the fragrance of her flower—the one that blossoms with a nectar that makes a simple drone want to tap. It leads him to their bedroom. He creeps to the door and falls to all fours. He peers around the doorframe and into the room, scanning for her. He sees her watching him. She is crouched behind the corner of the bed, and their eyes lock. A playful fight ensues, and this leads to a chase. He pursues his pussy down the stairs, into the living room, dining room—and some chairs were knocked over in his excitement to get at her—through the kitchen, and back into the living room where they finally take each other down on the carpet. There is a flurry of pawing, gnawing, licking, and biting: then, the sounds of animal copulation fill the rooms.

Day 14: Health and Fitness
The point of the day is to reinforce the importance of health and fitness. They start the day with an early morning run, five miles, then a light breakfast and sex. They move on to aerobic stretching and military calisthenics, sex, and then a nap.

Later that afternoon, they take a fifty-mile bicycle ride on the mountain trails. They only took one break, and that was to have sex in the thick of some large trees, brush, and ground cover.

That evening, they settle into a challenging yet relaxing session of sexcathalon. It is a game they created that challenges the participants to integrate sex with exercise. It has proven to be both intellectually and physically challenging, and good for their cholesterol.

They both subscribe to the idea that to maintain one's mental endurance and strength as much as one's physical endurance and strength for the purpose of pleasuring one's partner will never be considered hazardous enough to warrant a Surgeon General's Warning.

Day 15:
Her tour of astrology continues with Taurus, Gemini, and Cancer. (See day 9.)

Day 16: The Soft Touch
First he clips, files, and smooths her fingernails. Then he clips, files, and polishes her toenails. Then he moves to her pubes, which she keeps thick and high, and this is mostly by his request. He says he loves to pull her scent through her bush as he tastes her; besides, it tickles his face. He trims and shapes her bush with barbers' scissors, a straight razor, and some soapy water.

Finally, he arrives at her head. He begins with a wash and conditioning that moves steadily into a hot oil treatment and scalp massage. He ends the evening by brushing her hair until the stroke of the brush weighs her eyes down.

The last thing she remembered was that familiar calm that is the sound the stroke of the brush makes in her hair. It became a lullaby.

Day 17:
Penetration is her obsession today. She wants to feel the eye-twitching, waiting-to-exhale joy that good penetration is, and she wants it repeatedly over the next few hours. She wants to find that quiet place where a person's mind goes when the moment is right.

She trains him like her favorite dildo. She gives herself the head only, and then over a long period of minutes. She urges him to piston it slowly. She wants only slight pressure so that it can convince her opening to tighten to feel him. All at once, she gives him the command for more dick. She firmly grasps each of his tight ass cheeks and pulls him softly into her. Some more inches slide effortlessly into her. There is the joy. She loves to feel herself opening to his size. She will have him feed them to her slowly. He embraces her tightly, giving her his addition and some kisses for a brief moment, until she exhales. She then taps his ass, and he withdraws.

She repeats the process, adding the soft sweeping of his soft and swollen head from her clitty to her well and back, and more inches. Pull. Push. Tap. She repeats the process again, but adds a hard stab with only the head of his stressed tool, then the sweep, and the full length of him. Pull. Push. Tap.

The discipline is to remain focused on the goal even as her opening twitches in anticipation of the next series of stimulation, and specifically in spite of her young girls' pleas for immediate satisfaction. That young girl argument is strong. But the discipline for them both is to develop the strength of will to evolve every part of their selves/persons. This includes the sex.

So they nurture those young parts in spite of their ardent protests and continue. The soft sweep, the stab, the slow piston of every swollen inch. Pull. Push. Tap. She will repeat this process for as long as it takes to reach the goal. She will constantly build in technique and minutes until she finds that quiet place she was looking for. The eye of the storm.

Day 18: Discipline
He is feeling a little abusive.

He positions her nakedness on an iron canopy bed. She is on her knees. He binds her with white cotton rope. She does not struggle. There is no need for that this session. She will be his willing subject because he needs to do this. They have needed to do the many acts they have performed on each other over the years. All of these acts are necessary to the maintaining of their sexual sanity. These acts are performed mostly with the need of the experience to say what they do or do not enjoy. Some of these acts have been incorporated into their lifestyle, and others will never be ventured into again.

Her dark meaty ass is held high in the air atop her thick legs. The round bottom of a black latex butt plug peaks at him from between her cheeks like a dark playful eye halfway into a sly wink. The end of a thick black dildo hangs teasingly out of her vagina like a playful tongue stained in licorice. Her knees are dug into the mattress, and her ankles are bound by padded leather shackles. The shackles are kept apart by a two-and-half-foot metal rod, and they are attached by two-inch lengths of chain. Her back slopes down from the globes of ass meat at forty-five degrees and eases into her torso and face that both rest on a large pillow. A black nylon strap with Velcro fasteners on its ends keeps a thick black latex cock gag secured in her mouth. Her arms are pulled forward to the headboard, and each is secured at the wrist to a bedpost by that same cotton rope. Finally, her neck sports a slave collar that is connected to a chain that is fastened with police-style handcuffs to the frame of the headboard.

He introduces the sting of a leather strap to the bottoms of her bare feet. He does not engage her violently though. It is not his intention to cause her any injury or pain. He only seeks to create some motivational discomfort. So he proceeds aggressively until he can hear in her muffled cries that she is motivated.

There is another sign of how motivated she is. Every strike of the strap on her feet causes all of her sphincter muscles to contract against the phalluses stuffing them. The resistance urges the muscles to squeeze ever tighter in an effort at relief of sympathetic response. This energetic exchange makes all of those openings very wet and cooperative.

After a resounding strike of the strap on her feet, he pauses to admire his work. Her pussy had contracted so strongly during the treatment that it ejected the dildo. Still, though, it twitched in anticipation of being fed. He drops to his knees, places his mouth to her wet spot, and began the kiss. He makes sure to concentrate most of his attention on her swollen clitoris. As good as his mouth sounds like it is to her, he determines that her young girl is much too ravenous to be sated by tongue. He rises to his feet, positions himself, and slides into her every bit of dick he had available. She, of course, lets him know that every bit of his dick was just what she wanted. He, of course, then continues to give her some aggressive dick until he explodes inside of her.

He pauses to collect himself, then back to the treatment. He applies the sharp sting of a large flyswatter to the cheeks of her ass while asking strange questions like, who invented the semicolon? He used this method to wake her from her bliss, confuse her, and to let her know it is once again time to be disciplined. After some time, he abandons the flyswatter and retrieves and applies a broad wooden cooking spoon to her very alert buttocks until she lets him know that she was once again attentive to his method.

He throws his knees into the bed directly behind her. He bows to her sensitive ass and adorns it with kisses, gentle sweeps with his tongue, and firm caressing with his hands. His hands work their way to the butt plug and ease it out of her. She lets go a sound of relief as its fullness escapes her. That moment of relief is intensified when his mouth applies its soothing skills to her still-gaping anus. That simple feeling of relief was transformed into that kind of electric sensation that will leave a mouth wide-the-fuck open. He licked her stretched asshole until he could no longer stand not to be in her. He mounted her in one quick movement and slid his full length into her rectum. She, of course, gave him notice that once again every bit of his dick is just what she needed; accordingly, he continued to drop every bit of hard, hot dick into her ass for as long as he could stay disciplined to that pleasure. He would be on her for quite a while because his system was still recharging from her pussy. In hindsight, this is the reason he took her pussy first, so he could stay rigid in her ass until she begged him for mercy.

Day 19: The Moments
They hurry home to a shower and a meal. They sit naked and cuddled on the couch with a thin sheet for cover and enjoy a classic romance, a comedy, and a drama: *Porgy and Bess*, *Purlie Victorious*, and *Man Friday*. They enjoyed that embrace that they have become used to from each other until slumber had them both against its bosom.

Day 20: The Experiment
She lays him on a towel on the bed and shaves his pubes and anal area clean with a bowl of warm water, soap, and a straight razor. Once clean, she begins oral devotions. This naturally leads to the purposeful tonguing of his asshole and that until she converts him into a one-man choir who is motivated to sing them both into heaven.

Her sex is intuitive in part and whole. Her hand begins the expert work on his member that only his good right hand has ever been capable of. The other hand expands the treatment by adding a four-inch black latex dildo that she works into his ass when her tongue abandons it to suck and lick his balls and dick.

She continued this assault, keeping his eyes sedated, his mouth wet and only able to emit his pleasure song in desperate breaths, and his penis as rigid as a penis could possibly be without becoming a health hazard. Her treatment is precision. Its success requires she changes her tools every fifteen to twenty minutes. She graduates the intensity and skill level of her hand-and-mouth work to coincide with the promotion of the phalluses from the four-inch, to the seven-inch, to the ten-inch dildo that takes his breath away and makes him succumb to the treatment with that throaty whine that males emit.

He blew his cream through the air in milky streams that dotted his stomach and chest, the sheets and pillows, and the wall and floor. She fit her mouth over his still-ejaculating member and began to encourage it with a vigorous sucking. Her hand eased the dildo out of his ass while her mouth delighted itself with hard, wet dick. He let go another wave of semen with a groan that moved through his body like a tsunami. It washed itself out in one last great effort in her mouth.

She came to rest on top of him. They kiss. They hug. They fall to sleep.

Day 21:
He wants to kiss. He loves to kiss. So they sit in the balcony of a movie theater and kiss.

Her lips are juicy, so he licks them, pecks them, and presses his to them. He does not look her in the eyes. His gaze refuses to move from her lips. She knows he adores them, so she keeps them from him. She makes him fight for them. This raises his aggression level. Today, his assertiveness is the price of admission to her pleasure. Once he subdues her, she submits them to him. Her lips show their appreciation for his interest and energy by being thick, soft, and intelligent.

Day 22: Heavenly Body
She wants to masturbate. This is simply that day when no touch is more desirable than her own.

He knows this because he knows her eyes when they get so blank that only the most severe meditation is behind them. He knows her body when it moves with such determination as to be proof that she has a plan that day. But most of all because rather than the alarm clock bringing him from slumber this five thirty, Monday morning, it is the sounds she makes when her fingers are being especially good to her. It is that sopping and gooshing an orifice can make when it has been very well stimulated and every fluid in the body seems to want to congregate there. It is because of all this, and the body and mind being connected sympathetically, that she lets go the most stirring moans and squeals that she, at any strength, could not hold back; and anyway, she did not want to. She enjoys listening to her own pleasure. It is a dominating source of stimulation for her.

He wakes up enough to catch the last few minutes of her reveille. She pauses in those moments after, then rises and joins him in the process of readying for work. As he began minutes before her, he left home minutes before she should have. He worked the whole day with her sight, sound, and scent bound around his mind like a helpful string tied around a finger. It would remind him of what duty he has to come home to.

He arrives home and hurries through his routine of shaking off the work persona. He rushes up the stairs and to the bedroom to find her as he knew he would. She is on her back on the bed, naked, sweaty, and furiously engaged with herself. There is only the light of three basic candles in the room. There is one on each table on each side of the head of the bed, and one on the shelf by the door. She is concentrated. She is powerful. She is the source gravity for all things within the room, and all things in this system evolve around her and because of her. He is drawn to her.

He is first pulled into an outer orbit as he marveled at how magnificently the candlelight helped her brown light up the room. Then closer, and his marvel turned to excitement at the prospect of discovering some bits of that divine knowledge that is contained in that heavenly body that dominates his mind's eye. He seeks the knowledge of the whos, whens, whys, and wheres of his being. He believes the answers are within them both and can only be discovered by merging his intellect and hers. So he flies closer still until his body softly collides into hers. He cannot recollect at what point his clothes were burned off by her heat, but when they touched, he was pure.

He assumed a position in her orbit. For now, he well represents the element of passion that our moon incites in those spirits susceptible to emotion. This is a skill that her other necessary satellites cannot demonstrate. Still those others orbit about them: a four-inch black latex dildo with a fat head, a thick seven-inch heavily veined black latex dildo, one small vibrator, and a string of anal beads. He plays his position. He kisses her passionately on her mouth, and her mouth responds instinctively, accepting the passion.

He plays his position in veiling those inanimate satellites in his shadow. His passion covers them and masks their movement like the night sky does this earth's waters. He works to make them all compliant to the needs of the two. Once all of these items have become true to her form, she finds herself made a new thing. She feels reborn by that catalyst of divine no/ things that she and her satellites have become. He has played his position in obeying the laws that govern him, moving him slowly away, and those satellites caught in his shadow. Once again, they are on her periphery. Each settles into its place still brilliant from having been touched by her, and she shines brown in his mind's sky.

Day 23: Copulation
He wants pussy. He wants to get wet. He wants her under him so he can feel the enveloping warmth of her limbs. He wants to feel her exhalation warm his neck as it is forced from her center by each and every deep strong stroke he treats her to.

He wants to marvel at her profile as she lies on her stomach. The dark skin. The soft lines. The drowsy eyes. The drool puddle spreading under her face as saliva leaks from her mouth. She cannot close her lips around the sounds created by the force of the hot dick he is dropping into her from behind in a decidedly aggressive manner.

He wants her in his arms as he tours the floor. He wants her lips on his, her arms around his neck, and the weight of her body an inspiration to keep his machine in motion for their mutual pleasure.

He wants her from behind and bent over the back of the living room couch. He wants her from behind and standing in the hall near the bedroom. He wants her face-to-face while she stands against the dining room wall, balanced on her right leg with the left leg held vertically against his shoulder and pressed to her body by his weight.

He fucks her long, aggressively, and with a seemingly unquenchable energy for her form, her moans, and her scent. He takes her wherever and however he finds her, and she submits to him wherever and however he finds her.

Day 24: Black Light
She continues her tour of astrology with Leo, Virgo, and Libra. (See day 9.)

Day 25: Dive
They go out for drinks at a barely legitimate but popular dive of a bar that sports a live band that plays blues covers. All of the waitresses are working their way through school, and the bartender looks like he has spent at least some time in someone's penal system. Whatever is on the menu is not recommended; however, a man or woman on their knees under a table and only partially hidden by the tablecloth would not raise any unwanted attention.

Day 26: Shock Value
Another long yet typical day at the grind. You had your tea, your conversation, and your work. You had your conversation, your lunch, and your work. Finally, you had your work, your conversation, and the journey home.

He enters the home and relieves himself of his work baggage. The coat goes in the closet, and so do the shoes. He replaces the shoes with those fuzzy brown bear slippers that are the most comfortable he owns. He puts on some music, Dianne Reeves, "Bridges." He sits in the lounge chair in the candlelit living room and rides that beautiful music to a soft place in his imagination.

She enters the home thirty-five minutes after him. She gives her coat and shoes the same treatment, but opts to keep her feet naked. She notices him sitting in his chair with waves of that flickering candlelight wetting his sedated form. She notices the music. She loves that song. She stands and watches him for just a moment. The peace of slumber is on him. She can see that young man of so many years ago through its veil. He had the kind of dreams of life and love that a young man maintains. He will still achieve those goals, especially if she has anything to do with it.

She walks to him. She leans down and kisses him on his lips. His eyes open. Their eyes lock, and they kiss again. Her hand holds his and tugs it gently. They both rise. As they move to the stairwell, he breaks away to blow out the candle and turn off the music. She continues ahead of him.

When he enters the bedroom, she was in the bathroom. He could hear the soft hiss of the shower's waters. Its soothing rhythm adds more reason to his already drowsy eyes. He sits at the foot of the bed, lies back, closes his eyes, and lets that rhythm take him.

When he feels her hand on his knee, his eyes opened. She is already in her pajamas. It is a gray flannel jumper, the kind with the feet attached. She is still tying her night scarf around her head when she urges him to the shower. He yawns, then sighs, and then drags himself to the bathroom.

It was a chore to summon the energy to remove his clothes; in fact, he labors to turn on and adjust the shower, and still, he was near his end of will to get in and wash. He manages it, though, and brushes his teeth just for good symmetry. He drops the toothbrush into its stand, throws the towel and washcloths into the clothes bin, and crosses the portal into the bedroom.

She is naked. There is a large brown lifelike dildo protruding from between the squeeze of two bed pillows. Her mouth is on the phallus and treating it to her method as if it could appreciate her energy; and indeed, it seemed to.

His eyes move from her bobbing head and follow the line of her frame from her shoulders, along her back, to her ass. She always kept that ass in the air. There he notices a black latex nut-sack and the few inches of phallus that hung out of her ass.

Her left hand moves from the assist with her mouth. It creeps along the bed and rides up her left thigh to her wet spot. The hand begins a teasing massage on her pussy. The pussy responds by getting wetter. The hand then flips around her body, takes command of that nut-sack, and pushes those last few inches of latex dick into her orifice. Her mouth pops off its practice toy as if stunned by the rush of deeper penetration. She turns to him and says, "Come taste me, baby."

What do you do? The scene is every bit as exciting as one may imagine, and he has imagined such scenes with a dangerous frequency. When he imagines such a thing as a woman being pleasured by multiple men, it is always the figure of some woman he has seen somewhere that is both the student and teacher in this erotic scenario. The three males are always three versions of him. He cannot imagine another male as submissive and dominant, as passive and aggressive, and as unselfish and selfish as he can be for their mutual pleasure.

However, he has never imagined that his wife would enjoy such a session. He always accepted it as a natural possibility; after all, she is everything he is, and that includes that erotic animal. And though the male elements of this scene are two-thirds fabricated, the suggestion is real. For her to enjoy such a scene as he imagines a woman enjoys when he applies the pleasure, she must have three men. The fact of it begins in reason, for we cannot achieve what we cannot imagine. Once imagined, though, it is merely a purposeful action away from being a reality. And this is, for just a moment, a very uncomfortable realization.

He glides on to the bed on his knees and falls mouth first to her wet opening. She greets his effort with a moan that oozes from her throat with the power of a Gregorian chant. Her pussy accepts his mouth as if inevitable; and indeed, once she exposed it, his mouth was obligated to taste it.

She allowed his mouth to work to her satisfaction. No more than that because he will spend the day tasting her without redirection. She suddenly leans forward and pulls her ass from his face. He peers over her dark mounds to see her mouth pulling off her toy. She flashes him a smug smile then jiggles that phallus so that it bobs next to her face, then easily slides her mouth back onto it.

He raises up, measures, and slides his full and excited length into her wetness. When he hits bottom, she choked on her toy. However, he does not pause, and neither does she. He commits himself to feeding her young girl, and she to pleasuring her mouth.

He is on her. His animal is emerging, and he is on her. The force of his thrusts has knocked the phallus from her mouth. One side of her face is now pressed onto the bed, and her mouth is now full of the desperate sounds he is pushing out of her.

His animal is emerging. Her left hand strays back along her body to the phallus in her ass. She grabs the latex nut-sack and begins to piston its full length into her ass. Her ass accepts its size hungrily, and her mouth finds the motivation to exercise with the toy again. Her pleasure sounds grow. He grows with them.

His animal has emerged. He pulls out of her pussy while simultaneously pulling her hand and the dildo it wields away from her ass. He pushes his weight against her, forcing her body to the bed. He measures and drops his full size into her waiting ass. The dildo had fallen out of her mouth when he adjusted her body, but the shock of his insertion forced her to reinsert it to muffle her relieved squeals and cries.

His animal dick is so good; and as a matter of fact, it becomes that much better when she is enjoying her bestial impulses. He lets loose every hope and frustration, fear and conquest, in his effort on her ass. She fills her mouth with that latex and encourages his reaching his peak by humping her ass into his thrusts. It works. He fills the room with his joyous scream, and her ass with his cream.

She lives to feel his weight on her after he has exploded inside of her. She likes to allow it to linger until she can feel his heartbeat settle back down to calm. She wastes no time tonight though. She urges him off her by lifting her left side. He pulls out of her and rolls over to his back. She turns, throws her right leg and arm over his body, slides over, and mounts him for a sixty-nine. She still has his cream leaking out of her ass as she holds his hardened penis for balance and measures her ass over his face. He does not have the slightest impulse to resist as she fits her cum-filled asshole over his mouth. His devotion is slow at first, but then builds up quickly to its usual ravenous attitude toward pleasuring her. She uses his penis and the bed for balance as she hovers above him. His hands keep her cheeks apart so his mouth could work. She gradually relaxes her asshole so more of his cream would leak out into his mouth. She moves the hand that pressed into the bed to his hair. She grabs a handful of his locks and begins to wipe her asshole along his nose and outstretched tongue. She is now fully relaxed. She pauses long enough to allow him to squeeze his tongue into her asshole. She giggles when he begins to wiggle it inside of her.

She slides her asshole up to his nose and fits her pussy over his mouth. His devotion does not stop. Her left hand reaches out to the pillows and retrieves her toy. As he tastes her, she begins to squeeze it into her ass while simultaneously dropping her mouth on his stiffness.

The joy of tasting her is indescribable. The sixty-nine position especially adds a level of desire in him to pleasure her. He lives to have her on him. But when her mouth falls on his again-rigid dick and begins the work he had seen her practice on the phallus, he thinks the sky is falling. He thinks

114

that every molecule of oxygen has dropped to the floor, and that is why he suddenly had trouble breathing. Fortunately, it is just a professional dick suck.

Her mouth continues on him. His mouth continues on her. Her hand reaches to his that was kneading her ass meat and redirects it to the phallus. His hand takes command of the toy and works it in her ass with as much real dick energy as his hand could feign.

Her animal nears maturation. He could feel it in her method and response. Her mouth begins a lesson in licking and sucking that could only be described as masterful. He works his pelvis so his thrusts would coincide with her work. She grounds and mashes her swelling clitoris and wet opening on his lips and tongue with a growing aggressiveness. She meets the thrusts of the phallus with her ass, making certain she gets every bit of it into her.

The discipline, though, is the timing. Her mouth, her clitty, and her ass. Her mouth, his dick, and her pussy. They work separately, slowly tuning themselves to that perfect pitch. They work together in an orchestra of erotic movement. And their melody is nearing perfection.

When she lets her cream go, he presses his mouth to her opening so he can receive it. When he lets his cream go, she closes her mouth over his penis to receive it.

When they awoke some half an hour later, they were still in the sixty-nine position. He pulls the dildo from her ass, they fix the sheets and go to sleep.

Day 27: Personal Training

This is what he calls his inclination toward auto eroticism. He insists it is a necessary element in maintenance and further development of his erotic and sexual interactive skills. She, of course, believes that he simply enjoys playing with his dick.

Day 28:

They go to a bar known for its variety of martinis, as well as its up-and-coming money crowd. The total of this place is as full of people as those people are full of themselves. She and he sip their drinks together. They make small talk and share investment strategies with interested parties. They mix and mingle and find themselves flirting with the idea of ménage à trois action with the more tasty patronage. They satisfy themselves that they could, if they wanted to.

Day 29: Role Play
The stalker and the helpless housewife.
(Use your imagination.)

Day 30: You hang up!
He sent her flowers at work, then called to say "I love you."

He met her for lunch and treated her to her favorite meal, miso soup and a sushi/sashimi platter.

He met her at the door to their home, having cleaned himself and the house, cooked, and prepared the table for a candlelight dinner.

He prepares her for bed, tucks her in, then kisses her goodnight. He leaves the bedroom and goes downstairs to the living room. He uses his cell phone to call their home line, knowing she would answer. She is in bed wondering, *What the hell!* He sits in his executive's chair in the den, sipping herbal tea while they talk for two hours like two people who are just getting to know each other, and still working hard for that ass.

Day 31: The Good Man
She hosts a tea for some of her high school and college friends. It is a small six-person gathering featuring the five who compose the pack.

The aroma of sandalwood incense fills the room and is proof that it is cooking somewhere out of sight. The room is made to be intimate. There are only a few chairs dotted around an area of large sitting pillows. The area is highlighted by several floral arrangements, which add more natural color to the scene. The sound of classic jazz lies just under the volume of their collective voices as these friends recount, narrate, and laugh over the good old days. Their every comfort has been anticipated and accommodated for by the caterer, her husband.

He first serves them appetizers. Then the tea and a light entrée. Then finally, the dessert and an evening drink: screaming orgasms and/or Irish coffee. He was a one-man show in preparing the room, the mood, and the food and drink. He did all of this while maintaining the highest levels of courtesy and professionalism. He did all of this while dressed only in black tuxedo shoes, black socks and bow tie, and a black apron with white letters that read, "Cooks give good meat."

She received rave reviews and requests for his hourly rate.

Day 32: Man Thing

Today she wants to feel helpless, so she plans the right moment to challenge his masculinity. The moment presented itself during their "settling in for the evening" ritual. He was sitting naked on the end of the bed, and she was strolling past in only her panties. He was highly agitated because of a string of seemingly childish complaints she made. The first of these, she was inconsiderate enough to inform him of at his office, and that at nine fifteen that morning. That was the beginning of his incitement—the first button. She then took great care to continue the assault of passive button pushing so that he may not suspect. She continued pushing buttons throughout the day so that he may not have an opportunity to recover and think.

That first button, though, led to this moment. She pushes the final button she knows will encourage his animal response. She nags him about a single sock that was hanging just out of the dirty clothes basket. It does incite his animal response.

He grabs her, full of genuine anger and malicious intent. She struggles. He smacks her face and subdues her. He rips her panties off her while

117

she begins biting and scratching in some convincing mock resistance. He sits with her struggling body in his arms and throws her stomach across his lap. He weighs down her torso with his, locking her legs with his, and begins an old-fashioned spanking while cursing the most marvelous shit at her. He continues this until he believes she understands his position, that of pissed-off man, and eases off his assault.

He had good reason to relent; there was proof of her surrender. Her mind became compliant because her body was made subdued—that's a twist; anyway, streams of her juices trickled onto her pubic patch, and at one point, almost with every strike of his hand to her bare ass. Her moans oozed from her mouth, coating the floor in a sticky haze that seemed to cement his feet to its mahogany planks. The moment he became kind, though, she became spiteful, and again cut him with her words. She made sure to cut him deep this time because she needs him in her. She told him that he hits like a bitch and that she has had girls with strap-ons who have given her better dick. Damn!

Her betrayal of his kindness was successful. He flies off the handle and takes her aggressively in every way she imagined he would. She could not hold her energies at bay. Those willful currents of ethereal plasma overran her until she was as much a thing of singular purpose as he was. Though he did have a moment to think, and then especially enough of one to figure out her motive, he let himself go because he needed this kind of release as much as she did. Besides, not even him should ever pass on an opportunity to lay the pimp hand down. This way, there will be no doubt in her mind that she owns the tastiest dick in town.

Day 33:
He creates a home spa and treats her to a manicure, pedicure, facial, a glass of good wine, relaxing music, and a full body massage.

Day 34: Wet Dream
She greets him at the front door *buck naked*, which, of course, incites his immediate arousal. She begins undressing him until he is naked and wearing the face of anticipation. She takes his hand and walks him up

the stairs and into the bathroom. Along the way, she makes certain she keeps her magnificence in his full view while it moves like only feminine magnificence can. She can feel his dick stretching trying to reach her.

They enter the bathroom, and she climbs into the tub and pulls him in after her. She pushes her nakedness to his and initiates a kiss that has historically meant his orgasm would soon be crying for freedom. She prompts him to his knees. He likes where this is going and begins his oral devotions to her abdomen, hips, thighs, and pubic patch. She prompts him to his back, then crouches to him, kissing his mouth, neck, and chest. She then rises a bit and hovers over him, bracing her arms against the wall for support, and begins to urinate on his stomach, chest, and face. It trickles down his face and head until his upper body is wet. He and his shocked-as-hell expression lie still in her fluid. She then sighs, smiles politely, and turns on the shower. She lifts him to his feet, and he still sports that shocked-as-hell mug as they shower together.

Day 35: Darkskin

She used some spare time over the last two months to create an erotic portfolio. It is a simple "forget-me-not," from wife to husband.

She used three digital video cameras. She owns one, and the other two were rented. She also employed the help of a girlfriend of hers who occupies herself as a professional photo/videographer.

She wrote a script. She designed a set for each room of their home she intended to use, as well as for those few outdoor sites she scouted. She acquired all of the theme clothing she would need. She edited then scored the video with mood-appropriate music. She wrote every erotic story, poem, and advertisement that would appear in her mock magazine. It will be titled *Darkskin* because that has been his passion name for her since their first meeting. He used it as a greeting to get her attention as she feigned intending to ignore him as she and a girlfriend walked past.

She positioned the stationary video cameras, not to miss a thing. The videographer controlled the third camera and was especially careful to highlight that *thing* that he is most helpless against, her huge dark ass. She made certain that one full hour of this two-hour cinematic event was exclusively of her huge dark ass. It was dressed in only ass-friendly wear. It was blessed with oils and lotions. It was teased with a variety of girl toys. It was bent to every ass-stounding position she could manage, and then especially those that she knew would take him over the edge, like the lollipop. That is when she is standing, or on her knees, and her torso is bent to the floor. Her hips and ass balloon up, making the thing seem even more massive, and that is usually when his tongue falls out of his mouth and begins to lick and suck at her ass meat, pussy, and asshole.

She did all of this to create the thing that she knows he enjoys. She created the thing that will feed his addiction for a naked woman doing naked woman shit on video and in magazines. She created the kind of fantasy that would occupy her husband's idle hands time in a productive manner; that is, focused on her.

Day 36: Queen for a Day
He caters to one of the fantasies she articulated in the stories section of her magazine, *Darkskin*. It was a short erotic story about a woman's fantasy of what she would do if she were queen for a day.

He prepares this event with as much meticulous care to detail as she showed in preparing the magazine. This episode begins, as many of theirs do, with a glance, a touch, and a kiss. A caress and an embrace follow a pause that is just long enough for him to bathe and prepare her.

They dance slowly to the rhythm of anticipation, and the soft music filling the room has been ignored. She wears only her Victoria's Secret teddy and a blindfold. He is in an opened silk robe. They move hypnotically, as if they intend to mesmerize each other through the dance of their moving parts.

He lays her on a palette made of two large futon mattresses. They are covered with a very large copper-colored satin sheet. The palette is surrounded by chocolate- and vanilla-scented candles, and the sheets are sprinkled with honeysuckle and mint leaves. The lights are down, and the candles are lit. She lies blind and ready for the unknown.

He escorts two men, both perfectly resembling the type of man she wrote about. That is, they are both dark-skinned, tall, and very muscular with a better-than-average package. Both men are very naked and blindfolded, and both have clean, smooth, just-shaved genitals. He stops each at one of her feet, then prompts them to their knees. They are professionals. They have been instructed by him on what is to be done.

The first begins with a touch. The contact sends a chill through her. She knows it is not him, her husband. She cannot see, but she knows. The first's caress runs along her toes, from the smallest to the largest, and slowly down the length of her foot to the heel. As his hand passes softly along her arch, she felt the warmth of his exhale on the tips of her toes. Then the wet of his mouth. Then the stroke of his tongue as it moved expertly from toe-to-toe.

The second touches her, and his technique is similar to the first's. This one, though, prefers kissing and licking to sucking, and his hands are much more practiced in pleasuring feet. The husband begins simultaneously with the second. He lies next to her, presses his lips softly to hers, and his hand gently handles her breasts. His hand enjoys her in that very familiar way that she finds comfort in. He relaxes her with his voice, his touch, and his kiss. This combination is as soothing as all the memories of him they have established in her mind. He soothes her while those pairs of lips and hands kiss, caress, and lick her.

They three work her out slowly. They taste her with their mouths for an excruciating time. They sample her as if she is a rare delicacy to be savored; at the same time, they mold her by hand with a spiritual pleasure, as if they each were a mystic craftsman working with the ethers of their dreams. They work her out energetically so she can feel them in their collective nakedness of mind and body. She can feel their collective devotion to her pleasure.

He works her face and neck; they work her feet and lower legs. He works her shoulders and breasts; they work her thighs and hips. He works her stomach and navel; they work up her sides. They work her arms from the shoulders to the tips of her fingers. Each is on his side of her, and when finished with those digits, each slowly places her hand on his genitalia. Her hands instinctively adore their total package of soft balls and stiffening dick as if precious things. The feel of them, the size—they are so warm and playful. They softly kiss her shoulders, neck, breasts, and face while she enjoys the feel of their hot members pulsing to full size. Their growth forces the grip of both her hands open ever wider to accommodate their size.

He works down from her navel to her pubic patch, and finally to the insides of her thighs with the slowest, most intelligent mouth in creation. He maneuvers his hands under her knees and lifts them up while the male on the left locks and pins her leg down and away with his leg. The male on the right grasps the other leg by the ankle and pulls it open and down, leaving her wide open to her husband. He bows to her and begins a passionate kiss on the sweetest spot along the divine U, her clitoris, and vaginal opening. The two pairs of lips, tongues, teeth, and hands grow in their intensity to demonstrate their devotion to add to her pleasure.

She knows that she can have as much of them three as she can stand in any and every way she can stand it, and for as long as she can stand it. Her husband whispered this to her at the beginning of the treatment while they were warming her up. It is her day.

Day 37-46: Seven to Nine Days
She feels the need to refresh his appreciation for the female form and his devotion to satisfying that form.

She begins his seven days of devotion at her feet and ankles. His duty from sunup until sundown is to please her through her feet and ankles. He is allowed to use only those tools that God granted his person. They will not have any other physical contact with each other throughout this period except through the days' appointed area. There is no penetration allowed, and he is not allowed to touch himself at any time.

The seven days encompass the seven erogenous areas she created: feet and ankles; legs and hips; the ass and divine U (from the top of the crack of her ass, down to the pirate eye, around the fountain of youth, up to the clitoris, and ending at her navel); stomach and back; breasts; arms and hands; and neck and head.

He must be dutiful and efficient as well as passionate and energetic. He must be unselfish and giving of his self to achieve her pleasure. If he fails to satisfy her on any part, she will then have him repeat that devotion. She anticipates he may spend more than a day on her ass and divine U.

Day 47-89: Discipline

The disciplines are exercises he designed to make them more aware of the power of their senses while sharpening their senses and generating a greater appreciation for their senses and while enjoying their senses without becoming dependent upon their senses.

The disciplines cover a six-week period with each sense spanning a week in development.

The sense faculties he addresses are the physical, which would include sight, hearing, smell, touch, and taste; in addition to the nonphysical, which would be intuition. The former five, he places in the same category of *physical* because however different they may seem in their design and function, they all require the physical touching of some stimuli to some physical mechanism on or within the body in order to receive, decipher, and perceive information. The latter, however, the intuitive, is beyond physical description or influence because it is not a physical manifestation. He believes intuition to be a product of the divine consciousness. He specifically believes it is a product of God's all-knowing attribute for which all time past, present, and future are the same moment.

He begins with her sight. He deprives her of it for an ever-increasing period of hours every day for seven days. During this time, he applies a variety of stimuli that would allow her unbound senses to become more acute in recognition of a thing other than visible qualities.

The exercise is designed to enlighten the participants by creating circumstances that demand they expand their methods of receiving/ communicating information. The underlying idea is to create the basis upon which a couple can learn greater trust, appreciation, and understanding of each other. The overlying idea is to celebrate the animal ingredient of people, the body, its potential, and its importance as a first-step component of the physical/intellectual evolution of people. The goal is to learn how to overcome the body and its limitations. He believes this a necessary step on their path to graduation to the next phase of development of their intellectual/spiritual component.

He will address every one of those sense faculties in a like manner. He will work with the intent of developing their (hers and his) self-awareness to a point where they can begin to believe they can be free of their physical restrictions. They must develop the discipline to tune out the illusory effects of mind coupled with ignorance, and tune in to the all-seeing, all-knowing, all-capable no/thing that is the source of all things. Amen.

Day 90: The Animal

She is in beast mode. She wants dick. She wants it out, up, and in her. She begins by greeting him at the door as he comes in from work. She is wearing the most erotic costume God ever created: her dark brown polished with cocoa butter oil.

She leads him to the couch by the collar of his shirt. She turns to sit and drags him down to his knees with her. She places her right leg over the back cushion, and her left on the coffee table. She grabs a handful of his hair and pulls his face into her crotch. He jumps into his devotion energetically and with the type of practiced skill that allows her to relax into the moment and enjoy the high.

Once she is warmed up by way of an eye-twitching orgasm that he left no evidence of, she is ready to receive him. So she receives him on the couch in her pussy until his shirt and pants are soaked with his sweat as he explodes inside of her. She recovers, rises, and walks him upstairs by his tie.

In their bedroom. She releases his tie to allow him to come out of those work clothes. As he undresses, she poses, standing with her legs shoulder length apart and facing the mirror with her arms braced against the top of the bureau. Her face is pressed against the mirror when she looks back at him, winks, then makes that dark ass bounce. The response is energetic. He gives it to her with his tie hanging loosely, his shirt halfway unbuttoned, his pants fallen about his ankles, and one shoe on and the other not in sight. When he moans his genetic material inside of her, she allows him a moment to catch his breath and to finish undressing.

She leads him to the bathroom and starts the shower. Once they are both under the water, she wastes no time. She receives him in her ass in the shower as he attempts to wash away the day's grime. She loves the feel of how hard that dick becomes when he ejaculates.

They then remove themselves from the shower, and she takes him while he tries to get dressed into his house wear. She realizes he may be a little tired at the moment, so she excuses his lapse of judgment in attempting to dress. She takes him in a manner that reflects her silent argument, and in fact, the point of her action thus far, that his better duty today will be to remain naked and ready. She drives her point home by taking him first in her pussy, and then in her ass, and then until he is spent and unable to do anything but sleep.

She allows him his rest. In the interval, she prepares one of his favorite meals, curry shrimp and bay scallops with mushrooms, onions, and red peppers sauteed in Marsala wine, cream and butter, and served over basmati rice.

When he wakes, she has it waiting for him on a silver platter complete with a slice of German chocolate cake—one of his favorites—a glass of white wine, and a carnation. She then assures him that he would never taste it unless he gave up some superb dick; indeed, he knew that if he shows any resistance, she would dump the entire tray on the floor and not give it a second thought, and then she may still take the dick by force if necessary. She has done that before. So he resigns himself to giving up some superb dick.

She spends the rest of the night receiving him in the session's two preferred openings until his balls ache, and he falls to slumber in midstroke in her, and on her.

Day 91: Movie Date

He picks her up from work and drives to a popular adult cinema playhouse. They both giggle and wear goofy smiles because neither can believe they are about to enter into an adult movie theater.

They purchase their tickets and proceed through the doors and into the lobby. They proceed into the theater where the movie is already in progress. Although the room is small, and there are only a handful of others present, they still have a difficult time finding seats. They must maneuver a maze of three lonely fellows and a lesbian couple, all of whom have occupied some of the more acoustically correct yet private seating. They finally find some seats that are just close enough to the others to hear, and possibly see, what goes on in their lives.

Already the company they keep have relaxed into their moods. The silence of sensual discomfort is marked by a lack of obvious motion by anybody and the studied concentration of the eyes on the screen. This is easily replaced by the silence of sexual arousal, which is marked by the same studied, concentrated eyes, but moves along with some heavier, very audible breathing and obvious motion from everybody.

The images and sounds on the screen, together with those of their movie mates, all create such a lewd suggestion the entire room begins to feel a part of the film. The sound of their combined efforts seem to dominate as dialogue for what happens on the screen; at the same time, the action on the screen becomes a substitute for what they wish from each other.

Finally, he reaches for her breast. She immediately reaches for his crotch. They kiss. It is not so prolonged a kiss as to miss much of the movie, but long enough to realize that their lips have finally touched. Their hands continue to find all the right places to grope. Suddenly her breast comes out, and his mouth is on it. Then his penis comes out, and her mouth is on it. They expose each other part by part. Each part creates a higher step that raises their desperate energy. The desperate energy builds until it explodes out of their mouths in a song of moans, pants, and squeals. Their song joins with the others, and together they form an impromptu chorus whose goal is to sing for the forgiveness of lascivious energy and abandoned sperm.

Day 92: Pussy Chess, Not Checkers
Sometimes a woman has to remind her man and herself of what she is working with.

She picks this evening, the one that he has been planning for weeks in order to hang out with some of his buddies. He does not hang out with his male people very often, only once or twice every two or three months. He always has some surprisingly interesting story to tell, though, and always about some unlikely incident that occurred as they were out on the town. He always seems invigorated for days after one of their male bonding sessions. We all need those moments away from our routine to reestablish our perspective on life.

But fuck all that. Tonight, he is going to have to make a choice.

So he comes down the stairs, funky-fresh dressed to impress ready to party. He mutters something about what time she should expect him back as he glides down the stairs and bounces into that cool stride, like *ha-ha!* Then he sees her.

She is standing butt naked on a beach towel in front of the door. On the towel is a stereo remote control, a bottle of virgin olive oil, a small decoratively etched and frosted crystal bowl, and an open container of carnation cream. The lights throughout the floor are out except for the recess lighting above her head, and they are dimmed. They paint the space in energetic brassy, earth tones that remind the eyes and mind of autumn. Around her waist she wears a gold hip chain, and attached to this are his car keys. They sit nettled in her thick dark pubic patch.

She smiles a sly smile, then picks up the bottle of oil and removes the cap. She covers every square inch of her body with the oil. The oil is life. They both refer to it as nonprescription Viagra, or that topical stimulant. She picks up the remote control and points it into the dark of the living room. The system comes to life with Prince's "If I Was Your Girlfriend." She begins with an erotic aerobic stretching routine that was choreographed for the music. He still stands on the same spot at the bottom of the stairs and has not moved a muscle. The music mixes into JD's, "Extended Version," and her dance becomes hotter to suit the mood of the music. She hits him with a Persian belly dance that had to take at least some professional lessons to prepare. The belly dance moves into a New York stripper routine. The stripper set puts her up against the front door, the walls, his body, and finally on the floor. That set ends with her on her hands and knees, and she is bent into the most submissive Greek position anyone has ever assumed. The music changes again to Minnie Riperton's "Inside My Love" and eases their imagination back to passion. While she is on her knees, she crawls on all fours over to the crystal bowl. She pours the cream into the bowl, and with her huge black shiny ass raised slavishly in the air and shimmying from side to side, she purrs while licking the cream out of the bowl.

She makes certain, of course, to raise her head occasionally to throw him a playfully seductive glance as the cream rolls from the corners of her lips and down her chin.

He, of course, has already informed his friends, via cell phone, that he would not be able to make it that night.

Check, mate.

Day 93:
He sends her to a very highly recommended holistic health spa for some her time. His responsibility is to drop her off at 7:00 p.m., Friday evening, and to pick her up at 7:00 p.m., Sunday evening.

The in-between time, he spends enjoying some him time.

Day 94:
They begin practicing yoga and meditation and adopt a more holistic perspective of their being. This means practicing being less animal and more human. This means first becoming complete people. This translates into crossing the bridge to becoming both mentally and physically healthy.

The idea is to cleanse the mind and body so as to gradually remove all impediments to healthy being and thus, enlightenment. They train to develop the mind into the disciplined vessel capable of complementing the divine will.

Day 95: The Taste
He comes home to a note on the door that reads, "I won't be home until tomorrow, but I left you something inside to taste." Once inside, he proceeds as casually as usual through his home. He follows his nose toward the kitchen and whatever that deliciousness is that has it hooked; and it smells like curried something.

There he finds a tall dark-skinned Indian woman. She is barefoot with a gold toe ring on the second big toe of each foot. Both her eyes and past-shoulder-length hair are so dark as to make her chocolate skin seem to glow. She is wearing a very sheer white robe covering her voluptuousness, and her gaze is the type that takes the breath completely out of a man.

She steps up to him so that they are nose to nose and informs him that she will be his wife for the evening. She then proceeds to her wifely duties.

She relaxes and feeds him a light but energetic meal. She bathes, oils, and massages him. She talks with him. She laughs with him. She seduces him. She allows him to have his way with her until he thought himself sated. She then begins her treatment. She is highly experienced with all things sensual. Or more precisely, she is a professional practitioner of the sexual arts and sciences. She intends to leave him a dry husk of a man by morning, but one who is blissful.

Day 96: Candlelight and You
They lie naked in each other's arms on the couch in the living room. There are two glasses of iced lemon water on the coffee table. A rose incense is burning somewhere out of sight. The only light in the room comes from the mocha-scented candle stationed between their drinks.

They are feeling a variety of music by artists such as Anita Baker, Phyllis Hyman, Prince, Keith Washington, and others. This moment, though, they are riding the mood of the duet song "Nothing Has Ever Felt like This" sung by Rachelle Ferrell and Will Downing.

They know that these are the moments that mean the most. These become the most fundamental elements of the equation of their joy of each other. The sum of the equation is two. Two whole people into each other. Two whole people into themselves. Life composed of two whole halves that are the spirit. Life composed of two whole halves who enjoy their God moment. It is all love.

Day 97: Equilibrium
He wants her to see them from every angle. He sets up three televisions connected to three video cameras strategically placed about the room. In between the cameras are the various mirrors that are ordinary to their bedroom: the bureau, the headboard, and the dressing mirrors. Then there are those mirrors he installed on the ceiling directly above their bed. They are in the shape of a triangle the approximate size of their bed.

He wants her to see what they look like when they cook right. He wants her to see how magnificent her body is. She does not seem to have the appreciation of her body that he does.

He wants her to see them from a new perspective, not his, nor hers, but one detached from their biases. He wants her to see what he sees when she is in motion and her machine is operating at peak efficiency. He wants to see what she sees when he is in motion and his machine is operating at peak efficiency.

They burn. They shine. They warm the room with their exercise in the potency of the duel nature of all living things.

Day 98: The Past
They spend the day reminiscing about their childhoods and the day they met. They remind each other of those good things that make them smile uncontrollably and laugh without fear. They remind each other of each other's good times, and in doing so, they become sympathetically integrated into some of the happiest moments of their respective lives.

Each comes upon the idea that their lives and all of the joy therein were a preparation for the moment they would find each other and consummate a love that had always been since the beginning of things.

Day 99: The Present
They spend the day contemplating the moment. Who they are. How they are. Why they are. They remind each other that being together is joy for them, and being is joy for them. They remind each other that all they have is the moment, and each one builds upon the next until the great pyramid of their life is formed. This is a lifetime's task. This is part of what the pyramid represents, the dynamic of the living being—God as people.

Day 100: The Future
They spend the day seeing their tomorrow.

With full awareness of the divine wisdom that has already told the story of their lives, they map out their time together. They can see their spiritual growth and physical accomplishments as easily as their yesterday. They recognize that whether their remaining time together is another second or another hundred years, they will celebrate it by honoring their god through living with love, peace, and harmony.

Day 101: Game Night
Butt-naked Twister, nah! They never seem to get past the fourth spin before they are at each other.

Strip Poker, don't think so. He gets too serious about the cards.

Truth, Dare, or Consequence—that's the one. This is just the mental stimulation they need. They both enjoy asking the tough questions and coming up with a challenging dare. They both also look forward to issuing harsh punishments as consequence for falling short during the session.

There are sure to be inquiries into such subjects as the first dick ever sucked, and the first time with more than one person—and those are just her questions for him. Happy gaming.

Day 102-105: The Sophomore Diamond
First base: he picks her up at home. They go to the movies and share a popcorn and soda. They hold hands and smile a lot.

Second base: he goes to her place to watch her favorite movie, "Miracle on 34th Street," the original with Natalie Woods. She cries at the end, and he comforts her with an embrace. They kiss until they want to do more than kiss, but they know they must stop. So they stop, embrace, and enjoy the brown until it is too late for her to have company.

Third base: she comes to his place for dinner. To her delight, it is a light appetizer, a nice soup, a light entrée, and then dessert with sparkling cider. Everything is served with fine china, stem, and silverware. Before and during the meal, they talk and laugh about those amusing, though seemingly inconsequential, things that make the world go round. After the eating, the laughing, and the soft talking, they dance slow to soft music. They dance so slow the room seems overwhelmed by their mood and becomes sedate. The potency of their union woos the music until it lies on the floor next to them in passion's kiss.

When two are in love and appreciating the warm brown touch of the one who wants you as much as you want them, it's a beautiful thing. And things may go too far tonight because you want to touch her there, so you let her know it's acceptable to touch you there. That seems like a fair exchange; however, things may go too far.

You find yourself in that brown, that warm comfort moment, and you don't know when your clothes fell off. There you are, though, naked and in the embrace, and you think that nothing on earth or in heaven could be as soothing to you than the experiencing of this person. They nonetheless stop and mutually consign the inevitable to some very eagerly awaited future date.

Home plate: she invites him over for an equally elegant meal that neither of them are upset they never get to eat. He enters her home. There is a welcome hug and kiss that was like "the truth," and it lingered through those some minutes of small talk like the memories of good things do. She then passes him a cool glass of some refreshment, and the chilling dew that covers the glass only makes the hand that held it all the warmer. When their hands touch on the exchange, and his warmth mingles with hers, it is understood that there is nothing more to say or do, but to shut up and do.

Day 106: The Left

The left is a person used to enhance the pleasure of a male and female intimately engaged. The left is a person who is practiced in the intimate arts, and whose desire to facilitate pleasure is greater than any of the pair's reservations.

The couple. Their love and respect for each other is above the need for debate of any kind. They travel the path that living is stride for stride. They are open to the dynamics of each other.

They meet at the front door and share a laugh at how unintentionally precise their timing is. They enter and make themselves comfortable. They peel those work costumes off and lounge. They have drinks, and they have music: Patrice Rushen's "You Remind Me," among others. They have a conversation about back in the day when that song was new. They speak about what they were doing the first time they heard it, how it made them feel, and they have something to smile about.

They marinade in that moment created by fond recollection of the first kiss, the first date, that first "I think I'm grown enough for this" moment; after all, it is the one that precedes that first real moment.

They have a quiet contemplative dinner full of shy glances and coy smiles. They adjourn upstairs to the master suite, hand in hand like giddy schoolchildren en route to recess.

They disrobe each other slowly. The energy of this new thing has their minds so numb they could not rush through this step if they wanted to. They are naked. They embrace. Not one of them could have imagined that discomfort could be so erotic.

They move to the bathroom as one body with their tongues and hands steadily probing and exploring each other. He breaks their continuity to draw the bath as those she eyes watched. They bathe.

The hot water, busy hands, and soap were useless; they were still stuck on each other like tissue on honeyed fingers. They remove from the bathroom into the bedroom. They mount the bed. They have grown in desire, and their desire grew thirsty. So they wet it. They massage each other with a carrot and tea tree oil mixture. They kiss, caress, probe, and taste each other. She does her husband while he does his wife, consequently leaving the left to become their conduit to other pleasures.

The left becomes that new twist on the old recipe. There is nothing wrong with the standard dish, but when you add jalapeños, goddamn! It is not her place to replace either partner. It is the goal of the left to intensify those comfortable pleasures the couple has developed while introducing something new. The presence of the left is often as much new inspiration a couple can take.

So she nurtures these two. They touch each other with hands of hot familiarity. She touches them both with hands that though unfamiliar were sure. When they kiss, their lips seem molded for those spots, and each anticipates the service the other's lips could provide. But her lips could not be accounted for in so sure a manner, so the touch of them to either of their bodies is icy with surprise. When their tongues taste each other's primary pleasure parts, hers instinctively finds those secondary parts to excite. When she is on her back and he is on her and in her, the left incorporates all of the hands, lips, and tongue into service with her breasts, arms, legs, and whatever other parts of her body proper can be used to incite more pleasure. She is not the pleasure, though, she is to the left of the pleasure of those two. She will remain as pure as the showers that fall on a rain forest, and she will be that perfect conduit for that current of electricity that binds them.

Day 107: A Night of Debauchery

He introduced the subject to her one night during dinner. They spoke on it, supposing what would be involved, then laughed and forgot about it. He reintroduced the topic again some months later. This time, he had gathered some factual information to speak of, and he did so with a more serious intent.

She did not object to it, the idea of it, but to actually participate would be something totally other than what she had ever seriously considered. However, they are now walking through the portal of an establishment whose purpose is debauched pleasure. She could feel it the moment they entered.

It is more than the scent of the many floral arrangements and that soothing effect they always seem to have on one's person. It is more than the candlelight and the way those naughty shadows call to those erotic centers of one's imagination. It is more than the music whose soothing tones blend perfectly with those dim flickering candlelights and calming floral scents to become a subliminal suggestion of lust. It is even more than all of those pairs of eyes that seem weighed by some intoxicant—either alcohol or lust—and they are all trained on you, the woman, the man.

It is something in her and in him. It is as if every person here is a candle, and that active intellect—the flame, and they all seem to be illuminating the objects of their collective desires. For this moment, they all seem to be defining their being through the vessel of body. No words are spoken, and none were necessary. She felt it, and he felt it.

They were escorted by a very attractive and petite Asian woman wearing only a sheer purple teddy. She led them to the ready room. It is a large room with gym benches and lockers. There was a muscular black male sitting behind a desk at the entrance to the showers. They shower, then chose their costume. They chose naked. Naked is always a good choice. They stared each other in the eyes. They kissed softly. Then hand in hand, they walked slowly out into civilization.

Their presence is acknowledged by careful strokes of desirous hands as they move slowly down the corridor. They navigate through a gauntlet of people whose minds and bodies are engaged in some type of intimacy.

From parlor to parlor they strode. They see the spa room. There are seven bodies as wet from the waters of the hot tub as their own honest efforts at specific pleasures. They were at each other in as furious a manner as those jets that agitated that water.

They saw the bondage room where dominants trained their submissives to obedience. There was race play in progress. A dark-haired white female dominant costumed as a plantation mistress and her submissive—a lean, muscular, bald, and dark-skinned male were the players. He was on his knees and dressed only in a tattered loincloth. His hands were restrained behind him with period-appropriate shackles. He wore a collar, also period appropriate, and connected to it was a short chain that she commanded. She had just finished shitting in a dog bowl and stood over him with her ass at his face. She pulled her dress up, bent over, and pulled his chain until his mouth was wedged into the crack of her ass, and she could feel his lips and tongue on her asshole. He begins accommodating her with his oral devotion while she brags of how "this filthy nigger loves to clean my ass with his mouth." The audience of ten or twelve naked observers moaned their approval as "I Wish I Was in Dixie" played on a system somewhere out of sight.

They passed through the game room and a naked foursome playing Spin the Vibrator. That Pakistani girl must have gotten the point because of all the hard dick her mouth was pleasuring. There was a group playing Naked Baby Oil Twister—always a crowd favorite, and a Russian woman and Chinese man were playing billiards with a rainbow audience of four very naked and excited men standing around them. Apparently the wager is whoever loses must take all four men, mouth and ass, until they have all ejaculated; and this is not their first game; and as a matter of fact, neither is playing very well. Finally, they come around to the roulette wheel. There are four naked persons, two female and two male, lying on alternate black-and-red slots built onto a large scale replica of a roulette wheel. It is basically a large round bed that spins. The players place their bets, which can only be red or black, and the wheel is spun. When the wheel stops, the person who occupies the colored slot you bet on that is closest you must fuck.

Finally, they walk into the One World Room. It is a large circular room with an open granite floor. There are sheer multicolored curtains that hang from the twelve-foot ceiling, and they circle the room. There are four large wooden ceiling fans forming a large square above, and in the middle of those, a single vent. There are nearly one hundred vanilla-scented candles placed in wall sconces and floor stands throughout the room. There are large futon mattresses lining the walls, and they are all covered in jasmine and cherry blossom leaves and buds. In the middle of the floor are three large brass bowls on iron pedestal stands. One bowl contains a variety of condoms. Another bowl contains a variety of stimulants like yohimbe, Viagra, and Kankankan. The final bowl is a water fountain.

There are bodies at play everywhere. The bodies totally reflect the theme of the room. There seems to be a representative from every major world language present. Their play is simple, whatever pleasures.

So his eyes lock on hers. They kiss softly. They embrace and find a comfortable spot somewhere within the world to be free.

Day 108: Chairs

She has a thing for chairs. She does not know why, and he has stopped trying to figure it out. His duty is not to figure this one out, though, but to satisfy her lust for it. She has had him pleasure her at least once in every chair they own. There are those two or three that she finds uniquely tailored to be the most suitable for receiving her husband's adoration. These chairs are thickly padded for her comfort and low to the ground because she likes to watch him crawling to attend to her.

There is his executive's chair in his study. She often has him taste her pussy and asshole as she sits in this chair. There is the chaise in the sunroom. She mostly enjoys having him taste her ass in that one. Finally, the lounge chair in the living room. She will often have him sit naked at her feet as she sits naked in that chair watching Jeopardy! Then there are those bar stools in the basement. They sit higher than regular stools. She likes that because she really enjoys gazing down at him dominantly as he pleasures her feet and toes with his mouth. If he does a good job, and he usually does a good job, then she will sit in the stool so that her ass hangs off its perimeter. She then allows him to worship her ass. She has found that this is one of his better ass-worshiping positions.

There is her beanbag chair in the bedroom, and her latex chair in the basement. When she resorts to these, he knows she wants the dick from behind and aggressively. She will take it in the pussy or the ass, but normally, when she goes for these chairs, she wants it in the ass.

Then there is the old standby, the sofa. It is the kind of sofa that a person makes out on. It is not really good for sex, but you could if it were urgent. The sofa is where they cuddle, kiss, and all those intimate things couples do on a sofa. Mostly, though, they talk while they sit on it, and he always seems to find himself giving her a foot massage as they converse. She lives for those conversations.

Day 109: Domestic Service

He wanted to hire a maid for the obvious reasons. They often have long workdays, and because of those, they often do not have the time to attend to the domestic work associated with home ownership; besides, he wanted to try to seduce the woman into sex.

She objected for the obvious reasons. She felt they could adjust their schedules to allow for more time to attend to their home; at any rate, she knew he wanted another piece of ass in the house for his enjoyment.

So they compromised. They will alternate weekends, and whoever is on must perform their chores nearly or totally naked. This is her weekend.

She wears only a head scarf and slippers. He will swear on whatever one holds as sacred that there is no more intensely arousing a sight than a naked woman on her hands and knees, wearing slippers and a head scarf and scrubbing the floor, any floor, but especially the bathroom floor—he believes it may have something to do with the optical acoustics.

She should have a scrub brush, and she should not be aware he is watching as she stretches to reach some hard-to-clean spot under the pedestal sink. As she stretches, the ass balloons up and spreads open! And the titties are hanging! And both the titties and the ass jiggle with every stroke of the brush across that hard spot. And God do not let her look back at him with that look of surprise that the women in the movies always seem to have when they discover the pizza delivery guy is not wearing any underwear. But she must have a Southern or Latina accent when she says, "Oh! Meester, I did not hear jew come in." Damn!

Say When
(an extreme erotic tale)

I sit with my eyes closed and staring hard into the visions being replayed in my mind. *That bitch*, I think, but choke back the words. Even in this state where I nurture tender malice, I find it difficult to speak its influence. It pains me to realize that those hard thoughts are mine. They are though. And since born, I must parent them until they mature.

I have studied her over the last several weeks. I observed her schedule and took note of her habits. She leaves home at twelve fifteen in the afternoon, and usually returns by eleven forty-five that night. She will enter through the front door, turn to lock it, then proceed through the dark house into the living room, where she will turn on the stereo system. She will then move without hesitation to the kitchen. The light will pop on in the refrigerator, and she will reach for the rice milk. After pouring a glass, returning the container, and closing the refrigerator door, she will walk to a chair in the living room. This very chair I now sit in. She will sit in it sipping milk and listening to her mind fade in between the notes of the music as the music weaves itself into the dark fabric of this room.

11:41 p.m.
It is a warm night. It is humid, as it always is the beginning of July. But then it could be below zero, and I think I would still sweat as profusely. My nerves get to me easily. That is why I never gave any serious consideration to engaging in criminal activity. It is amazing, though, how easily a person can be influenced into a change of position. Even so drastic a change as to become criminal minded.

I have been completely naked for a half an hour. All is quiet here except for those things that go bump in the night. The sounds an old home makes when its frame adjusts to pressure changes always sound like footsteps to me. Add a good bit of darkness, and the scene becomes motivation for chilling imagery.

The leather of the chair grips my moist skin, and it squeals when I adjust myself. It is odd. As mean and uncomfortable as heavy thoughts are, I seem to produce them in an easy stream. The chair becomes increasingly more comfortable as it molds itself to accommodate our combined weight. As much as I believe those thoughts, and in fact, this whole scene is beneath me, they move me. I don't mean to sound like a snob about it, but the line between what I imagine and what I live is a means of identification. It verifies that I am the person I believe I am.

I touch myself, moved by base thoughts as the dark of this room touches me in an effort to motivate some part of my higher spirit. Dark is cosmic melanin that is the blessing of night. Dark matter is the ethereal essence of the divine consciousness. Therefore, it knows all. It seeks repentance of my contemplations.

I am no stranger to this home. In my pursuit of her, I have made myself a fixture within this space. I have the key to gain entrance. There is always a window open or a door that is unlocked. Civilization has its perks.

I know these floors and these walls. I have studied this place. I know the sight of her. She is five foot eleven inches tall, one hundred sixty-three pounds, and an uneven percentage of that concentrated in her ass and thighs. Her hair is in twists that would hang midway down her back, but she often maintains them in some coiled or braided style.

I know her flavor. One evening about a month ago, I went through her things when she was away from the home. It was all standard but for two discoveries. She kept a briefcase in her immaculately kept closet. It had a combination but was unlocked. She must have been in it recently. I opened it and found a nice variety of dildos and vibrators, two butt plugs (small and large), a string of anal beads, and a tube of lube. I don't know why, but I removed the anal beads from their container, held the string by its metal loop above my head, raised my face to it, and slowly lowered the string into my open mouth. I swear, no matter how well you clean those things, you can't get all of the ass residue off.

I know her scent. The second discovery, I came upon in the bathroom: I was going through the clothes hamper looking for soiled undies. As I moved about socks, towels, and some Hanes briefs—white, with a faint skid mark that was too long not to need an explanation, the scent of something like honeysuckle but a little too sweet caught my nose. It guided my hand expertly. I grasped them, removed them, and pulled them to my face for a deeper inspection. A strong inhale. The scent of pussy, I think, is why there are so many drones in a hive. It greatly intensifies that natural nonphysical, nonintellectual connection that males have to females. We task to become covered in it, in fact or by association. In an effort to realize this, a male will become like a drone if it is necessary to the task. I took the panties and retreated.

I returned the very next night. At 11:45 p.m. She opened and entered through the front door. She did not turn on a light but proceeded through the dark house into the living room where she dropped her handbag on the coffee table and turned on the stereo. It's a Bose system that fills every corner of the room with Marion Meadows's "Forbidden Fruit." She then moved to the kitchen for that glass of milk.

She passed within inches of me as she moved to the stereo. The familiar scent of her body lotion caught my nose. It is still too sweet. I watched her as she stood before the open refrigerator door. Its light brightly illuminated her figure. She wore white Reebok sneakers and a set of green scrubs. They are the type medical staff wear in hospitals. Tonight her hair is out and pulled back into a ponytail. I only caught a partial profile as she retrieved a glass from the cabinet. She is beautiful. It is the kind of natural beauty one imagines when viewing the busts of queens of Africa's antiquity. The kind of beauty that can motivate a boy to become a man. She poured her glass of rice milk and walked out of the kitchen as the door closed on the refrigerator's light.

It would be difficult for any amateur to know the dynamics of whatever activity they are engaged in. It is the professional who knows what to anticipate and how best to respond to the unanticipated. It is the professional that can establish themselves as the center of a situation and control its flow. Tyrannical control is sometimes necessary.

I moved with the fluid pulse of the music. I wrapped my left hand over her mouth and my right around her body, pinning her right arm against her side. We paused.

I did not hear the glass hit the floor and shatter, scattering its pieces to unseen corners of the dark room. She did not feel the droplets of milk that freckled her legs and feet as they bounced from the floor helplessly into the air.

The moment came upon us in a hurry. Neither of us moved. Neither of us breathed. The moment began to stretch, winding its hungry mass ever tighter around our emotions with every passing second. It allowed us no fresh movement of thought. And I suspect, our last thoughts could not serve as advice for now. There is instinct, though, and it shouted, *Act or be consumed.*

She began to struggle fiercely, using every bit of physical strength she had at her disposal. I kept a firm grip over her mouth, muffling her screams while dragging her into the living room toward the tall leather chair. She bit at my hand, but I adjusted my grip. She kicked at me, mostly missing, but what little contact she made only managed to slow my progress. The chair came closer. She punched and scratched at any part of me she could manage. If I were affected, the tranced determination that shrouded my face would not show it. At the chair, she focused her last bit of energy on becoming as relaxed as she could. It would be easy; she was exhausted from the struggle. She earned a moment of relief. Her deadweight caught me off guard, and I stumbled to the floor before the chair and on top of her.

I lost grip over her mouth. She screamed, but the moment also caught her unprepared, so the sound was too weak and unsure to displace the waves of music or to penetrate the walls. With the fingers of my right hand, I formed a pincer around her esophagus. She gagged. I secured my left hand over her mouth and, with some aggressive pressure from my right hand, pulled her to her feet as I rose.

I turned us both and fell forward into the tall leather chair. I moved my right hand to her waist. Her throat was pressed against the firm top of the chair and sank into its cushion. She could probably feel the resistant oak frame of the chair pushing against her throat. It sounded as if it made her respirations more difficult, but not impossible. I kept her mouth silent with my left hand while her body stretched to the floor, held helpless by my arm's grip around her, and my weight.

Again I leaned my naked and excited body on hers. I stood and prompted her to do the same with a demanding tug at her torso. She complied slowly. I prompted her to place both knees into the chair's soft seat. She complied. I did the same but positioned my legs inside of hers and pushed hers solidly against the unyielding walls of the chair's sides.

Suddenly I felt the cool of liquid running along the thumb of my left hand. I pressed my body onto hers, pressing her breasts deeper into the chair's back cushion. She began to cough. I still wonder about that moment. I was not giving a command or preparing for one. I felt passion and wanted to express it. So I held her tightly. We paused in that moment.

A steady stream of cool liquid began to wet my hand. I retrieved one of my tools from the coffee table next to the chair, the duct tape, and with one smooth motion, I covered her mouth from left to right. During the transition, I think she thought to take the opportunity to scream. And that is the difference between the realized results of the amateur and of the practiced; the tyranny of the practiced discourages rebellion even when the moment is in the oppressed's favor. The thought fell from her mind to her left eye, condensed, and rolled down her face and over the gray tape that now covered her mouth.

I tried to calm her. My voice became melodic, almost like a song. She seemed too overrun by the energy of the moment to know that she was responding like a robot to the commands I issued. She moved nervously like someone who had never known the experience of being forcibly detained. The culmination of her compliance found both of her hands bound by bright yellow nylon nooses slung around the sides of the chair. The yellow rope extended from her hands and securely down the leather of the rear of the chair, where the two separate lines came twisting together and disappeared under its seat. They reappeared at the front of the chair where each wound around a leg, then up to nooses tightly secured at her calves.

She heard me. I know she did. She had to hear my breathing, my movements, and the desperation that motivated them. She had to hear me moving around her just beyond her peripheral vision. I maneuvered clumsily about the room, taking care not to be revealed by the telling pale blue moonlight shining through the skylight above this chair. She had to hear me bathed in guilt and lascivious intent while I bound her like a package and paused. The still of the moment lasted all of a heartbeat.

She felt his hands on her ass. They gripped her cheeks lovingly then slowly rose along her hips to her waist. They came to rest on the waistband at the small of her back just under the shirt.

There it was. That instance where a person's labor comes to fruition. Only when the fruit is tasted can they say if it was worth the effort. He was attempting to rip her pants off. The power in each attempt shook her body to its whim until the material weakened and split. He tore them completely off and discarded the rags to the floor. Those powerful hands then took a grip at the back of the waist of her panties, a pair of the same kind he pilfered, and with barely an effort, split them to the crotch.

The sound of the tear made her heart pause and the lump in her throat expanded. The shadows of the trees coming through the skylight refused to sway despite the force of wind pushing them. And she could swear that when her treasure was exposed, he went cold and froze to the spot. The attention of time itself was drawn by that ominous sound, and nothing in all of creation could move until its echo faded.

What would be worse, knowing what violence is to come, or knowing what violence is to come and not being opposed to it? She feels enveloped by him. His energy, his method, and all else he has brought to the table serves the wants of this scenario. It is his contribution to the game. How deliciously it all makes her tingle. They need each other in order for either to reach their potential within the continuing saga that is the story of them. The stalked and the stalker. He needs her to be the helpless victim, and she needs him to be the violent intruder. Mutual consent is implied upon initiation of the act.

Insertion. It was hurried and strong. It flowed from her excited opening to the depths of her chasm and back repeatedly. It flowed like harsh and intense words being sung over the poetic melody and rhythm of the moment. He serenaded her with it. He pounded her with it. He tortured her with it for twenty minutes without pause. He is no superman, but strong emotion nurtured to this extent acts as a shield against the senses and, most especially, tactile sensitivity. It numbs one's ability to sense reality because the mind is focused on a fantastic idea. What perceptive ability is left is experienced in what seems a single breath—a single breath where a person can perform well above the standard of their personal reality.

At some point, though, the moment fades. The only words left, if they can be judged words, are those sounds of desperation moaned over the melody life makes when its children interact like this. He hears that melody being played by nature's orchestra. It overcomes his moment—his solo exhibition of percussion, thinning it and making it comply to the standard of the song.

From the point he came back to awareness, to the point the greatest part of his rage subsided to anger then to passivity as it was ejected into the head of a black latex bag—ribbed and unscented—took not more than two minutes.

He moved about her like trash, as if he were ashamed of himself for what he was. He moved like a nigger, as if he were ashamed of what he had allowed himself to become. He gathered himself and dressed in a dark corner. He cut the ropes that bound her hands—carefully, apologetically, and disappeared into the dark.

I watched her for days afterward, hoping to witness the effect the session would have on her countenance—knowing that my power moved her. A part of me wanted to see her in dismay. A part of me wanted her to experience the unchecked shock and emotional turmoil that is notorious for creating perpetual victims in similar circumstances. A part of me wanted her to lament for what had supposedly been taken from her, and concede defeat. Because of my desire to participate in this development, she now possesses an insight of herself and of the power the mind has for self-determination. I wanted to see her soak in it. I wanted to see it run in streams from her every orifice as it inundated her body. I desire nothing less than the satisfaction of victory.

However, for those days I watched her, she seemed unaffected. Her countenance was as it always was, mostly pleasant. When her husband arrived, it would change slightly to pleasantly smug. There was a question in her eyes when she gazed at him. It seemed a question she was hesitant to admit was necessary to ask. So she did not ask, but left it spoiling on her face. Other than this, she was unaffected.

She did not inform the police of the offense. Neither did she inform her husband, Mark Anthony Nelson. The fiend timed the meeting to occur during one of her husband's short but frequent absences from home.

Her husband is a very successful entrepreneur. He devised a system of holistic health and fitness that actually worked. It became largely successful. As a result, when he is not working the center, he is attending or speaking at workshops, seminars, and conventions all over the country. Lately, his time has been occupied with the opening of a new center in New York, New York. His business trips usually last but a single day. There are times, though, where he may be absent for a two- or three-day stretch. He always keeps in touch by cell phone, and he always comes home to Philadelphia.

Whatever inconvenience his business put on his life was compensated for by his love of his work and lots of money. A disappointing addition to these reasons occurred only in the past year. He cherished his free time, she cherished hers, and they always spent it on each other. Since the New York project, he has had very little free time to spend on himself or her. Naturally, she understood the situation for what it was—the realizing of a dream—and did not interfere with any childish demands. Occasionally, though, she could not help but to distract him with whatever interaction she determined was mutually therapeutic. All work and no play would not do.

However, the circumstances would not support long evenings out on the town or weekends out of the country. In fact, those circumstances worked well as fuel for their imaginations. The task became to devise a way to enjoy what little time they could still share together in as constructive a manner as they have become accustomed. Their custom itself is not tame. It is only governed by statuettes concerning public decency and their imaginations. This new fuel, though these diminished moments they have to share with each other, they burn like rocket fuel.

They put their heads together and came up with a contest. The objective is to bring something new and hopefully surprising to the table with each meeting. *New* means new to you or your partner, and *surprising* means likely to surprise even the author. They have been playing for months.

Something incredible happened within those months. They finally met each other. I don't want to sound ridiculous, but their story is unspectacular. They saw each other for the first time in high school. He attended Central and she Germantown Academy. They were both members of the track-and-field programs, and they both excelled. She first caught his eyes during their sophomore year when she blazed the track in the two hundred meters, setting a school and meet record. He drew her attention when he swept the discus, shot, and javelin, setting school records. Neither bothered to speak, but they did notice.

They met again senior year at an SAT prep course. They recognized each other. They made those knowing smiles that become aggravated by necessary small talk. They kept each other in good company for the duration of the course, and they hesitantly parted ways when the course ended.

They both scored over eleven hundred on the exam. He went to Drexel for engineering. She went to the University of Pennsylvania to become a doctor of orthopedics.

He continued in athletics, joining the soccer team, where he did well. His interests in physical fitness grew, and by his junior year, he took on classes in sport management. He graduated with a BA in engineering and a certificate in sport management. The day of his graduation, his mother gave him a hug and asked to have the parchment that represented his degree. It was scrolled and bound with a blue ribbon. He smiled as he slapped it into her left hand. Her right hand rose and in it was a similarly scrolled piece of paper. He unrolled it and read it. It was the deed to a six-unit building in West Philadelphia.

She bought it in 1987, when he was entering high school. She used the money she was saving to buy a new car and the money his father, Christopher Nelson, had been contributing since their separation and divorce. The real estate market was very buyer-friendly at that time, especially in the area around Forty-Fourth and Chestnut.

His father was physically and emotionally abusive to his mother, Patricia Marie Little-Nelson. She was like the many other people who become trapped in a situation. They were betrayed by their own perceptions and self-image. They did love each other though. They were good friends and made good partners in the business portion of the marriage. Socially they enjoyed many of the same activities and genuinely enjoyed being in each

149

other's company. All of this and their son, Mark Anthony, made the low end bearable for many years.

Christopher crossed the line one day in June of 1981. He came home from his office, and as usual, everything seemed fine. He once aspired to be a professional football player, but it turned out he was better with numbers and economic theory than he was at scoring touchdowns, so he became an accountant/financial advisor. There were hugs and kisses for the family, some laughs, and the discussion of whatever issues had come up. During the discussion of some forgotten issue that they disagreed on, his voice became gradually louder and his posture more aggressive. He had a notoriously volatile temper. It always resulted in her being struck and oftentimes repeatedly. Mark Anthony had witnessed it for all eight of his years. This day, though, something was different. Mark Anthony rose from his chair in his room where he traditionally retreated to when his parents had their evening talk, and proceeded downstairs to the dining room and the spot of the commotion. He stepped in between his mother, who was on the floor crying, and his father, who was standing over her yelling.

Christopher paused. It was the kind of pause that you see in someone who is truly taken aback. He regained himself, then slapped his child to the floor. His mother screamed. Mark Anthony, with only a single tear running out of his right eye, stood up and regained his position between his mother and father with a determined countenance and posture. The word *motherfucker* had just left Christopher's lips when he punched his son in his face, knocking him unconscious.

When Mark Anthony regained consciousness, he was on a stretcher being escorted by fire rescue personnel. There were many police officers around, and his mother was speaking to some people in suites. He did not see his father, who had already been taken to the district. He suffered a fractured jaw. His mother did not press charges although the district attorney did. His mother spoke on his father's behalf in court. This and the facts that he was a business owner and had never been in the legal system for any reason earned him leniency. He was given two years probation, ordered to undergo a psychological evaluation, and required to complete anger management training. He was not to be within one hundred fifty feet of his wife or child, and she was granted an immediate separation pending divorce. He did not challenge. Patricia Marie and her son left the home and went to live with her mother in North Philadelphia.

Their home was left to Christopher by his mother who had died five years earlier. His mother also suffered at the temper of his father, and he and his siblings were witnesses. It only ended when his father one day left the house for work and never returned.

Mrs. Nelson loved her son, her daughter-in-law, and her grandson. She and Patricia were very close. She was part of the reason why Patricia did not leave Christopher before Mark Anthony was conceived. Mrs. Nelson detailed Christopher's pedigree and history. At the end of it, Patricia understood that the one she loved had at least an issue that would not be easy to remedy. She understood that if what she had for him was love, then she would have to endure for a period of time until he came to another understanding of love. Other than his understanding of the time. He was shielded from his mother's love by questions that he asked and could not ask about his father, and he did not receive the satisfactory answers. Patricia's child was not part of that arrangement though.

Patricia did not allow the PFA (Protection from Abuse) order to be in effect a day longer than it took Christopher to complete his anger management training, which took a year. She and Mark Anthony picked him up on his last day, and they went out to have dinner as a family for the first time in over a year. Patricia did not request child support or alimony from him, nor did she allow the court to impose any. Every month, though, she would find five hundred dollars transferred into her account. She also received notice from Oppenheimer Investments updating the summary of a college fund in her son's, Mark Anthony, name. Its inception date was October 19, 1973, the day after they discovered the pregnancy.

A year later, Christopher bought a row house two doors from Patricia's mother's and presented Patricia with the deed. He was saving for a home for his family in Chestnut Hill. He and Patricia had always talked about living there. But he knew that she wanted, and now needed, to be close to her mother. He eventually sold his childhood home and moved to Moorestown, New Jersey.

Christopher and Patricia remained loving friends from that point. Christopher and his son eventually got past the emotional toxins immediately created from such an interaction. It took some very open and painful discussion about blocks of his childhood that had no closure. It took the revealing of person and self, what he had allowed himself to become, and what he could yet become—father to son, man to woman—to close those ugly chapters of his past. Christopher eventually came to understand love.

Her name is Tyre Lana Diop. Her father is from Senegal, and her mother from South Philadelphia. They met at the birthday party of a mutual friend held in a banquet room at the Four Seasons hotel. They began a friendship that evening that has lasted over thirty-three years.

Tyre Lana is the proof of it. She was born January 26, 1973. She has two siblings, Jeffrey Abdul, her younger brother, and Tyre Aishe Diop, her older Senegalese sister.

Her father, Abdul Diop, owned a successful import/export business. He dealt mostly in textiles and art. Her mother, Lana Denice Smith, was a middle school teacher. She later earned her bachelor's degree in English writing, then a master's degree in education administration. She worked as a professor of English at Community College until Tyre graduated high school. She has since followed her passion of writing and makes a comfortable living at that.

Her sister, Tyre Aishe, is the elder by three years and lived in Senegal with their paternal grandmother, Tyre. Her mother died after being struck by a speeding vehicle a year after giving birth. Abdul managed as best he could, but the strain of nurturing a newborn and a fledgling business were too much. His mother insisted on caring for her granddaughter. So

Abdul left his daughter in his mother's care while he built his business. His pursuit of growth led him from Senegal to Boston, and then to Philadelphia, where he established himself.

In the summer of 1986, Abdul brought his wife and child to Senegal to meet his side of the family. From the moment they stepped off the plane, Tyre Lana was enraptured. She has only just gotten to the point where she can articulate what it was that she felt then. "It was warm," she would say. "It wasn't the sun but like the gaze of a thousand eyes from a thousand lifetimes ago. And in their eyes was the loving recognition of a parent to a child, like the divine to the person and the person to the divine. It was love."

Her grandmother's name was Tyre Mana Cofe. Abdul was her third boy, and he has two sisters, one older and one younger. His elder brother, Mansa, picked them up from the airport and delivered them to their mother's home. The reunion was emotional. Although he had been back to visit several times, that was the first time he brought his wife and child. They remained in Senegal for two weeks. Lana became unusually familiar with her grandmother. It was unusual because in such a short time, Tyre Lana had cleaved to Tyre Mana as if she were born to her. When they left, there were a lot of tears, and Tyre Aishe was with them.

It was a difficult adjustment for everyone initially. There were the common barriers of language and custom, but those things could be easily explained and forgiven. Aishe's English was very good, but she had a heavy accent. What could not be easily explained or forgiven was the amount of attention Tyre Lana began to miss from her father. In retrospect, she understands that her father had a great responsibility toward his elder daughter. They all did. But an adolescent is not understanding of suddenly not being the only daughter. She made things more difficult than they had to be. Her selfishness even began to drive a wedge between her mother and father.

The cure was realized the summer before her sophomore year in high school. She rode her bicycle to the school track to practice. She was good

153

in the two hundred meters, but had never placed or won. When she arrived, Aishe was there and just finishing her warm-up laps. Lana tried to avoid direct contact with her sister, but Aishe was insistent. Lana began and finished her warm-up and drills with Aishe as the sole spectator. When Lana began her practice runs, Aishe joined her on the track. Aishe was an accomplished runner in Senegal, a fact their father neglected to mention, but concentrated on her studies in botany and herbal medicines. The herbs she grew, she used to relieve the arthritic condition of Tyre Mana. This is why she did not want to leave Senegal. Who would care for mother? She detailed all of this to Lana as they ran together and gave Lana some advice on her form, running style, and most especially her vision. "One's vision of oneself," she would say, "is the complement and motivation of one's skill. I like to see myself as the wind. Nothing is as swift as the wind. The heavens are my corral, and when they open, I want to touch as much of the earth as I can before I lose motivation. So I run fast." Naturally, Lana felt her sister's advice was out of place, so they raced. Aishe beat Lana by such a distance that Lana felt dumbfounded rather than disappointed. Aishe's last words to her that day, "Vision, sister. Let your ability catch up to your vision."

They practiced together every day they could that summer. Aishe was attending a center for holistic studies in New Jersey and would be attending University of Pennsylvania in the fall for biology. Lana became better focused, and with that focus came better satisfaction of her pursuits. And best of all, the sisters became sisters.

And that bitch did not even bother to acknowledge me. What I did to her in that chair. How I moved her in that chair. Rather, she went on like business as usual. I can respect her cool. She is not easy to shake up. But the nerve. The fucking nerve of her to behave as if mine was not the winning method.

I felt compelled to take another turn, and I would not be satisfied by the slight humility I dealt her that first time. This time, I would calculate more diabolically what spices my method should contain to dislodge that word stuck in her ego. This time, my nerves would not cause me to pause or to suffer remorse. This time, I will hear her confession.

I was able to manufacture an anger that carried me through the days until that moment where once again her husband would be attending to some out-of-town business. I was able to nurture it to that moment at eleven forty-five, when she entered the home and proceeded about her usual routine, curiously, without the slightest deviation. However, rather than her work costume, she wore a black business outfit. It was a skirt with matching jacket, a beige blouse, and short-heeled black pumps with ankle straps.

I struck through the dark, grabbing her firmly by the throat with my right hand and slammed her back hard into the nearest wall. Something bounced from the wall and hit the floor beside us. She fought back, striking me with a fist across my jaw and several kicks at my legs and groin area. I struck her hard across her face with the open palm of my left hand. She slowed but fought on, apparently not yet affected by my tightening grip about her throat. I struck her again with a solid blow to the stomach. This was enough to relieve her of what inspiration urged her to fight, and enough to scare the oxygen from her lungs, letting her body collapse in my grasp.

When she came to her senses, she was gagged by a strip of the same kind of gray tape I used during our first meeting. Her right cheek was pressed firmly against the polished wood floor of the study where that chair sat. Both of her arms were underneath her and stretched along the floor. Each of her arms was ridiculously bound by plain thin brown rope, and each to the inside of its corresponding leg—elbows to knees and wrists to ankles. Her back rose into the air on a forty-five-degree angle, curved soft, and wide at her ass, then turned down into two dark thick legs. Her knees were pressed into the boards of the hardwood floor. Around her neck was a length of thick brown hemp rope. It was doubled, and the soft flesh of her throat lay on the loop at its bottom. The length circled her flesh until it came together and corkscrewed from the base of the back of her neck to my hand that held its commanding end.

My foul attitude pushed me into her with a spiteful vengeance. It pushed me into her pussy, and her pussy held as sour an attitude as I. It frothed, foamed, farted, and boiled. It perspired a creamy attitude over my latex-covered member. It coated it, possibly in defense of its sensitive components and possibly initiating a diabolical offense of its own—an offense that salutes a war of attrition.

I drove my length deep. From the pee-pee slit until my balls smacked her clit—and hard, so that her body rocked and shook violently with every thrust. I worked so hard that I activated combinations of muscles that would inspire a new category of aerobic workout. I worked so hard that personage rage found itself idea to idea with that personage compassion and proceeded to beat it down.

I would not relent. I was every bit the growling, drooling, scowl-faced madman that haunts only the best of sexual fantasies. I rode her hard until holes were worn in her knees and streaks of blood stained the floor. I rode her until her eyes rolled back into that frenzied white that a feeding shark's becomes. I rode her until her breathing had become so sporadic and shallow that I began to wonder if she were still in the world.

I worked that delicious dark pussy until a piece of my anger ejected in one large boiling mass into the pocket of red latex made available for that duty.

I pulled out of her and threw that bag off. I quickly replaced it with another of the same sort—bloodred, studded, and cinnamon-scented.

In the interim, she had not regained her senses. What power of anger I lost in that first ejaculation was quickly regenerated through the intensity of the moment, and my member became incredibly stiffer. Incredible in that iron can only be as hard as iron can be. It cannot become more so without becoming something other than iron. My penis had reached the limits of the capacity of the many cells within it and began to exceed them. Perhaps this was a natural phenomenon that occurs when an organism is stressed to its peak. Then perhaps it was the force of will.

When I pulled that first condom off, the silken dark flesh of my member twitched then expanded as if inhaling. I stood for a moment and watched it in near amazement. It seemed as if it had been lifetimes since the last occasion I'd seen it in this kind of majesty. My relationship of that time had been very user-friendly, but I had not had this kind of inspiration to push its potential. There it stood, however. Its kind is older and more mysterious than the columns of the temple of Karnak at Luxor. At a time of its greatest expression, it was more visited by curious and eager admirers than the Empire State Building.

It is beautiful. I watched it and the full dark ass lain beneath it. Both of my hands instinctively reached out and grasped that ass by each high plump dark cheek and pulled them apart, exposing her anus. It was an angel's kiss. A dark orifice covered by shadows and the intent of our debaucheries. A sensitive organ whose body was stressed against the force of my tongue's query. There is no greater beauty in all of nature's creation, nor any greater taste than helplessness to a fiend.

I enjoyed the sight of her sacrificially helpless and at my command. It made me quiver. I did not prepare her with any more lubrication than my tongue left glistening on her asshole. There was no time. The moment the inspiration hit me in the brow, it was simultaneously felt in my package. Such a moment must be seized, not intellectualized, and certainly not forgiven. It was an inspiration grand enough to motivate an already-stressed penis to evolve like an erotic Pokeman. It stretched that red glove that suffocated it to its breaking point.

I forced its swollen candy-coated head into her nearly dry anus. Not bone-ass dry as the wave of the previous interaction caused her body's sympathetic reactions, one of which was the secretion of fluids out of every pore and into every orifice.

Still, the shock of so great an object being pushed into an unprepared opening, oh my. As its soft head pushed past her resistant sphincter, she became more aware. As the impossibly fat end of all of that dick rushed in behind it, awareness came to her in bushels.

Her reaction was a throaty moan that was just short of a scream and muffled by the tape. Only the low hum of what sound was greatest escaped. That I choked off by tightening the rope. A single twist of the hand that shrank its fibers into her soft flesh. I then gave a fierce tug on its end that suddenly lifted her face from the floor and, just as suddenly, dropped it back in place with a thud.

The only leniency available was that found in my initial inability to push that tool like I wanted. Without some type of additional lubrication, even the most eager penis would find only discouraging discomfort in forcing such an issue. Her body, though, whether wiling or not, accommodated the will of the moment and produced more than enough lubrication to make the siege mutually comfortable.

I threw length after length into her hungry dark hole. Gradually, the discomfort of the first insertion faded from her brow. Gradually, the natural joy found in feeling one's muscles relax and submit overcame her. Her gluteal area, her body proper, her mind—all of these overcame her and became her. One unit of flesh, consciousness, and will submitting to the force of the power joy.

She ceased what struggling she could manage, and her eyes regained their normal gaze. She was focused. She was psychically that canal that accommodated my sex. And the more fiercely I pushed my energy into her, the more she craved. The craving initiated a sympathetic reaction in her orifice. Her canal began to massage my member with the soft stroke of its silken walls. Her canal began to suck at the sensitive shaft as it withdrew. Her canal created a vacuum within the chamber that my mean tool invaded. A chamber that I gradually had insufficient power of hip to pull completely out of. As a unit, she stroked, sucked, and tickled my principle until what rage there was drained into it, and through it, to be lost in the ethers of time contained in the head of a red latex bag.

I paused for several moments over her. My dick still throbbed inside of her with the waning pulse of the power that brought me there. I exhaled sharply. I slowly pulled out of her and stood over her. I stared down at her, still trying to manage my breathing. I could not help but to superimpose some sore image of my own past over this scene. And despite my knowledge of the differences that separate the moments, guilt plagued me. It came upon me with the same force I applied too precious.

I walked to that executive's chair and sat. I sat and watched her. She is beautiful. My breathing had calmed. That feigned anger had transformed into a real remorse despite my best efforts to deny it. I watched her dark tortured body illuminated by the pale moonlight shining through the skylight above. I cried.

As the tears rolled slowly down my face, I noticed that great dark form of hers poised so slavishly. Her skin's the color of the finest smoothest walnut. It is Africana skin. It refracts this light in a pale shade of blue that is typical of her level of melanin. That vision on this mat of pitch she leans against is ghostly. It is like looking at a life-sized black light poster—the ones from the seventies that depicted astrological sex positions. All she needed was an Afro.

From that chair, I could see her sphincter still twitching from the shock of the abuse. It was relaxing to normalcy, but still sported a nickel-sized cavity that shone on her brightened cover like an eclipsed sun in the afternoon sky. I watched it shrink, slowly regaining its composure and, as slowly, closing the portal that my method excited. Slowly but certainly condemning that mean energy, I abandoned within her to rigorous rehabilitation. In the morning, it may appear as a smile.

I loosened her ropes and faded from sight on the passing notes of "Lonely Woman" by Ornette Coleman.

Empathy moved me chaotically like some airy thing at the mercy of whirlwind forces. They bounced me from questions of morality to those of spirituality to those of the simply social-legal. From pillar to pillar to yet another pillar of reasoning or antireasoning, I was ricocheted. And I felt remorse. To the extent of my ability. To the extent I was sorry it had to happen. And therein was my shield against the tempest. No matter the apparent beastly and cruel nature of the act, it was necessary. And necessity dictated the moment.

I left her as she was—on the floor, half naked, and her sex abused. Her husband would have been returning by nine this morning. I think of what word she could say to ease the predicament. I laughed thinking that she would finally have to humble herself.

She woke and heard him downstairs at about 9:23 a.m. that Saturday morning. He proceeded through the floor along his normal routes. He found it to be as ordered as it usually was. Everything was in its place with the exception of a framed picture of him and her taken in Bahia, Brazil. It hung on the wall between the living room and kitchen. It was not there. Other than this, the place was as it should be.

His route finally took him upstairs to his bedroom, where he found her still in bed. He stared at her lovingly for a moment. He had already removed his shoes and wore only black dress socks. He walked to her side of the bed, as is usual when he finds her there. He knelt to the floor, leaned over her, and placed a soft kiss to her cheek. She stirred from her feigned sleep and opened her eyes only enough to see him.

"Hi, baby," she whispered in a raspy morning voice.

He responded in kind with a soft, "Hey, kid," then stood and moved about the room while removing his clothing.

She enjoys watching him undress. She loves his body. In her opinion, his form is the model that all males should aspire to. He is six-foot-two-inches tall, two hundred ten pounds, and 6 percent body fat. He is a vegetarian and so is she. He sports the same walnut-colored cover as she, and like her, his hair is in neat locks that hang freely from his head.

He is sculpted. There is not a part of his being that he does not work out. His physical practice, though, is the more immediately obvious of the group: mind, body, and spirit. And for her, he is physically delicious.

He unwrapped himself. He first unbuttoned and peeled back his white dress shirt, revealing his bare stomach and chest. She stared at his waistline and followed it from his left side to its center. She could see the dark coarse hairs reaching out from under his belt line. She followed the hairline as it traveled up his center crease and over his deep navel. Her eyes rode over a smooth and well-defined eight-pack of blocks that rose and exploded into a thick ripped chest. He threw the shirt off his shoulders and allowed it to fall to the floor. Her eyes reached his neck and were studying her favorite kissing spot—the one that takes his will to resist from him—when the shirt dragged her attention down his massive shoulders and arms and splashed to the floor in a bunch.

He turned away from her while unfastening his belt and undoing his pants. He always does that, and she would prefer he didn't, but it is a habit of his. The pants dropped around his ankles, revealing his bare ass and legs. She was not surprised he was not wearing underwear. He wears them nearly exclusively during his workouts and rarely for any other occasion. His ass, although slightly rippled with strands and knots of muscle. They convulse as he removed each foot from its sock and pant. He turned to her and paused. He sported a quizzical countenance, as if he were not completely certain he were completely naked.

She loves that picture. Nothing is more inspiring to her beastly impulses than a naked and well-built man standing poised for the unknown; and the dick, especially with the dick in full view.

Only her eyes moved as they washed over him from foot to head, from head to face, and from face back down to that head. He was half hard, so it hung, but it hung thick. His balls were shaved bare, which is the way she likes them. He is the perfect size; he fits everywhere comfortably. It is his skill when pushing that thing, though, that often graduates him to honorary big-dick status. And although they both know that she has the occasional craving for the feel of the actual big dick—an appetite she developed at the university—they have found great freedom in the comfort of each other.

He walked into the bathroom, brushed his teeth, and rinsed with mouthwash. He trimmed or cut whatever hairs had grown too bold, then started and finished a shower.

He reentered the room as naked as he had left but without the smell of business clinging to him. He moved about the room from station to station. He lotioned, moisturized, and deodorized. He noticed she followed him with her eyes around the room. The difference was in her eyes—those soft brown eyes with the half question and smile shining from them. When he finally got in bed, she was already turned to his direction.

He settled into the comfort of the cool sheets. He smiled at her as if he could not read the intent that was plainly written on her face. He snuggled the sheets around himself and closed his eyes. Her left hand first found his right arm at the elbow and ran a course up to his shoulder. From the shoulder, it strayed to his bare chest, then trickled down across his abdomen and belly button. It paused when its fingers first hit the ruff of his pubes, then continued its trek until it found his sex.

His penis seemed to waver between conscious and unconscious like a fiend on a heroine nod. It leaned lazily to whatever degree her playful hand suggested. Her hand made at least one hundred eighty degrees worth of suggestions that playtime was just beginning. The penis had the only eye in the room that could not see that.

She used her careful hand's grip on the dick as an anchor to pull her head and torso to his. Her lips kissed along his chest and kissed it like a newborn thing. Those tender lips then followed the example that hand made. Those lips found his drowsy sex and, with profound word of mouth, began to rouse it.

The energy in her method spread like a virus from his loins. Every pulse of his blood carried its influence. It overtook him in less than seven heartbeats.

Gradually, the feel of his member being licked, pulled, stuffed, stroked, and sucked into that cavern of warm, soft pink flesh, guarded by tooth and governed by tongue, overwhelmed him. Tooth, what's rough posture let loom the tense thrill of what inquisition like punishment could be administered for any sudden moves; and tongue that frisked, cleaned, dressed, and questioned the alleged.

He lay in the cut and endured this treatment as reparation for some heinous deed done; or perhaps for the sake of sanity, as she finds its practice meditative. He endured obstinately to his he-will. It is that part of him that will resist an outside influence. Its strength was gradually failing, though, because of the concentration of heat upon his member, the intimidation of rows of sentry teeth, the prodding and coaxing of tireless tongue and lips, and the thrust of an inquiry that was sometimes long and drawn out and other times moved in dizzying speeds and direction. He endured, but she would not be denied.

Her left hand began a massaging barter with his balls and assured them that should they cooperate, a mutually beneficial deal could be struck. The left testicle was hesitant, but it always is. The right agreed on the condition that the anus was part of the deal. It only took the persistent and gentle stroke of a single digit across that asshole and the slow torturous insertion of that same digit as coercion, and all at once, his house fell apart. He resisted no more. The proof was in his bellow as it echoed off every wall. He had not ejaculated, but she knew he no longer had a line of defense.

By this time, the sheets were thrown to the floor. Her knees were pressed into the mattress, and the poetry of her dark form dominated his view. Her thighs stretched from her knees into the air to form a tight round ass. The ass sloped down into thin waist, toned back, and warm swinging breasts. As they swayed with the rhythm of her method, the large dark leathery nipples tickled his thighs. Her head hung over his crotch with the right arm bent and resting along his stomach while holding the base of the shaft of his swollen dick.

His sedated eyes rove her form. They moved from her head bobbing slowly above his groin and over her strong but femininely soft body. His hands immediately began to roam. The left moved along her right side and came to rest on her ass. The right played in her hair. It found inspiration and griped a bunch of it and pulled it away to expose her face. He wanted to see her work. She did not disappoint him, but intensified her method so it left his mouth as wide open as his eyes and libido.

His sensitive digits did not rest though. His left hand continued to feel along her like he were a blind initiate and she were an ancient parchment written in braille and containing the answers to the mysteries of life. His fingers rode over her soft round ass and down her thighs. They probed her form like it was new. Slowly his fingers walked along the back of her knee, her calf, and her right ankle. They rest for a moment then moved slowly back along the path until it came to rest in a grip on her ass.

It was right about then that her will and diligence came to fruit. His body convulsed terribly. He felt his genetic matter being pulled and not ejected from his shaft. The mouth that housed his member created that very same vacuum whose pulling force drew his potential from his balls in an incredible hurry. He choked back a scream. The shock of the assault caused his testis to produce greater amounts of material than he had previously surrendered. The wave left him breathless.

When the moment faded, she raised her face from his crotch and kissed his belly. She stared at him with glossy lips and a trickle of cloudy liquid driving to her chin. She smiled then rose to her feet and disappeared into the bathroom.

His penis enjoyed glory, proud glory, until its vitality faded and left it a tubular heap of dark flesh shrinking into passivity. His eyes became dull and lazy. His respirations calmed to normal as did his body, whose inflamed nerves still ticked and twitched from the waning force of energy applied and lost. Sleep came so easily he was not aware it had him until he woke up later that afternoon to the aroma of cinnamon oatmeal and a fruit bowl with a variety of berries, banana, kiwi, and mango being presented to him in a tray with a glass of water.

This is exactly what brings me here tonight. She has denied me one time too many. She has denied me the satisfaction of experiencing the win. I will have victory. She will say the word tonight.

11:44 p.m.
And the images of what I will do to her and my right hand have me high. Masturbation has definitely gotten a bad rap. This shit is good. The security lights burst to life as her car pulls into the driveway. That light is dimmed and tinted red as it bleeds through the crimson window coverings. The effect lit up the room as if a flare had been ignited. As the light faded, my eyes drifted left. On the bookshelf along the wall, I spy a large wooden sculpture in one of the compartments. It is the Ghanaian Sankofa. Then darkness.

The moment is upon me. The possibilities of the next bit of time fill me with motivation. My entire person becomes hard and ready. I will disappoint no one tonight. Me, the dark, and my wife knew this was coming.

11:45 p.m.
And the dead bolt's mechanisms click and turn. She enters as usual and proceeds along her usual route. I assault her, ridiculously at the same point I had two times previous, and brutalize her slightly worse than on that occasion. She fought harder than she had any of those times, and she resisted the application of my treatment with more ardent urgency, but fell nonetheless.

This time, after taping her mouth, I dragged her ass upstairs to the bedroom by force of her hair. I ripped every article of clothing from her body and laid her on the bed. I produced nylon ropes I had prepared the day before. I bound her unforgivingly to the bed first by pushing her head through the center bars of the footboard and securing it with a headlock of my devising. It is made of two one-and-one-half-foot pieces of two by four. Their flat sides are joined at their ends by two half-inch by twelve-inch machine bolts held by washers and wing nuts. Once tightened about her neck, it is impossible for her to pull free of the bars. Also, the sharp corners, dents, and scratches I decorated the boards with would be quite uncomfortable to struggle against. I then bound her arms behind her back and at her wrists. I tied her wrists with rope then lashed and secured the rope over the wrought iron crossbeam of the canopy. This made it necessary that she stay on her knees at all times, or the weight of her body could dislocate her arms at the shoulders.

I began the assault from the preferred point, the rear. I engaged her with so much more spite and aggression than before that I was not aware I was capable of losing myself so completely to the beast. I worked her pussy with strong strokes that if prolonged had to jar loose some vital organ. I worked her pussy until her cream—the proof of the effectiveness of our method—caked and gathered about her opening and my loosely swinging balls, and at least a stream of cloudy liquid oozed down her inner left thigh. I kept it up until I exhausted two condoms in my efforts to make her say "when."

I began to express myself into her ass with as much discontent as I had in her pussy. I had to do so with a blind eye to the blood-streaked scars created on the surface of her neck from the headlock, and as deaf an ear to the muffled sounds I wished were both cries of discomfort and defeat.

Suddenly the mirrored door of the large walk-in closet to my left began to open. From it strode a rather long fellow of at least six foot six, very dark-skinned, and massaging an already excited piece of dick meat. But "piece" is much too misleading. He had a major portion, an unfair allotment, an uneven allowance of dick that he obviously treasured.

He approached us as if following a script. He smiled pleasantly at me before taking his position before her. He knelt with his left leg standing at a right angle and the knee pressed against a bar of the footboard while the right knee was pressed into the carpet. That dark tool of his rose and pointed tellingly at her face like the needle of some divine compass revealing the direction of heaven.

His right hand grabbed at a bunch of her hair and pulled her head up forcefully against the restrictive blocks until the full of her face was in his view. Her eyes tightened, and her face became bitter with the sudden surge of pain shooting through her neck.

It was then that I noticed or even cared to notice her countenance. Her tear-filled eyes were barely buoyant over her face wracked with all the contortions of the accelerated thought that this combination of interaction can evince. Her eyes found mine, and what motion I had left in my hips ceased. What ill intent I still hoarded began to evacuate with every exhale. I found myself, suddenly, the shamed prisoner of my determination to win.

The inevitable questions concerning my behavior would come. However, the most pressing question was, who the fuck is this guy? He certainly was not part of my equation. With that thought and a now-deflated inspiration, I thought my only recourse was to retrieve my pistol from the closet and shoot this motherfucker. The instant I began to pull my now-flaccid penis out of her ass, he ripped the tape from her mouth with one unkind motion. The tape had hardly been removed, and she was already barking at me. I did not move, of course. I could not. I was still trying to catch up to the situation.

"Fuck me, you limp bastard!" she shouted.

She then committed herself to repeating the command but in various profane combinations until the newcomer had heard enough. While still controlling her head by her hair, he issued a sharp slap across her right cheek while tugging violently at her hair, calling her a bitch, and ordering her to shut the fuck up.

We both felt the shock and indignity of it, she and I. But while it froze my tongue, it emboldened hers. She responded in form with a "shut me the fuck up, you black motherfucker." The "motherfucker" had barely left her mouth when the length of his tool disappeared beyond her thick lips, distorting the sound of the insult. He held her head aloft by the hair.

His thin hips pulled that dark length back some inches then slowly slid it forward into that wet cave until she gagged and choked. She squeezed a cough around his swollen sex as streams of thick saliva escaped from the creases of her mouth. He jerked her head back and informed her politely that she had better not bite his shit. After this warning, he reeled in half his length, leaving a full six inches for her to pleasure. And she did—greedily, savagely, and like a person who fiends for the feel and taste of dick. She worked as if this was the icing on a very carefully prepared gourmet cake, and she would show no shame of indulgence of such rare and sweet slices of being as this.

She growled and moaned at it. She hissed, spit, and barked at it. It fought back with parries and thrusts. He stabbed and smacked her about the face and mouth, with it leaving wet sticky trails as proof of each strike. He offers her mouth his heavy balls as a treat or a distraction. Either way, she attended to them with suck skill that he felt moved to massage his stiff twelve inches as she washed his balls in her mouth.

This went on for several minutes. It is amazing how conscious of time you become when the situation demands it. I was counting seconds and then seconds into minutes. This went on until I felt quite sure that he had taken up enough of my time. But the force of this situation—this stranger using my wife's oral skills for his pleasure, and my being dumfounded at what to do about it. Both of these oddities combined to reduce my participation to that of a slightly interactive voyeur. Or even worse, no more useful than one of those toys closed up in that briefcase.

The more intently I observed this scene, the more I became caught up in the ultimate absurdity of it. This situation, some would call sick, I simply could not call. I could not name it like one could a familiar noun. This lack of distinction forced on my senses by the unknown answer to the question of her, by the shock and wave of this stranger, by my desire to serve the illusions I have conjured—especially to serve the illusions, all of these conspired to disarm me, defuse me, and completely disallow me from acting on this situation. I could, however, react, but with some very limited range of intellectual motion controlled not by me, but by the disembodied will and hands of those whose purpose, intent, and motivation are momentarily so much hotter than mine. In the end, it was I, the beastly aggressor, who became no more than a device to be managed by the will of my intended, though pretended, victim.

However, these are all so tasty, satisfying visions. And especially to this extreme degree. They incite my mouth to water as my eyes are fixed on the spot of the action. The thrill of the session overrides my reservations, and my hips begin to push my now-growing member into her craven opening. That motion proved just enough to satisfy the momentary needs of her starved ass. I gathered this from the hungry way she opened to me and how anxiously she met my thrusts. Then those soft sighs of triumph that she pushed around that thick organ stuffing her mouth were proof she was aware of how bold a maneuver she had successfully executed.

I was so moved the word *when* was on the tip of my tongue. I was prepared to shout it out loud enough to bring a grinding halt to this game. I wanted to believe it was painful to witness this scene, but it was not. Not my person, ego, nor self-image was damaged in the creating of this scene. In fact, I felt a great deal of relief.

She and I have, and continue, an open dialogue about our respective sexual histories. Whatever is revealed is most often very detailed so as to give an honest and clear picture of the events. I believe we are both very confident that there is very little of each other's past and current lusts and desires that we are not aware of. And whatever has not been revealed is but a question away.

She and I had a very decent beginning. It began with honesty, and that honesty only became more pronounced as our relationship, then marriage, progressed. Since this game, though, Say When, our most guarded desires are surfacing. Those taboo thoughts that would once cause a still tongue and tight lips now move us to reach out to each other by telephone, telegraph, or carrier pigeon in the effort to share with each other the latest inspiration.

She knew of my hesitance to become more than mildly aggressive with a female. I knew how stimulated she becomes when confronted by aggressive males with large penises. This scene was inevitable in some form or another if we were to survive. So I could not say the word. Though, I could allow myself to enjoy the freedom of the moment.

This entire scene ended in a collective psychic scream. We had reached the climax of expectations. We came in succession. Her tonsil and tongue tricks drew streams of his hot cream into her mouth and onto her face and hair. They drew the air from his body in one powerful pull and nearly drew the color from his frame.

She seemed to find an extra-internal charge and motivation from the fruit of her labor. The movement of our collective effort became concentrated in her mind until it exploded from her body in all directions. She let go a sound that had to be what a banshee is supposed to sound like. That explosion of sound triggered the simultaneous release of juice from every orifice capable.

The combined influence of their energy invaded me through every receptive sensory organ and corrupted me from the inside out. I could conceive of anything more exciting or more completely fulfilling than the fact of us; we and him, they and me.

Before me lay the chrysalis that I battled to break open so that I may become everything we both needed me to be. I drove on that hole until I drove no end of verbal babble from her throat. The dude cheered us on. The final moment came when she called to her god as my energy invaded her. It washed through her and cleansed whatever ill energy had been created for the cause.

When the tide receded, I unbound her, and we lay on the bed in the glow. The stranger retrieved his things from the closet, washed, dressed, said his thank-yous and good-byes, and found his way out.

In the morning, I was again greeted by breakfast in bed. It was a fruit, soy protein, and herb smoothie. Her attitude and manner were as friendly and lively as I'd ever seen. We talked, laughed, and shared a shower. We hugged and kissed then shared a sixty-nine and a fuck. We cleaned the house. It was not a top-to-bottom cleaning, but more of a wiping and arranging. We went for a drive and found ourselves roaming a furniture outlet near Reading. That afternoon, we walked South Street, licking from our respective water ices. Hers was cherry and mine mango. We caught the first show at the Laugh House, then afterward retreated home to relax. That night, we talked over cups of chocolate coffee and then mostly about what new drama had developed at the hospital where she is a doctor of orthopedics. We spoke on topics great and small without touching on the topic of the moment. We fell asleep having exhausted our periphery need to know.

That Sunday, we stayed at home. This was our first weekend together in nearly a year. I woke up with the sun. I put on a purple satin pajama set Lana bought for me and moved outdoors to the gazebo. I performed a Tai Chi workout then meditated. Afterward, I moved to the kitchen to prepare some tea. She was in the kitchen wearing a brass-colored Chinese-style silk robe and already had two cups of rose hips and peppermint tea at the ready. We both walked out of the kitchen hand in hand. We moved through the patio doors, into the backyard, and made ourselves comfortable in the swinging love seat on the gazebo.

"He's a doctor," she suddenly started.

"Known him long," I responded.

"Since Penn," she says and pauses. Life is moving around us. Birds are singing. There are a couple of squirrels playing on the tree limbs just twenty feet before us. The air is warm, and the breeze is right on time. She takes a sip from her cup. "He's safe," she finishes.

"What's he do?" I add, then gave us a little push so as to create some motion. I was interested in the tea, but being with her is more soothing than that brew could hope to be. I take a sip nonetheless.

"Pediatrics. Do you remember that banquet we went to at the Wyndham about two years ago?"

"Yes," I injected and began to stroke the soft but scarred skin of her neck. I tenderly kissed the scar and hugged her tightly, whispering, "I'm sorry." She acknowledged me by rubbing my knee and smiling. She continued to speak though.

"At some point that evening, I introduced you to a couple, Simon and Marie." She paused to hear my acknowledgment.

I gave her an "all right," but I really did not recall. It was a medical banquet, and she introduced me to at least one hundred people that night.

"She's a lieutenant with Philly, and I work with him, I said," and another pause.

"I guess" was the best response I could muster.

"Anyway, that's who he is." A natural break in the conversation that I took advantage of. I prompted her to sit across from me so I could rub her feet. She did, then continued, "Why did you take my panties?"

"I thought it would be a nice touch. Something a stalker might actually do." And with that began the foot rub.

"You thought you were going to win, didn't you?" she suddenly offers.

"I thought I had you," I responded stoically, fighting back some arrogance, but eventually lost to a sly grin.

"You did. I wouldn't have thought you'd go there. I know you're sensitive about those things," she says. Her eyes do not leave my face, though my face is busy on her foot. I know her needs, though, so I look up from my duty and make just enough eye contact to satisfy her. Then I go back to work.

"Yeah, yeah. It was difficult, but—," I start and don't finish because that middle toe annoys me. I take it in my mouth and show it who's boss. Honestly, there is a method to this madness. That particular toe is strategic. As I grip it with my teeth and begin to massage it and the gaps on either side with my tongue, I hear her gasp and feel her adjust herself in her seat. There is a nerve in the area of that toe that goes directly to her clitoris.

"I appreciate it, baby. I really didn't think you would go that far. I almost said it," she began as her pleasurable discomfort intensified. "That first session caught me completely off guard. I knew you were going to do something, but I never figured on that." She now completely relaxes into the seat and my method. She is warm. I move from the seat on to my knees in front of her.

"When did you know it was me?" I said it with a level of suspicion for the answer, but I really had no idea.

"When you hugged me," she said.

I smile as I reflect on that hug and how revealing it actually was. My foot rub and toe suck have matured into full-blown oral devotion. My worship moves up her ankle to her calf, where it runs into an obstruction—her robe. My right hand pulls the end of the belt that was loosely knotted, and it fell apart. I pushed the robe to the side, exposing her bare thighs, crotch, and front. Then back to work.

"You know, I didn't think that would be too much. But live and learn," I said it with no real concern for the words other than something to distract her, which is part of this practice. My mouth was adoring her inner thighs.

"That's why I like playing with you, baby, you're full of surprises." She is in the moment. Her eyes are shut and in REM anticipation of what dreams may come.

I pause, "Well, good. I like playing with you too. And the next time, you will say *when*." I give a quick kiss to her bush. I bend her right leg at the knee then push it open and against the back of the chair. This better exposes my treat. Then I smile and add, "What's with all the dildos?"

"Well," she starts, "you're busy a lot, and I'm horny a lot, and even if you weren't, I've got to have them. That's something else I was introduced to at Penn." She smiles. "Do they really bother you?" she adds in a genuinely concerned tone and face.

"No, they don't bother me. They did remind me how much we still have to learn about each other, though." And I take my adoration to the next level. I use my tongue to gently sweep her labia, then softly kiss the clitoris. Then that slow and gentle licking again before I drop my tongue to her opening and insert my tongue.

"Ahh!" was her response, and it was accompanied by her right hand gripping the rail on the frame of the back of the chair and her left finding a grip of my hair for support.

I sneak in a sarcastic "what was that?"

To which she replied quickly but in a whisper, "Nothing."

"Good, baby"—she squeezes out coldly between the heat my mouth is causing her. She forces on that smug face she always wears when she's got some shit up her sleeve—"because you're next." She dropped it like it was hot.

174

My tongue froze deep in the pussy. I didn't even bother to pull it out when I asked, "Next for what?" which of course was mostly a mumble.

"To enjoy my toys," she declared now as sober as if my treatment had never affected her.

I cut her off with as much "please pardon the interruption" as my face could handle and said, "I don't do toys, babe." And between you and I, audience, I mean that shit.

"Not yet, you don't." Now both of her hands have gripped my hair and are in control of my head. I allow it. She adjusts herself to receive my full treatment. She is square to the seat, the robe is completely away from her body, her legs are bent and raised up so that the bottoms of her feet are rested on the back of my neck. She uses them as extra pressure to push my face more securely into her crotch. And my mouth is working expertly. Then she says, "When's your next business trip, baby?" Then that damned smug-ass smile.

Well, I pulled away, stood up, retrieved my cup of now-cool tea, and adjourned to the house.

"Hey," she shouted after me, barely able to fit it between her laughter.

I gave her nothing but my back. And I'm certain it was convincing, so I smiled and chuckled as I approached the patio doors.

"All right," she blares. "That's why I got the dildos," she adds, then begins to rub her clitty with her left hand while fondling her left tit with the right.

I look back because I know she is doing something provocative. I see her working and laugh out loud while just on the inside of the patio doors. I shout out, "You're nasty."

She looks me directly in my eyes, moves two fingers from her clitty to deep inside her well, pulls them out, and raises them to and into her mouth, where she sucked them clean, pulled them away, and mouthed these words, "You're next."

I smile and disappear beyond her vision.

To be continued

Peep Show
(a love story wrapped in an erotic tale)

April 23, 1994: Forty Deuce

"Have you ever been to a place like this before?" This is Ellis, but his friends call him El. He lays the question out in a voice that is nighttime-radio personality deep, but curiously no more soothing than the rattling engines of the city's fleet of Grumman buses. He generally speaks with an ease that makes him seem more bored than interested with the moment.

"Nah. I heard about them though." This is Kevin. His voice has been known to cover the range from his early morning Barry White to his late afternoon Chris Tucker. Despite what dress his voice may be wearing at a time, it has been known to reflect and evoke the range of emotion a person can qualify for. Generally, though, it is as warm as soft brown skin.

In a New York City breeze, a mixture of odors competes for dominance across their path. The smell of coolant is leaking from the radiator of a yellow cab gagging on its own carbonous poison. The aroma from piles of black bagged trash festering on the curb is intermittently disturbed by the passing waves of sweet burning incense and fragrant oils coming from the Muslim's table of goods. That spot near the 1 and 9 train entrance on Forty-Second Street and Seventh Avenue, where the vagrant sleeps, adds a colorful yet brief mix of stale urine and old sweaty cloth. All of this is unbelievably forgivable against the abundance of odors from tired sweaty bodies whose deodorants have mostly failed, and those conflicting cheap perfumes whose charge on the olfactory is heinous.

The traffic light turns green, and a chorus of engines growl together. The sound of motion is proved by the sticky rotation of poorly retreated tires, blaring horns, and the cordial salutations of drivers:

"Moo dat shit out da way!"

"Fuck you!"

The various paces of feet with and without soul. The bits of idle chatter from indistinct couples and groups. The muffled conversations of characters trying their best to sound shady. These are all sounds that can be found in any city, but this is a voice of Manhattan.

"Girls—all nude, all night. Check 'em out." These are the words of a special kind of solicitor. His job is to provoke those with disposable cash to dispose of it in this or that establishment. There are a remarkable many who may be on the bubble where wanting to enjoy a hard-on while gawking at naked and unfamiliar females are the issue.

Two pairs of rubber-bottomed feet trot up a flight of cement stairs, leaving the street noises to the street. The vender continues to solicit an audience, "Girls: all nude, all night. Try 'em here."

"You never been here before, huh?" says El as they climb the stairs.

"No!" Kevin responds.

They turn to the left at the top of the stairs as the heavy-bottomed music of a rap song pounds the walls and ears with the voice of Method Man, "They want their titties sucked. Ice cream."

"Just do what I do," El assures his partner.

"How much?" says a voice that is obviously unconcerned and just able to penetrate the music.

"Five," Ellis responds as the dry flip and unfold of a bill whispers under the noise. Coins hit a surface with a sharp thud, then are slid across into silence.

"Five," Kevin repeats and invokes the same response.

The music seems to have gotten softer as the theme shifts from rap to house. A door creaks open amid the flurry of sound while another opens silently. They both close with a thud and are latched shut. A coin drops through a slot, obliging the response of a mechanism. A dark window swiftly opens.

Peach-colored light invades the dark of the cramped booth through a small window. It is ten by eight inches big and about an inch and one half thick. The platform of the stage is higher than the floor of the booth whose ceiling is about seven feet high. The window is strategically placed about chest high.

Womanly smells flood in with the light. The scent of a woman is motivational, and then especially when she is excited; and the scents of many women are maddening, especially when we are incited.

There are three girls on the stage. One is taller than average, about five foot nine inches with dark skin like stained mahogany. She is thickly proportioned at about one hundred and seventy pounds. Her hair is in a very tight finger wave, and her eyes appear unnaturally light. She is at least a forty double-D cup, and they are fabulous.

The other is about the same height but thin and brown-skinned. She has much smaller perky breasts and a tight athletic body. Her hair is combed back into a ponytail held with a black scrunchie.

The third is white-skinned with straight dark hair partially curled near the ends. Her nice breasts have some sag, and the nipples are dark and thick. Her hips are wide and full, and her small waist and abdomen show signs of a recent pregnancy—there is that wrinkled pouch of skin resting between the navel and the pubic patch.

The thin girl is kneeling down and talking to a voice out of the dark window at the last booth to the left.

"You tippin'?" Darkskin says to Kevin.

Her voice has expectation in it and enough energy to make her seem concerned. She smiles lightly and rests her weight on her right side, as if to repeat, "Well, are you tippin'?" The shadowed face she spoke to stutters and begins to choke out a response. You could hear the blush in his voice.

Then suddenly from the left, "Come here, girl. I'm tippin'. Fuck the dumbshit!" This voice is assured, springy, and almost comical. Her attentions are drawn. She steps to that booth and bends at the waist, talking into the opening.

"You know the prices?" she asks.

"Shit yeah! I made 'em up," El responds, and she smiles.

"I think I'll start off with one of those big-ass breasts. Can you hoist that big motherfucker up in this window so I can lick on it, please?" El requests. His face, eyes, and mouth are reaching out like an actor in a Burger King commercial trying hard to convince any observer that you really can have it your way.

She pushes out some breathy chuckles, and her smile spreads to her eyes. His hands hung over the edge of the window just under her hanging udders. They were clasped together as if in prayer, and a five-dollar bill folded along its length was sticking up between thumb and forefinger. With the laughter waning but the smile still present, she kneels and raises her left breast to the window.

"No, no!" El insists, "Give me the right one. It's bigger." He is still reaching, and his face is at the peak of craving.

Her expression suggests that comment could almost have been funny, or embarrassing. She raises the huge dark breast to the window, and her eyes peer curiously into its shadows.

"You tippin', honey?" says the white-skinned woman.

He spends the last bit of time watching this female go from standing in front of him to on her knees having her breasts licked by his friend. He could see her looking down and smiling pleasantly while holding up a big soft-looking titty. He starts to feel a little as if he had been wronged, but live and learn.

"Yes, I'm tipping," responds Kevin.

"You know the prices?" she asks.

"No," he retorts.

She has a classic north New Jersey accent—the Hollywood version. Her eyes are dark brown, and her lips are thick, full, and filled in by some berry flavor. The thin girl has gotten up and walks behind the Italian toward the booths on the right side.

"It's two dollars to touch anything. It's three dollars to kiss on my tits and ass, five dollars to tongue my asshole, and ten to lick my pussy. So what would—," she begins, but the window closes abruptly and cuts her off.

The vibration from another booth's door closing is felt. Kevin pulls another token from his pocket and quickly raises it to the slot as he hears a muffled "oh goddamn!" coming from El's vicinity. The token drops.

The Italian has stood up but was still in front of his window. Darkskin is now standing with her ass pressed into her window. Her hands are gripping both gargantuan cheeks and pulling them apart. She is breathing through clenched teeth, and little passionate oohs leaked from her mouth. The thin girl is at the last booth to the right. A white hand decorated with some gold rings comes from the shadows and kneads and tweaks her breasts.

"What would you like?" the Italian says it with a smile while bending down so that her tits hang in front of the window.

"Let me feel your titties." Kevin's statement comes out with the tone of a question. He pulls two dollars from a neatly folded wad of bills and hands them to her.

Suddenly, "Man, hold up! Hold the fuck up!" El's voice becomes excited, and Darkskin is pushed away from the window. As his hand extends, his ring finger slips just enough into her opening to wet up to the second knuckle. El's voice comes through the window as Kevin's hand grips one of the Italian's swaying breasts. "Man, you better eat that pussy!"

"Man, I—," starts Kevin, but is interrupted.

"Man I what?" insists El as he quickly sniffs then sucks clean the glazed finger. "I didn't bring you all the way up here with me so you could feel on some titties. You could have done that shit on the block. Eat that pussy! Eat that ass! I don't care what part it is, but put your mouth on it." El is not the most serious guy walking, so he sings most of these commands. He then directs his attention to the Italian. "Do you want your pussy eaten?"

"It's up to him," she answers.

"It's up to you. Look, dog, it's me and you up here. All that anybody knows is what you tell them, ai-aight. I'll even pay for the shit. This is your motherfucking baptism. Do well, my son." A strong-looking long dark arm extends from the window, holding a ten-dollar bill. "Here!" El commands.

The Italian reaches out and takes the money. The thin girl has her knees resting against the wall, and the same decorated white hand is pumping three fingers into her pussy. She takes dollar bills from the dark inside the window every three or four thrusts and drops them on the floor at her feet. She already has quite a nice pile as the sound of another token is heard dropping into her window's slot.

"So what's it gonna be, honey?" the Italian asks Kevin.

The jeweled hand to the right retracts with those three fingers, and they disappear into the dark. The fingers reappear after about five seconds and rush back to the thin girl's wet opening.

The Italian's eyes are dark against her white skin. The swaying motion that has her breasts rocking pendulumlike about her chest has fallen to her hips, and both move to the music's groove. For the first time, he notices that her bush is crowded with thick black hairs. And oh, how he likes hairy crotch.

"OK," Kevin finally responds.

She smiles as she turns her back to him. Her hips and ass are made of a fine combination of muscle and fat knitted together loosely. Her ass is thick and wide like a heavy-bottomed European woman's. She backs up to the window until its edges frame her ass in like a Renaissance masterpiece, then she spreads her legs shoulder-width and bends to touch her toes.

Saliva begins to involuntarily wet his mouth as his pulse speeds and his hand strays instinctively southward to his tightening denim crotch. He moves clumsily toward the window, bracing his left forearm on the wall beside it and almost tripping over nothing. Most of the light coming from that room is blocked out. Only dim fringes of light around the edges of the window and at the V left by her thick thighs and pubic patch shine through. Those lights against her white skin and in that shadow make her ass seem to glow like a beacon.

He leans forward now with both forearms pressed against the wall. Her scent runs up his nose. A woman's scent; hers is a combination of pussy, ass, and remarkably, pears. The scent of pear is obviously a body lotion women use. Her scent, though, has such an influence on the male body because its effect on the male mind is deeply genetic.

He inhales deeply, pulling her aroma past his throat and fills his lungs with her. He kisses her right cheek and pauses. His tongue falls slowly out of his mouth. He extends it fully and flattens it while pushing it against her long labia that were covered by thick dark hair. A long slow stroke glides upward, feeling animated curly pubes that straighten against the force of his press. He then pushes his tongue deep into her well. He immediately feels her hole is thick with that cloudy nectar. The taste of pears contributed nicely to a full-flavored experience.

The scent of a female's ass can do things to a male. While he tastes her pussy, he could not help but to be distracted by its call. He allows his tongue to stray high. It rides across the smooth ridges of her sphincter.

"Yes, honey," her voice sings as her hands come down over the base of her spine and grip tender ass flesh, spreading it. Her dark sphincter stretches until it opens. She wiggles her ass, making the flesh ripple and jump. His tongue probes wildly as if offended by the motion, and his right hand caresses a dick that he thought could not get any stiffer.

"Suck on my asshole, honey!" Her commands hit him between the eyes like a bolt. He begins to lick and suck slavishly at her treat as her voiced excitement, however mostly feigned, begins to rise. The window closes.

"Ah fuck!" His frustration needs no explanation. However, he is new to this kind of interaction, and he is now within the wave that has consumed so many in addiction.

Hurried fingers pull tokens and loose change from his pocket. They miscoordinate and drop the coins to the floor. He picks up the tokens and pushes one into the slot while placing the two others on the window's ledge.

The Italian is on her knees, and she puts her face up to the opened window confidently. "What do ya want?" Her tone and grin are very much knowing.

"Can I finish licking your ass and pussy?" He does not know he sounds like a child asking for seconds at a dinner table.

"You don't have ta ask permission, honey. But I will have ta charge ya again," she relays.

Almost before the sentences end, a ten-dollar bill materialized between thumb and forefinger.

"Honey, you can taste all the pussy n' ass you want." She then takes the money and stands, assuming her previous position.

For the next one hundred twenty seconds, Kevin gives his oral devotion to a strange but appreciative ass. As the window closes, his nemesis became an unmanageable zipper. Finally, it moves, and a soft white wall of cotton stretched against the force of erection teases his impatient hand. The window closes, and he quickly retrieves a token from the window edge and throws it in the slot. It opens. Another ten dollars jumped from his hand to hers, and her timely encouragement fuels him.

"Eat my pussy! Eat my pussy!" she commands, sounding as if she were gasping for air. He complies, and with the energy that only a new trick could muster.

"Ooh. Eat my motherfuckin' pussy," she again commands.

He complies, and then some. His hand finally solves the maze of Hanes briefs. It finds his warm throbbing dick and pulls it free. It stands flat against his T-shirt stressed against the elastic waistband. It is pulsing with the rhythm of his heart and jumping slightly with each rush of blood. He takes his tool into his hand and begins to stroke it expertly. Men are always more adept at autoeroticism than most will admit. His palm is a comfortable place. His thick brown takes its position in his palm as if molded for the station.

"Stick your tongue in my ass. Stick it in!" she commands.

His body is leaning and braced by an arm. The back of his head moves in slow circles while his tongue guides itself between thick warm ass cheeks. His tongue strolls along straight dark hairs tainted with her scent. A tear of saliva leaves a streak down her right thigh, running from a dark tough-skinned sphincter easing open.

"Tonguefuck my ass! Stick it in! Stick it in!" Her voice is excitement.

There is scarcely a sound in his head but her voice. His eyes, though, are full, and his nose is crowded with an aroma he had barely noticed until now. It was a scent like lingering bits of mild tempered feces escaping from her anal tract and finding refuge in his throat, lungs, and mind.

She rocks slowly with her ass bobbing before his face. A small dark spot grows wide, shrinking slightly, then widening again as her muscles relax. He presses his face to her ass and inserts his tongue into her opening anus.

"Aaah! Aah, yes!" she cries.

His right hand commits to rhythms gaining speed. It is a feeling like relief coupled with desperation. Trained fingers feel along his long shaft, independently pressing and teasing sensitive spots in conjunction with a palm that snugly cradles his member. From base to bulbous head, his hand slides, coaxing his excited balls to end the desperation.

The window closes. He forgets the fifth token. His left hand drops and pulls down the elastic, freeing the entire length of his dick to his influence. His mouth has fallen open, and his eyes become lazy. He stands barely balanced and shrouded in a dire need to release this energy.

Thud! Thud! The banging at the stall door startles him out of his trance. He pauses.

"Kev. Come on, man!" says El, sounding very impatient.

He does not know whether he should continue his moment or tuck and exit. His eyes are opened and attentive; the shock of possible discovery sobers them. The shadows in the booth seems to become lighter. The music begins to pound on his ears, and he could hear the opening and closing of the stall door next to him. Through the seams around the door, he could see the movement of forms. Then the sound of a coin falling down a slot. "You tippin'?"

The Party:
"Damn, that bitch was fine. Did you see her?" El says it as if Kevin were not in the room with him. Kevin knows not to answer but to allow El his rant. However, he shoots his friend a cross-eyed gaze and a mouth twisted dumbly to one side from the passenger seat of the car.

Ellis is a tall fellow. He is six feet six inches tall and rather hard-looking, though not disturbing in any sense. He weighs about two hundred sixty pounds. His hair is a low Caesar fade and always neat. His eyes and skin are both pecan brown, and he suffers some epidermal conflict. It is nothing a better diet could not control though. His face, as already alluded to, while not in the running for the next EM (Ebony Man) supermodel hunt, is quite pleasant. He has puffy cheeks and a heavy solid-looking chin. His dark eyes seem to be set deep into his skull. The ridge above them that becomes his broad and contemplative forehead protrudes farther than expected. This makes his eyes seem deep and mysterious.

"I know ya saw her, but did you see her? Man, every time I think that I've seen the finest piece God ever built, another break the mold bitch just twists my whole shit back to some other shit. Ya na-wa-ta-meen," El's voice is more intense than the situation desires. She was nice though.

The bright city lights flash along glass and metal in motion. The city's sounds are shut out by American construction. 12:15 a.m. reads like a beacon on the dashboard clock. Hot 97 is the radio station, and BDP's "My Philosophy" is playing. The car is a 1993 Eagle Talon: black on black with a five speed manual transmission.

"Kev, did you see those titties? Oh, I knew I had to lick on those bad mu'fuckers," El says, managing to split his concentration between driving and recalling the titties. This in itself is complementary of his driving skill. Plenty of people have crashed their vehicles because they lost focus just thinking about a titty.

Flashes of memory impose themselves on Kevin's mind, causing a sympathetic reaction.

"Did you see the ass?" El says it desperately with a tone almost impatient for a response. He cuts his earnest gaze away from the road and to Kevin's face and repeats in a near whisper, "The ass." He finishes with the same sentence Kevin has heard him use a hundred times, "See, if I could find a woman built like that, I'd stop fuckin' around."

The imagery Kevin recalls is like several movies playing at once and on the same screen, but each remarkably distinct. Kevin's dick also remembers the scenes and rises to attention.

"Yeah, she was nice," Kevin responds plainly.

"Nice? Pss." This is El's cue to talk about every piece of ass he's ever seen. He relishes these moments where he can recount what he has seen, and where, and especially how it affected him.

The conversation journeys them down Forty-Second Street to the West Side Highway and south on the highway toward the World Trade Centers.

"Where are we going anyway?" Kevin finally asks. His thoughts have settled with his erection into the soft cushioned seat. He trusts El's driving and is staring blankly past the West Side Piers to the Jersey skyline across the Hudson River when he asked the question.

"I think maybe we'll go get a drink. Chill for a minute," says El, finally relaxing into a night mood.

"Sounds good to me," the words move out of Kevin's mouth casually. The peep show was foreign to him. However, he has been comfortable with a warm and quiet drinking environment for some time.

Kevin is six foot five, two hundred twenty pounds. He is wearing a low fade with shadowed sideburns that connect with his thicker beard and mustache. However, his face is usually unshaven, and his facial hair normally growing wild. Aside from this, his skin is smooth, blemish-free, and the color of most African Americans, like burnt bronze. His cheeks are not as prominent as El's, his chin not as heavy and sturdy-looking, and his eyes are not as dark and mysterious. His bone structure is lighter and more fluid, though, one portion of his physique flowing smoothly into the other. His forehead is high and round, and the muscles usually stay tense, making him seem, at the very least, troubled. The ridge of his nose seems to take forever to form its quickly cascading slopes into its puffy base. His ears are not as attention-seeking as El's, whose are large and protrude out from his head. Kevin's are small and lie flat against his skull.

The trip lasts about thirty minutes and traverses the Lincoln Tunnel and unfamiliar routes on streets in slightly familiar towns.

"What time is it?" Kevin asks, but then remembers the clock on the dashboard that blinks 12:47 a.m. "Where are we?"

"Jersey," El responds.

"I know we're in fuckin' Jersey. Where in Jersey?" The car glides quickly past Kevin's "what am I, fuckin' stupid" response and along potholed streets with here-and-there trash along the curbs and sidewalks. Mostly brick housing lines an avenue that is reflective of any commercial district, and people mill in groups hidden by doorway shadows or highlighted by street lamps.

"Jersey City," El says it while turning left and parking behind a red Pathfinder in front of a bar. Both sides of this street and across the boulevard are lined with vehicles. They exit the car casually, lock it, and meet on the curb. A white Lexus cruises by, bumping Redman loudly. It slows briefly then continues on past the light at the corner and down the boulevard.

There is a large neon sign on the building that says in red script, Billy's Bar and Grill. The front is bricked up to the knees then becomes vertical wood planks. Above this are two large windows separated by a sturdy-looking wooden door with a diamond-shaped window at face height. The windows have large dark curtains covering them and a green neon sign shouting Guinness.

El opens the door and enters, but holds it ajar briefly for Kevin. Sly and the Family Stone greet them at the door with verses that bend time, "I want to thank you, for lettin' me, be myself, again." The music comes from an old jukebox sitting to the left of the door against the wall. There is a long wooden bar with a brass foot rail and a slick marble top directly to the right of the door. The wall behind the bar is mirrored, and in front of it is a better-than-average stock of liqueurs. There is a hanging rack full of an assortment of glasses over the end of the bar farthest from the door. There are many stools with lazy-looking flat asses resting on them. There are tables with couples of varying genders lining the wall across the bar and down into an area that ends against a wall with a windowless door in it.

They walk down the lane between the bar stools and tables. El seems to greet anyone he can make eye contact with. He nods to a group of old-timers in brown leather jackets, Kangols, and cowboy hats, and then to a fellow about his forties in a plain brown suit sitting at the bar listening to the music and smiling. He smiles at two fortyish women sitting at a candlelit table, sipping at large glasses of something, and looking as fiercely attractive as that age can when properly maintained.

El signals the bartender. "Ice tea please."

The bartender looks to Kevin, who raises a brow and flashes his eyes from El to the bartender and back, then responds, "The same."

190

The bartender nods and begins work. He is a pleasant-looking guy with a normal build and a slight gut. He is about El's complexion, five foot ten, and wears blue denim overalls and no shirt with his mustache. He sports a low Afro and a decent physique.

They walk to the door at the back wall. There are two small round tables on each side of the door. Both tables have three chairs and a too-small white tablecloth set square on their surfaces. El knocks on the door lightly. Kevin begins to feel eyes on his back. He turns his head slightly to each side with the kind of inconspicuous motion that proved he did not expect anyone to notice. The room's population is busy inside themselves and does not seem to have the urge to notice him. He hears the door open.

A mad mixture of dim colored lights squeeze through the crack the opening door made and pushes it wide as the room inhales the two. "Apple Strudel" by Up, Bustle and Out comes like good news through the room's sound system. The gentleman guarding the door is large. He is wearing a tank top T-shirt, dark blue jeans with some logo embroidered on the side of his left leg, and some beige boots. His hair is in long clean plaits that hang about his head. He is about El's height, with twenty pounds, and he works out a lot.

"Big Boy," El says it in a low shout, and in his hand is a bill indistinguishable in the dim light.

The guard takes the money, hardly moving anything but his arm. "What's up, brutha?" he says.

El does not respond but continues walking past him with Kevin in tow. The entrance is bent to the right and opens into a large area littered with people shadowed in dim red, orange, and yellow lights. El stands at the opening, surveying the room. To his left, there is a small table with a man and woman sitting, holding hands across the table's surface and talking. Everyone is well-dressed, like they came from somewhere else. Kevin is on El's right. The stage is at the front of the room nearest the street. There are two brass fire poles. One is in the middle of the stage, and the second comes down in the middle of a group of three large round tables crowded with smiling faces. The place is filled with a mixed crowd of men and women of mostly their thirties and forties.

All of the tables are taken, and the walls are crammed against the backs of chatting bodies blowing smoke and leaning against the influence of the drinks in their hands. There are three other bodies whose look is similar to Big Boy's, and they are cautiously moving around the room. Teams of girls wearing only G-string panties, slippers, and carrying trays of drinks, weave between hard, calloused, cheap-feel hands, "my dick is hard" grins, and painful joy-joy faces expressed with eyes that cannot cut through their cover of silky female earth tones.

"Yo, there's a lot a ma-fuckas in here," Kevin says, seeming astonished.

"Yeah. It's not usually this crowded. It's a party. The owner's birthday." Kevin acknowledges the information with some interest, enough at least, to make its telling worth El's while.

The flashing colored spotlights change from their autumn mood to a big blue that paints the entire room. A siren begins to blare. Its pitch starts low then rises and falls continuously. The room seems to grow darker. Several bright pulse lights come to life from points around the ceiling and add waves of flashbulb brilliance throughout the room.

"Eh! You want a seat?" An unknown voice off El's left. The couple at the table was rising, and the male looked at El for a response.

"Ah, shit yeah! Thanks," El says, smiling.

The guy was impressive. He is six foot nothing, well-built and brown-skinned. The woman is magnificent. She looks like a nineteen eighties Gladys Knight, but not a day over twenty-five. Everything on her was tight—her body, her manner, and the dress she wore. They both smile pleasantly while gathering their things.

El and Kevin take a position to the side of each chair to guard the gift from the others that were standing about. El and the guy nod to each other as they pass, and El places his hand on the back of his seat. Kevin raises his eyebrows, and he smiles lightly at the couple then turns to sit. El's left hand touches Kevin's arm. He turns to respond. El's jutting chin directs his attention to the retreating couple. The guy's lady, Ms. Gladys, has an outstanding package. Her calves are toned and muscular as are her arms and shoulders. There is a long slit up the dress that exposes nearly her entire right thigh up to her ass. She is athletically thick and muscular with barely a waist or any sign of excess fat. She has a dark cover that reminds a male of his spiritual purpose—to become one and at perfect peace—and an ass to be worshiped. Her ass pushes against the dress like two helium balloons pressed together and barely held down by the weight of the material.

There is enough of a pause between them to be grossly telling of the obvious; the female form is motivation for life; and what joy of living there is, governed by her being.

"Ya know what I'm thinkin'?" El asks rhetorically.

El's question interrupted Kevin's vision, which included him on his knees kissing said ass. He knows his friend well, though, so he responds, "I have an idea."

They sit as the couple disappears around the bend. "Sunshine and the Rain" by Joi is lumbering through the sound system. A waitress appears through the swaying and bopping bodies. Her skin is tinted blue by the light, and she carries several drinks on her tray.

"Ice teas?" she asks.

"Yes, thank you," El's voice is as polite as hers. He accepts the drink and reaches for his pocket. Kevin pulls out a twenty and drops it on her tray before El's hand can complete the reaction.

She smiles and begins to place the second drink in front of Kevin, who reaches for it. She is about five foot five with a medium frame and that very light skin that is often mistaken for white. She has small but impressive breasts with nipples like large pencil erasers. She has a diamond stud in her left nostril and a hoop in her belly button. Her hair is dark and is in locks that hang in front of her face and down her neck. She is wearing a red thong that her ass and crotch frame in with untold delight. All of this in conjunction with her pleasant attitude and the effects of the alcohol posed a powerful lobby for a male's continued attention.

"Will there be anything else?" she asks.

El gestures to Kevin with his eyes. "You eatin'?" is the unspoken question. Kevin frowns, slightly shaking his head negatively.

"Nothing then," responds El.

"OK. If you need anything, just call." Her voice is as lighter than her skin. She spins and walks to another table where she leaves drinks and collects more money.

"You was jerkin' off, wasn't ya'?" Though dealt with a smile and meaning no harm, the accusation flies across the table like a wad of phlegm. It hangs off Kevin's nose.

"When?" The obvious next question as Kevin builds his defenses.

"When you were in the booth at the peep show, man," El's words push a button forcing Kevin to rerun the event even as his mouth denied the charge.

"Hell no!" Kevin's face is reaching for a look that would reflect innocence.

"Son?" El's face is a comical accusation.

"Hell fuckin' no!" Kevin finds flared nostrils, a tight wrinkled brow, and eyes that strain to stare down his guilt.

"Ma' man, look'e here. You took some long moments to come out after I knocked. And I know the window was closed because the white girl was at another window talkin' to some other dude." El leaves this statement and his sure countenance in the air to marinade.

A quicker heavier beat fades in over the speakers, softening El's voice. Two bikini-bottomed women ooze down the fire poles from dark holes in the ceiling while four others appear on the stage. The crowd roars. Kevin's expression is trying hard to seem as if his attention had been taken by the excitement. His body betrays his thoughts, creating an erection in the tight confines of his pants. His face becomes flush from the reaction.

"It's all right, ya' know." This is El's consolation.

Kevin's head bounces to the music's beat as pulses of light make his image as extreme as a picture negatives.

"I must have beat my shit for the first lot a times I went. Ya can't help it, man! I'd like ta meet the nut that won't beat his meat, ay-aight! Ya got pussy, ass, and titties in your face. The girls are fine. Oh! I'll work my shit, ay-aight." El's voice is deep, and it carries. He turns some heads with his testimony of his love of voyeurism and masturbation. The listeners seem as amused as El sounded, but Kevin somehow misses the joke. "I'll work my shit till the mutherfucka' break . . . or somethin'. I ain't really tryin' to break it, but for real. Psss." He finishes with a slick grin and his heavy laugh. He glances at the table before them and finds two of the five pairs of eyes occupying that spot staring back.

"You go on and work your shit, baby. It's all right," says the mouth under one of the two pairs of eyes as the mouth under the pair next to her begins to giggle. One of the three males sitting at her table turns to her, and he is obviously annoyed. He then turns to El, then back to the show.

The woman looks to be of medium stature with a well-oiled and blemish-free brown shell. Her hair is in a very complicated pump with gold and silver coloring highlighting the many corkscrew locks hanging about her face. Her friend is the definition of petite. She is maybe five foot three and one hundred pounds. Her hair is similar to her larger companion, but much less complicated. She has a brilliant smile; in fact, it is infectious. She has a small mouth with tight thick lips and such large breasts they will constantly call a person's attention away from her face.

"You don't have ta worry about that, sista'. I got things well in hand." El's excitement of having a new playmate got the best of him, and he offers the woman his hand for a pound.

"No, that's all right, baby. I don't need to touch your hand," the woman says and withdraws herself from El's offering. She then offers him her fist "Give me one of these." Her girlfriend is beside herself with laughter.

"Oh, that's it!" says El, as if throwing in a towel then touches his fist to hers.

"Oh, you got a big ol' hand. What size shoe you wear?" They three break out in laughter.

"Do y'all have ta talk about this shit now?" Kevin says, now infected by the other male's level of annoyance.

El intercedes as the women put on a very "well, excuse us" expression. "Nah, nah. Just lettin' you know that it was all right, that's all. This shit's between me and you," El assures.

"And us," chimes in Ms. Petite, and they two find yet another reason to keep their personal good time rolling.

"Look," El says, staring Kevin in his eyes and pauses, then, "all right?" El again assures his friend, and his expression is no disguise. He is sincere.

"Baby, don't you worry about it," the woman directs herself to Kevin. "If you want to work your shit, you go, boy!" She and her girlfriend give each other a high five.

"Yo!" her companion shouts just loud enough for them to hear. He seems vexed. He turns to her. She looks back at him with a puzzled gaze.

"What!" she blares while staring the dude straight in his eyes. "Never you mind what I'm doing," she continues, "you watch the titties." And her chin juts out toward the two jiggly girls on the tables just fifteen feet away. Ms. Petite chokes down a laugh with her drink. El sits high in his chair. Suddenly he appears to be slightly more serious than he has been all night, but with an amused look that spoils his stoic cover. Kevin submits to their silence.

The music stays fast and heavy. Many are standing and dancing in place while still more practice moves that were *the shit* while sitting or holding up the walls. The pole dancers keep crowds around them as they performed. The four from the stage are now on the floor and dancing. Each dancer is involved in a box-in containing four to six guest bodies each. Some are male, and some are female. Every one of them feels inclined to remove at least their shirts though. Kevin's interest parts from El's, who after the interesting dialogue seems content to watch asses float by and throw glances at Hip Chick and her petite friend.

"Yo. How is Lauren?" El suddenly questions.

"Lauren?" Kevin repeats as his eyes catch a bouncing group of dark shadowed bodies. "She's fine," he answers, but wonders why El would all of the sudden pull her name out of a hat.

Those bodies were near the stage. He watches their Afro forms slick with sweat and blue light blink in the flash of the white strobe and darkness. The pulse of the lights on their images became hypnotic and drew his mind away from the music, and back.

"Yo. I'm a take a walk," he says with his eyes and mind still preoccupied with the sight of that crowd.

Kevin stands and begins to weave his way forward through a mass of bodies against the sidewall and to the right of his table. Smiles and some polite words are exchanged as he passed strangers who either thought they knew him or wanted to. He slowly makes his way to the front of the room by the stage. The place is humming with the sound of voices straining through the music, light yielding to dark, and the smell of consumable toxins working on excited bodies.

He stands watching the group with the same kind of eyes that many could not take off the various now-supernatural performers who once played the world-famous Apollo Theater. Eyes that are still young enough to believe in a dream, and still hungry enough to believe they could pursue that dream. They sway, bounce, and shout on cue with whatever song was playing. And every song seems to be their song. Their manner holds a rhythm like of uninhibited love of living. It is as if every motion was one that was conditional upon the next, and each individual's part is necessary. He wants to know what they felt like. He stands and watches. In one eye plays his experiences, or lack thereof; and in the other plays the imagery of what could be. He despises one for no simple a reason than boredom and reaches out for the other with no greater purpose than discovery.

"Excuse me," a soft voice from behind suddenly cuts in, "do you want to dance?" She startles him, and it shows.

Kevin turns to his right, and his eyes fall to a face brilliant with a smile. She is tall, about six foot one. Her cover is very dark and even toned with very naturally dark eyes. Her mouth is just wide enough for her semiround face and sport-thick succulent lips painted in a light cocoa shade. She is wearing tight-fitting blue jeans, white strap sandals, and an oversized white buttoned-up dress shirt that hangs loosely about her torso. Her hair is a wonderful low Afro. She is thick like someone who has lived with thick all of her life and knows how to wear it. Her upper frame is solid enough to support her huge breasts, forty-four-E, he estimates. All he really knows is they are huge fucking titties.

"Yeah," he quickly responds. "Yeah, I'll dance." And he smiles as he walks to her and takes her hand, leading her out to the dance floor.

She moves ahead of him as they approach the middle of the floor where the crowds of dancers have amassed. As she passes, he saw just how well she fills her jeans. She has strong-looking thick calves that rise up to stronger-looking thicker thighs. Where her lower back meets the belt of her pants, there is a gap where her ass has pushed the material away from her body. Faces jump out at Kevin's eyes as they walked between the bodies seated and standing. The faces are mixed, but all had a tightened brow, focused eyes, and a twisted mouth. Kevin reads their faces easily. It is a language he could understand. Each one is a statement to the effect of "goddamn!" or "oh shit!" There is no debating her effect; she moves the room.

She leads him to the dance floor, bouncing as if possessed by rhythm. His eyes are on her, then on the crowd around them, and then back to her. She turns smiling and engages him. She pulls close at first, then moves away while her body jerked and swayed in rhythmic bliss. Kevin keeps up as best as he can but finds himself at a loss for dance steps. She notices his lack of prowess and takes control of them. She grabs him by the collar with her left hand and pulls him to her while spinning him. He lightly bumps one of the male dancers from the crowd behind them. The dancer does not seem to notice and keeps pace with his group.

Every movement she makes causes her breasts to jiggle. Their size cannot be hidden even by the size of her shirt. The friction of her movement causes the nipples and the little bumps within the areola to rise. The shirt molds to them and puts them on display.

They face each other. She rides his body up and down and side to side. He is impressed. She turns her back to him then pushes her ass against his crotch while bucking like a donkey. Despite brandishing a stiffy in his pants and the succulent body of the woman who caused it, his attention drifts to the group in front of him. She is before him, but before her, bathed in light and fantasy were the nearly naked mob of dancing bodies. Kevin's hands are on her hips. She stands erect then takes his hands and pulls them up to the gap between the buttonholes of her blouse. She then moves, both of her arms are above her head. One arm is cradling Kevin's head next to hers and the other is bent behind her neck.

"Pull it off!" she whispers.

He could feel her bare warm breast flesh moving under his hands like something alive. However she moves, they move, and his hands ride with them. He begins to undo the buttons and discovers that they are pasted on—Velcro. The tear seems to lower the music. It was like the entire room is listening to the ocean through a conch shell, and he could see the mouths of the enthralled hanging open.

She and he move seductively in a tight rhythmic circle as Kevin clears the open shirt away from her front. By the time they go one hundred and eighty degrees, each hand is full of her huge chocolate udders.

They are as thick as she is. They are the size and shape of summer watermelons and must account for no less than one quarter of her body weight. They are the color of an early Saturday morning summer thundershower; that is, so deeply warm and brown that you press your body into them hoping to be shielded from all else but the sound of the rain hushing the earth and the beat of her heart. Her nipples are easily the dimensions of the cap from a fingernail polish bottle, but half the length. The areolas seem to spread to form an area that appears like shiny black oil spills capping the undulant glory that is tit.

They spin slowly like two live mannequins in a Macy's display window. Kevin strokes and kneads them as they make their rotations. He lifts them slightly in his arms and separates them, then lets them free to bounce and sway as she commanded. He then puts each hand under its respective breast and points them at the watching crowd threateningly. The nipples and areola play like the large penetrating black eyes of a predator hypnotizing its prey through the dim light. The spectators are immobile.

Her moans are low but seductively audible. He can feel her sound as it rumbles through her body. He comes out of his trance when he realizes they have been joined by two of the male dancers from the circle nearest them. One is wearing a nice pair of casual pants, comfortable-looking loafers, and no shirt. The other is wearing black leather pants with beige and black Gators, and no shirt. They are both average-looking guys—one red and the other ash brown, and both sport mustaches. They press in on her from her sides, locking her in a triangle. They bounce in place. Mr. Gators relieves Kevin's left hand of its heavy burden, and Mr. Casual has effected an affectionate hug around her and Kevin.

A topless barefoot woman nearly Kevin's height and honey-colored and a short chubby guy with glasses join them from somewhere out of the audience. The tall woman wears only a smile with her tight-fitting jeans and pointy perky breasts. The guy is in what is left of a business suit: pants, shoes, and a saturated white dress shirt with no tie. Tall Chick maneuvers around the small group in their rhythm while Short Guy jumps right in and attaches himself to thickness's ass like a chubby pimple. As Tall Chick makes her circle, she touches each man as if inspecting him. She stops behind Kevin.

He feels her body press to his from behind. Her thin fingers slide under his shirt, and her soft lips start a kiss at his right earlobe and finish at the soft base of his neck. He sucks air slowly into his mouth, and it sounds as if he is leaking. The circle is tight. Her right hand creeps down his abdomen and burrows under his waistband. The circle is energy. Her hand finds his erection and grasps it tenderly. The circle bounces to a rhythm not found in the notes of the music. They seem to create a pulse for the music to follow, and the music does not resist, but envelopes itself in their magic. This is what Kevin feels he was looking for—a moment of complete freedom.

After some time, Kevin's attention is drawn by a tap on his shoulder. He turns to see El, who seems to have noticed the woman's hand down his pants, and smiles.

"Hey, hey! But we gotta go," El says it, looking again to the foreign hand probing under the denim, then to Kevin's eyes, and laughs softly.

"Now?" Kevin blasts.

"Yeah now. It's important," El says, then strides off toward the exit.

Kevin reluctantly dismisses himself from the group and makes his way through the crowd after El. He finds him standing on the curb in front of the bar.

"What was the rush?" Kevin says, still fixing his clothing.

"Hey, remember that lady we were fuckin' with?" he starts and leaves just enough space for his friend's response.

"You were fuckin' with," Kevin injects and with some attitude.

"Well, whatever. She thinks a brother got talent. I gotta go represent." The way El smiles after the statement, the way anyone smiles when they think they are sure to get some sex, one would think the whole world was a groovy place to be.

"What about the guy she was with?" Kevin says in a tone that still shows his disgust for having to leave the dance floor and that friendly warm hand.

"Brutha, I don't know, brutha, I don't care. We're going to my house after I drop your ass off," El says it as it starts to drizzle.

Ms. Hip Chick pulls up in a green Toyota Camry, and Ms. Petite is in the passenger seat. "Up! That's it"—then as Ellis notices the extra body—"oh, oh, I hope she's coming too. God, please let her be coming too. Bro, let's go." El eagerly points Kevin in the direction of his car. His excitement is not contagious.

The ride home is big with the sound of rain hissing on the pavement.

At Home:
Calm; it is the even hush of rain striking a roof. Each drop impacts the surface and breaks. Its pieces coalesce with other whole pieces and form a new body. It rolls down the grade of the roof following a path that could only be predicted if you were water. Each will mingle with others until they congregate in a pool within the partially clogged gutter. Some will be pushed over the lip of the gutter and will fall hard on the window ledge below. Their impact adds a sleepy pulse to the already biologically hypnotic rhythm water has. None of them will enjoy it though. They are each so supremely compliant to the divine that fracturing a body does fracture the movement of will. Each piece instinctually continues its quest to get back to the greater source.

An erection is a most beautiful thing. *I love my dick* echoes thickly in the front of his mind. His mouth hangs slightly open. His breaths are slow and even. His lazy eyes are full of his long excited brown penis. His dick is charged by the images in his mind.

Images as sharp as razors blink into reasoned reality. Each has its time then fades into another. They are some of the faces, the bodies, and the moments he has captured on memory. Such beautiful women, and all of them for their own reasons. All are random participants in his fantasies, and this night has created a lot of motivation to fantasize.

His right hand glides slowly along his long shaft while deft fingers massage live areas. His fingers and palm work in concert, forming combinations that only his right hand would know. Above his head, the trees make faint shadows through the skylight window. The black of the room manipulates the moonlight, bending it around his young frame. He is on his back. His knees are fanned out, and the bottoms of his feet are together. His head and shoulders are propped up on pillows, and the comforter lies bunched beneath his knees supporting them.

He moans softly. The images quicken as he becomes absorbed into his world of reason: A woman walks along the sidewalk on Whitehall Street at South Ferry. She wears a rust-colored silk jacket and matching skirt with a vanilla-colored linen blouse and two-inch black heels. She is caramel-skinned with big dark brown eyes. Her hair is blondish and is in a neat high wavy Caesar fade. He is naked, but the few other people who dot the street do not seem to mind. They are all busy juggling multicolored balloons and riding unicycles.

She walks into his arms where he stood at One State Street Plaza, and at his whim, she begins to struggle. She pushes him away and turns to run. He grabs her with both arms and spins her so they are face-to-face. He kisses her neck. She pushes him away with her left hand as her right hand becomes full of his loose hanging balls and thick erection. He pushes her firmly to the glass wall and, with both hands, pulls her blouse open. Her huge and perfectly symmetrical baby-oiled breasts bounce free of their constraints. She stares at him with innocent wide eyes.

She is naked. She pushes him down to his knees, and the scene shifts. She raises her left leg and rests her foot on the mattress at the foot of his bed. His mouth sucks and laps madly at her moist sex. A thick patch of pubes descend to her crotch from her outy belly button. Her pubes have been cut into the shape of a crooked arrow, like the I in St. Ides beer, and the point of the arrow ends at the thick hood of her clitoris. Her clitoris itself protrudes from its housing like the leg of a twelve-year-old boy squeezed into the leg of an eight-year-old's pants. She runs her hands along his head and neck, teasing his senses with her long fingernails. "Such a good man," she says, "to take my cream on your face." She then moans a squirting orgasm of her thick cloudy flow onto his face.

She is on her knees on a bed of hay, and he is standing behind her. Her body is hunched forward, so her naked torso rests on the soft fiber pallet, though her face rests on a pillow. Her ass is in the air and waiting for his attention. Her ass is a conglomerate of tight even-toned skin, thick muscle, and soft fatty flesh. He pushes into her. She gasps, then smiles, and a family of barn mice applaud. Her shiny oiled ass ripples continuously as his bare pelvis meets it with powerful thrusts. There are two horses to their left, murmuring something about it not being the motion in the ocean, but in fact the boat. His rhythm quickens. She arrives loudly, then begs, "In my ass, baby. Please fuck me in my ass." As he raises his engorged tool and presses the swollen cum-coated head against her sweet-smelling virgin puckered asshole, his version of Aristotle appears in robes and says, "That's the shit right there. But, dude, a girl?" He shakes that image away like one would the image of an Etch A Sketch, then pushes in slowly.

Back in the world of fact: His right hand tightens around his dick, simulating the snug fit of her rectum. His left hand massages and caresses his balls. He loves the way he looks in the moonlight. Two fingers stray to his asshole and gently rub along it. He sighs as his hand begins to piston along his swollen penis. Moans leak from his mouth as a silky layer of sweat breaks out over his face and bare chest. His eyes shut, and his toes wiggle as if nervous. A sudden bolt of energy blinds his mind's eye and seizes him. That picture of her is lost. Streams of energy leap from his excited dick into moonlit darkness. A thick warm wad of pearly sperm splatters on his chin and mingles with the dark curly hairs of his thin beard. His session leaves a trail from his chin down his chest and stomach to his sticky sleepy hand. He raises his left hand to his face and breathes in deep, adoring the smell of his balls. He reaches beside the bed and pulls a towel from the floor. He wipes his face, body, hand, and now-relaxed penis clean of all evidence. The towel falls to the floor. His eyes catch the moon ducking behind black and gray clouds. Through the skylight, it does not seem so far away. He falls to the lullaby of rain melting on the roof and a rhythmlike tapping on the window's ledge.

June 13, 1994: Dreadlock

> So full of artless jealousy is guilt, spills itself in fearing to be spilt.
> —Shakespeare (from *Hamlet*)

The room is dim and spotted with colored spinning lights. Ganja and the sounds of reggae music fill the spaces and the patronage's imaginations with exotic thoughts. Idle chatter rises and falls under the waves of music. Four naked women twist and gyrate in a seductive and lively manner on a runway. The bartender is shuffling drinks to the crowded bar while topless waitresses serve tables, private booths, and stage customers.

"Good evening. What can I get you?" sings a voice from behind.

Kevin turns in his chair to the face attached to the greeting. She is a short woman. She is about his complexion with small perky breasts, and each handful sports a silver hoop through the nipple. She is in fair shape, which means she does not go out of her way to exercise but is obviously not lazy either. Her eyes are chocolate against the brightest white, and they are as widely opened as her mouth is stretched across her face. Her mouth is gloriously wide with thin but very soft and smooth-looking lips.

"Water," he responds as plainly as that refreshment is uncomplicated.

"That's new. But there's a two-drink minimum," she adds with a smile then waits.

"Double water on the rocks," he says with a voice and countenance as if he meant no levity whatsoever.

She shakes her head in mock pity but shapes her face to show that she is somewhat amused. Kevin smiles and turns his attention back to the runway.

Next to him sit three guys who seem to be acquainted. They are dressed as the gallery is—boots or sneakers, logo-riddled jeans, shirts, and jackets, and some jewelry. The one closest to him has an accent that is possibly Caribbean, but he is probably African. The others are Americans. Before them sits a woman. She is thin and brown-skinned like a wispy stalk of dark bamboo. She is leant back on her right elbow, and her legs are open wide and pulled back into a crouched position. She massages her clitoris with two fingers then drops those fingers down to her wet hole and back again. From these males come a mixture of remarks ranging from compliments, which struggled to be as polite as they could be, considering their diminished state, to lewd suggestions that very much were generated by that same state. She smiles them away.

"Ya know, you're very talented," says one of the Americans, not even taking his eyes off her pussy to address her.

"Yes. I know," she says and continues to wink her glistening snatch at her captivated audience.

"Think you could do that with my dick up in ya?" he says it then grins slyly as his friends back him up with pats on his back and laughter.

"I'm sure, but I'd rather have that tongue, big man," she quickly retorts.

Her expression is manipulation. She contorts placing both of her ankles behind her neck and shoulders. Two fingers from her left hand fill her ass while two from the right fill her pussy. Silence jumps from their arrogant masks, and *shit!* reads on their faces like the terms of a surrender. The African begins to caress the dark silky skin of her ass and thighs. She pulls the fingers from her wetness and relocates his hand to her clitoris.

"You gonna take care a this, big man?" she says to the larger American. It was a definite challenge. She knows you cannot talk too loudly about your magic stick in such an establishment as this without eventually being asked to pull a rabbit out of your hat. She hunches her ass up and spreads its cheeks as far as they would go. Her tight asshole stretches until it opened just a peak. Their mouths gape slightly, and their eyes take on an intoxicated look. She has them.

"Go ahead, man!" says the smaller American. He is brimming with anticipation of the act and probably trying hard not to be the one called upon to represent their collectively misrepresented interests. The African continues to massage her clitoris while she fingers her pussy and asshole. Bills are exchanged. They are a grip of single bills and are showered upon her by the African and the smaller American, but the larger American passes her a twenty then bows to her.

Across the room and to the right in the far corner is a young lady giving a lap dance at a table of four men. The table is small and square with one small glass bulb full of burning wax. It offers only a dim gift of illumination. Even though there are slight light and shadows, Kevin could see that there is penetration. She faces him and kisses and licks his forehead tenderly as she ride slowly on his tool. His dick is stretched from the unzipped cave of metal teeth that spread wide enough not to catch anything sensitive like skin or hair. She is the color of desert sand with a head full of neat long dreadlocks that are just darker than her skin. She wears a garter on her left thigh crammed with bills of varying denomination. She caresses his face and body, and her teasing rhythm trains him. When she slows, he would raise another bill to her. His three friends look on. One is jerking off and looks as if he were about to blast.

"Your drink, sir," the waitress says and places a napkin on the table then the glass on the napkin. "Don't take it to the head too hard," she adds as Kevin places a ten-dollar bill on her tray. She spots it as Kevin raises his hand and pushes the air between him and the tray; it is a recognized signal for "No change necessary." She smiles and fades away slowly. Kevin smiles after her in response to the sarcasm of her previous comment, then lets go a loud and obviously manufactured belly laugh. It would have been more amusing if it had not drawn the immediate yet brief attentions of the bouncers and some patrons. None of them seem amused. Shorty snickers but continues to move away.

He spies another waitress at a table in front of Shorty. In one hand, she balances a tray of drinks, and in the other, she cradles a man's head as he hungrily nurses on her right nipple. She smiles a lot as she gazes down at him. It is a sincere smile. It is the kind of smile a person shows when they truly enjoy the happening of the moment. She allows him some time to satisfy his urge then pulls the tit from his mouth and grasp. He seems to plead with her for seconds as he places some bills in her garter.

She says some words that put him on pause, then they both smile as she walks away toward the bar.

The music has suddenly caught a different attitude. Buju Banton's "'Til Shiloh" begins rumbling through the system. Bamboo has moved closer to the edge of the stage nearer the seats. The African is licking and nibbling on her tits, and the Americans have switched places. The smaller seems a lot more eager to worship her pussy than his friend. She seems pleased in any event. Kevin wonders if it is because of the men attending her or why they attend to her.

Kevin turns back to the stage and notices one of the women have left. Two are moving about, entertaining customers seated around the stage, and Bamboo is still busy with her customers.

Those little colored dots of light chase each other around the room like wild fireflies. The music grows less intense. Kevin's eyes seem to have become fixed on a stain on the stage floor.

I don't know who my mother is, he suddenly thinks as his eyes shift from that stain to the ripples the low-end bass makes in his water. Mother *is not who she is but a means of identification for me, her child. Additionally, it is a word that indicates to the world she has borne a child. But it is not who she is.*

A curious thought? A curious thought indeed. One whose origins he cannot name. Perhaps it is the culmination of some intense subconscious deliberations being offered to the conscious for further investigation, or as an answer to the question he has yet to ask. In any event, he was sure that she wouldn't agree with him being here.

My mother is pristine against these women, he thinks, *but then, she is my mother. Some of these women have children. They are someone's mother.* He interrogates himself as his eyes are now fixed on a spot of light against the wall behind the bar that does not seem to move as wildly as the others.

It shimmies like a star and in a tight circle, as if in a slow orbit around some unseen solar system.

He finds himself wondering what brought these women to this. He thinks the most romantic scenario would be that some had fallen on hard times and are making the best way possible until they could pull things back together. Maybe some feel they have no personal attributes that could free them from this life and are wishing for some cavalier person to rescue them. The truth, he realizes, may involve hard times, but is rarely romantic. Some do it because they like to do it. Some may enjoy the power they wield in these scenarios, and for them, this may be the only scenario where they get to feel powerful. The possibilities are many and varied.

He thinks about the thin girl (Bamboo) and the three guys. Throughout the discourse, she knew what they wanted. She also knew what she wanted. She was aggressive while seeming passive. They were passive while seeming aggressive. She cut right through their bullshit with that hot pussy knife. Females need a hot pussy knife when dealing with childish males, and hers was glowing. Those three paid for their humility and hers. All the while, she laughed at them. The incredible part is that they felt empowered over her because they were able to handle her body. This satisfies some part of them that will later praise her as that bad-ass bitch, and they may never realize what had passed.

The only thing that had any value in that exchange was each of the participant's self-images, and they exchanged those for something of no value, the dollar, because they have subscribed to the illusion of its worth. This is capitalism, and this type of establishment is an icon of this kind of capitalist exchange. For each of the participants, it was just business as usual, which is sad enough. Add to that, though, the diminishing effects on positive perspective of female to male or male to female, which, of course, is the most damaging effect this type of barbarity can have on a culture of people.

Two or more people accept that their mutual worth is only as potent as the currency that is the bartering tool. Once accepted, the medium of exchange becomes more important than the people who wield it. Those intellectual lines that once defined a person's self-image are crossed by bridge of motivated hate. The hate is the product of a satanic social system of order toward the persons who are to be enslaved by it, and the potentially enslaved assimilate this mind-set and direct its destructive power toward each other by reducing each other to things to be bartered for.

Cultures of people accept the means of their eventual physical and intellectual downfall. There is a time, though, when the aggressed upon do realize what a dire situation they find their cumulative lives have come to. At that point, rather than abandon what vehicle brought them to such a disreputable condition, they revel in it. They celebrate it. They honor it with whatever brand of perversion can be committed upon self and another, and this with a great deal of mutual consent and trust among the actors to do whatever is in their respective and selfish best interests of the moment. This kind of capitalist establishment destroys the bond of familial trust that once made us tribes people of a most powerful order. Furthermore, with every willful turn, it sinks those actors and the community proper deeper into a manufactured, though nonetheless real, hell.

This stage is the remnant of a diabolical system whose patriarchs designed it to be a reflection of their mind-set and perspective of the world. It feeds on the hopes, dreams, and especially the potential of those females and males within a people. It reduces a whole half of the life dynamic to a whore, and the other whole half a whoremonger. And once subscribed to, there can be no trust between the only two elements within a people that can right the wrong. The people's spirit becomes fractured and unable to will positive action; the culture then follows, becoming fractured and unable to reflect positive action. The existence of such a capitalist establishment in one's neighborhood is an indication of how far you have fallen.

The music becomes louder, and the rippling water less interesting. A Latina strides across the runway in front of Kevin. The thin girl has left the stage, and her three victims sat drinking and bragging. The Latina walked to the end of the runway and crouched before two men in business suits. They smile a lot. The other three women busied themselves moving from one end of the stage to the other. They were all black women. One of them looked like she had recently been pregnant. She had that same thick wrinkled pouch of flesh that sagged below her belly button—a sight he begins to believe has become disturbingly too common as of late. She was very pretty, though, and otherwise nicely built. Each of them in turn would find her way to Kevin, who would politely smile them past.

"You OK?" the voice came from behind. Kevin turns to see the dreadlock girl from the lap dance in the corner standing behind him with a tray full of empty glasses and money.

"What?" he responds, sounding more startled than hard of hearing.

"Are you OK? You looked like you were deep in thought," she says then smiles a most pleasing smile.

"Yeah, I'm fine. How are you?" his response is in the midst of thinking that he is sounding and looking too green. He thugs up his voice and relaxes into the chair.

"I'm fine. Do you need another drink?" she says and smiles with her entire physique. That is, her posture and manner were soft and agreeable. He felt compelled to trust her.

"Umm. I'm not much of a drinker, lately. This is only water," he says then passes her the glass. She takes it and places it on top of some bills on her tray.

"I don't drink much either. Would you like more water?" she questions, throwing her friendly gaze deep into his eyes.

"Yes," he responds in kind with his mouth and eyes. He cannot help but to stare in her face, she is stunningly beautiful. Her skin and features are of a quality one would think she lived in a salon, but she is spoiled by no type of makeup. She is a natural beauty.

She smiles and walks away and around the stage, taking other orders. To the left, a woman performs a table dance for two guys. The bartender is laughing with some customers sitting at the bar. The bartender is tall and thin with a Caesar fade and a goatee. He is easily about his thirties. The dreadlock girl approaches them, and she and the bartender stand talking while the men he addressed bend their necks to study her form.

"Hey!" suddenly demands a voice from above.

An excellent right foot adorned with a gold band on the index toe rests below the voice. Kevin's eyes rise up silky dark calf and thigh to pubes cut into a thick knotty question mark. She wears a gold stud in her navel, a small gold hoop in her left nipple, a gold hoop in her right nostril, and a bald head. She is food for thought. Her cover is very dark; that is, so deep brown as to be nearing actual black. She proudly sported the chiseled look of a middle-weight bodybuilder. Her eyes seem black through the shadowy space separating him from her. She is magnificent. They stare for a moment.

"What's the question?" he finally asks, gazing at her pubes.

"For you? Can you handle it?" she responds. There was a truckload of passive aggression with the response, and she stared deep into his eyes and never blinked.

"Ya don't say!" he squeezes out while trying desperately to maintain his composure. He does not feel he is a punk, but these new environments and people of late are taking him places he had not accounted for.

She crouches to the floor and rests on her open left palm. Her breasts hang like dark chocolate drops with ebony kisses for nipples. Her mouth is small with thick, puffy, smooth lips. Her nose is the perfect size and shape to be called cute, and her forehead is broad, round, and smooth. Her kind expression sedates Kevin, easing him into discourse. He thinks that she probably has the only head and face in Manhattan that could wear a baldy that well. She smiles.

"Yes, I do say. Would you like anything?" she asks as her eyes visibly fall to his crotch then rise back to catch his eyes.

"Like what?" he says, staring back into her steely glance like prey staring at predator. He is not certain which one he is at the moment.

"A regular show? A lap dance or table dance? A private show?" she offers, still smiling.

With every experience, Kevin's respect for scenarios expands. He has watched its actors at play. From what he could gather, the experience was akin to having one's brains sucked out of one's head, but curiously no one seemed to mind. Most males never see it coming because their eyes are full, and some blood has left the brain. Other males avoid it out of ignorance to what is going on. It's called dumb luck. Still others see it, recognize it, and embrace it for their own reasons.

"How much?" he almost whispers the question. He spoke softly as if someone nearby might hear him through the music and realize what he is bartering for.

"Your drink, sir," sings a familiar other voice.

Kevin turns to see the dreadlock girl placing a glass of water on the surface before him. He pulls money form his pocket and fishes out another ten-dollar bill and places it on her tray.

"Thank you," he says, smiling pleasantly into her eyes. She meets his gaze; then the two women lock eyes briefly. The dreadlock girl then turns away and begins to distribute drinks to other patrons.

The Riddler chimes in, bringing Kevin's attention back to that transaction. "The price is dependent upon service requested, but I'll hook you up." She does not seem to be able to discourage that smile. It is pleasant and confident. It works with her eyes and all of her parts in a concert of physical beauty. Her music is hypnotizing.

"A hookup, eh?" He does not know how to respond, and it shows. His pause lasts longer than a person who is accustomed to such goings-on. Her smile now becomes knowing.

She stands straight. His eyes lock on her studded navel then sink to the question. *Can you handle it?* It bounces around his mind, and he begins to wonder about its relevance. There was a time he said he would never get involved in such acts. He thought it behavior that was beneath him and subsequently never gave it any serious consideration. And for that time, that was the right answer. This time, though, he finds himself on foreign ground. His experience in this world cannot support such an opinion. Not that a person must suffer hell to be informed it is an undesirable condition, but that a person must have lived a life full of the range of experiences required to have an understanding of why such a state of being is undesirable. Those judgments he clung to for that time not only came from a place of his personal ignorance, but were in part handed down to him by others who had lived, learned, and formed their opinions. Ultimately, he discovered he must walk this path and face whatever consequences and repercussions will materialize with as much conviction as the knowing. He must know if he can handle it.

She smiles and turns to walk off the stage. Her ass is taut dark globes of muscle. It shimmies and jiggles as she strides. "Follow me," she commands.

As if I wouldn't, he thinks. She throws that ass around like its old money at a charity fund-raiser. She did not even bother look back. She walked off the stage and around the left side of the bar to a door. She opened the door and disappeared. Kevin felt as though he should be insulted. She was so confident that he would follow. He thought to return to his seat or even to leave just to spite her, but he could not gather even a mustard seed of determination in that direction. As he approached the door, he passed the first waitress, Shorty. She was taller than he thought. She was at a table serving drinks to a couple of guys. She stares him past with a smile.

Through the door, the light turned amber, and the air was moving. The music was audible but muffled as it pounded through the walls. There was a corridor along the back wall of the bar with four doors lining the left side from end to end. She stood in the third doorway. He approached, and as he did, she fell into the space. He followed.

The door opened to a room—seven feet wide, eight feet high, and ten feet deep. It was well lit with a metal-framed bed pushed against the far wall, a metal filing cabinet at the head of the bed against the wall, and a wastebasket in the corner to the left of the door. She walks past him and closes the door. Only the heavy bottom of the music could be heard. He stepped away from her and put the wall closer to his back.

What the fuck am I doing? he thinks while looking her over. Onstage in the dim light, he could see that she was exceptional, but in this well-lit room, he had no words to describe her magnificence. This of course raised the same type of question, *What the fuck is she doing here?* However, the best he could do was to try to think clearly.

"Have you decided what you want?" she says in a less-commanding tone but while moving closer to him.

"No," he responds. He is unsure if he were responding to the menu, the situation, or his life.

She moves in closer and wraps both of her arms around his waist and presses herself to him. Her warm breasts flatten against his body. He responds instinctually by wrapping his arms around her as gently as he embraces any female. His mind is speeding as she starts to speak. Thoughts flash through his mind, creating a video for what she describes. Her words become the subtext.

"Well, a straight-fuck is one hundred dollars," she starts, but what she says does not seem to fit her face. "If you want a dick-suck with it, that's one sixty. A dick-suck alone is fifty," she continues. "If you want some ass, that will be two hundred," she pauses for a moment, then, "and if you want to be a special friend, well, that's negotiable." She finishes by rubbing along the stiffy pushing against the front of his jeans.

He is high on emotion, and his condition shows. She pulls him away from the wall and spins him, putting his back toward the bed. She then pushes into him, coaxing him to back up. He looks down into her face for some relief. Above a sly smirk, her eyes cast a subliminal suggestion; in a room where she has probably fucked, sucked dick, and taken it in the ass, he cannot be her judge—she is innocent.

Her lips press to his as his calves stop against the bed's metal frame. Her hands crawl under his shirt and survey his abdomen. Her soft fingers caress the tight muscle along the small of his back. She nudges him, and he falls to the bed. He lies with his arms up as if surrendering. His mind is no longer racing, her kiss stopped that, but he is still numb. She crawls on top of him, straddling his waist. Her hands glide up his body to his face then along his shoulders and arms. Her hands press over his wrists, and her weight shifts forward. She places a gentle kiss on his chin.

"What do you want?" she whispers in his left ear.

"I have a buck, twenty," he says and pauses.

She licks his lips as he speaks while her bare ass begins to bounce and sway slowly along his crotch.

"Give it to me please," she lays it out politely.

His right hand flies to his pocket and pulls the wad of neatly folded bills free. He knew what he carried in that pocket, so he did not bother to count it. He passes her the whole bunch, and she secures it in her right hand.

Her tongue attacks, leaving a moist trail from his lips to his neck, where she nibbles and sucks lightly. A moan leaks from her throat, and he begins to wonder why, but then realized he did not care. His dick is stiff under his left pocket. Her hips rock forward and back, scrapping her hood against the tight denim over his dick. Her moans grew louder. Her crotch falls on his and mashes her moist box against it. She rises slowly, steps to the floor, drops the money, and kneels down.

She unfastens his boots then removes and drops them to the floor. She swings his legs around and pulls him to his feet. Her hands flash across his belt and zipper, and his pants fall to the floor around his ankles. She anchors the pants as he pulls his legs free. His stiffness makes his silk boxers stretch like a tent. She begins to nibble and lick at it, moistening the material. She handles it gently with her hands while her mouth attacks it angrily, but carefully. Sleek fingers creep up his sensitive thighs to the waistband and yank his boxers around his ankles.

She pushes him roughly to the bed, and at once, he feels his scrotum sack being inhaled into her mouth. He thinks that this has to be the same sensation as being electrocuted. His eyelids flutter uncontrollably, his mouth twists, and some saliva begins to leak from the right corner, his body lightly convulses, and a sound like he has never made before creeps from his gut and out of his mouth.

She lifts his legs aloft by his boxers. It is as if his ankles are bound by silk shackles. Her soft hands push against the backs of his thighs at the knees and press them against his body. Her tongue starts at the crack of his ass and glides up until it tastes his puckered asshole. His legs lurch forward suddenly. She catches them and halts their progress.

"Keep them back, baby," she commands in so sweet a tone he nearly mistook it for a request.

He does not bother to remove his head from the pillow as he wraps his hands around the backs of his knees and pulls them back securely. She pulls the boxers from his ankles so he can open his legs wider. Her lips and tongue then begin to lick and suck on his asshole and loosely hanging balls. All he is capable of is gagging out grunts and moans while holding his legs open and back. Her hand begins to slide along his stiff member as her mouth consumes it. In her mouth, he feels the wet of saliva and her tongue while one hand jerks him off and the other cradles and massages his balls.

Interest finally gets the better of him. He raises his head to see the action. The view between his legs is a fantasy in his eyes. He watches her mouth slide up and down his dick, coating his sensitive tool in silken saliva. On the rise, her lips close to a kiss at the tip of his swollen head. A snaky tongue presses against its thick shaft then slides down to his sensitive sack and back to the head. His breathing becomes a mixture of deep moans cluttered with rapid pants and silent openmouthed screams of delight. Perfect teeth gently nibble their way from the head and down the shaft to the balls. Her left hand is masterfully riding the length of his slick thick-veined dick. Her trained tongue draws each testis past cocoa-painted lips into the warmth of her mouth. Underneath his overwhelmed expression and moans of approval of her oral method, a slender dark finger, with nail painted black and filed to a point, penetrates his twitching anus.

He did not know how to feel. He wanted to move. His hand was close to her, he could reach and push her away. As the thought passed through his mind, her mouth, tongue, and hands became more intelligent and began showing mastery of his pleasure. Bolts of energy began to rock him. He felt her hand working his sex and deftly coaxing the semen from his balls. His balls were again captives of her mouth; and the combination of tooth, tongue, and lip provoked a sundry of responses in his mind. His mind was full of the images of her mouth handling his sex, of her finger pleasuring his ass, and of her. He felt he should scream a word of protest to at least sound imposed upon by this treatment, but it was good to him. It was good like things that are tenderly coveted for a time, then experienced in an explosive moment.

Her tools then became more intrusive. That finger begins to work his anus as if it were a little dick, and her mouth and hand intensify their search for sperm. The suction from her mouth suddenly seemed to reach directly into his balls. An uncommon high begins to graduate to the sort of experience that has had others chasing that dragon for the rest of their lives. He will enjoy having been in the company of that beast tonight.

His ejaculation freed his voice from being the exclusive spokesman of animal sounds. He spat out an "oh, shit!" as the first wad of his cream rose and landed on the wall behind him. Her mouth and face caught the rest as she devoured his juice and menaced his sensitive part. His arms relaxed, and his legs fell free—one to the bed, and the other rested gently on her shoulder and back. For a moment, the room seems still. His eyes are closed, and flashes of light create splashes of color through his eyelids. The pulse of the music suddenly fades back in.

Her laugh is barely audible because it is muffled against his body. He feels her lips kiss the insides of his thighs, and her loving hand gently strokes his still-live erection. He feels the ghostly imprint of her finger still pushing into his rectum. It twitches. She slides his leg away and stands.

His eyes open to the sound of a dry sliding. The cabinet drawer is open. She removes a fifth of some whiskey and takes a mouthful. The liquid rolls around her mouth then she swallows. He stares. She removes a piece of gum, unwraps it, and pops it in her mouth.

"You ready for more, baby?" she questions, barely acknowledging his gaze.

She is the most exciting woman that he has ever experienced. She is regal feminine dominance, like the women of his African ancestry that he has observed or seen the likeness of in some history book.

His sex remains at attention. She then pulls out the always-recognizable square of a sealed condom. She tears, opens, and removes the latex helpmeet. She bends to him and places the red latex disc on the head of his penis. With a pump of her fist, the condom bled down his length, coating his tool like a piece of candy. She crawls over him and straddles him as before. Her forehead and nose are lightly pressed to his. Their eyes are locked.

He does not know how, but somehow, she seems to know him like the master knows the layman. Her experience gives her intelligence on what he will do and say. Her experience goes deep into the psychology of men. At any time, she may find herself as their mother, a friend, a slave, a master, though mostly the master.

The head of his stiffness is at her opening. She rocks on it, allowing the tip to slightly penetrate her opening, then she pulls away. Their gazes penetrate into the reflective place where a person hides a part of their self. She continues her motion on his head as she continues her probe in his mind. He feels her moving on him and in him. His hands rise, one up her thigh to her ass, and the other along her midsection and back. Soft dark skin and strands of muscle tighten at his touch.

"Put ya fuckin' hands down, sweetie!" Her honeyed command is full of threat and carried on a whisper. He complies hesitantly, but quickly, and allows his arms to fall to his sides.

"You don't move, baby. I got this," she speaks, insisting the words with her eyes into his. He blinks twice, and it works as a sign of comprehension.

The intensity up till now was in his anticipation of something more than slight insertion. His anticipation gave him energy. It made his balls tingle and his dick hungrier. He thought to push into her, and the urge found its way to his pelvis, where it would have acted had she not warned him not to move.

Their eyes are latched. As her face rises, her eyes tow his and pull his head from the pillow as his hungry tongue reaches for hers. She feeds it to him passionately, pressing his head back to the bed.

The thump of the bass on the walls keeps the pulse of seconds, but time has lost its relevance. He measures in images dominated by her face and form. They are pleasant images. Their eyes are locked. He is now certain he is the prey.

Her pussy crept like the rays of the smiling sun along the length of his twitching member until she made it brilliant. The pleasure of being warmed encouraged his hands to forget her orders, so they rose up to her again.

"Put 'em down!" her voice jumps at him suddenly. "Keep fuckin' with me, and I'll have you moanin' like a little whore in here."

He almost cannot believe she said it. She was not angry. Her voice was not harsh. She was calm and did not even pause from her work. He got the impression, though, she meant it. He is briefly tempted to test her conviction, very much with the idea of being thought disobedient, and that with the idea of finding out just what she could possibly do to him to make him moan like a whore. And he has never heard a whore moan, but he does not believe he wants his first audio confirmation of it to be his own voice. So he complied. He lay passively on the bed with a hard dick and a ready mouth both at her disposal as she did her work.

Her energy rose. Her grind becomes an exercise in control. Her vaginal muscles contract, squeezing on his resistant tool as she rides up his length. She relaxes her opening when she feels his puffy head at her gate. She pauses, then allows it to glide softly and easily along that length until she has all of it inside of her.

Her lips intuitively walk up his sensitive right side. They seem to know that area behind his right ear and down to his collar is especially hot for him. Her lips do not linger there but move on to his waiting mouth. Though in the discovery, they do hesitate after he gasps and clutches the sheets into his fists. When her tongue invades his mouth, it reminds him of her oral treatment; it is highly skillful and aggressive. She repeatedly uses his tongue like a little wet dick as she licks and sucks it. Her tongue wrestles with his in a cage of teeth and cognac-tainted saliva as her ride becomes more urgent.

His eyes shut. A ball of energy is building in his sack. His toes have gone mad. His voice is again lost to desperate babble, and his muscles burn and tingle from the pulses of energy radiating through them. The conclusion of the moment is upon him. He fights it because he must; after all, no one wants the high to end. But it must. He was stone-faced until she played her ace.

She kept his hands at bay until this moment. Now is when his fetish becomes the tool to his unraveling. She whispered in his ear the words he longed to hear, "Grab my ass, baby." They are simple words with little meaning in the context of things, even sex. To a worshiper, though, and then one who has been denied the pleasure of the object desired, the words become a divine command. Both hands immediately fly up to her ass. It was soft, but massive. His hands rove over the curve of her hips and up to the small of her back. The tips of his fingers zippered into each other and rode down the crack of her ass until each hand was full of its heavy buttock. Her voice remained all aware, and it seemed to mingle with her gentle kisses and intellectual touch until they became the same powerful force influencing him to submit.

His eyes open. He feels the sperm fleeing his balls like students do the last class on the last day of school. They bully their way through his penis and into the condom. He feels the pool of energy relaxing into his navel and groin. He feels her lips tenderly on his forehead. Her eyes smile into his, and she rises to the floor.

"There's a box of baby wipes in the drawer," she says while picking up and counting the money then moving to the door. Kevin watches her. She opens the door. He stands. He glares at his erection as if stunned. She blows him a kiss and disappears behind the closing door. The music flooded in briefly then was again dammed to a muffle as the door closed.

God, she is nice, he thinks, and again notices his rubber-coated erection. He looks to the cabinet. It has three drawers. The top drawer is partially open. That is where the whiskey and condoms are. He pulls open the second drawer. There are a variety of dildos, vibrators, and lubricants lying in confusion at the bottom. To the back of those was a black nylon harness, the type a female would use to simulate the action of a male. He closes that drawer and opens the third.

"Eureka!" He retrieves the box of wipes and sits on the edge of the bed. He looks down to see his dick staring up. He grabs the condom by the tip and pulls it off. Milky liquid trickles down his erection as he drops

223

the condom to the floor. He then remembers the wastebasket and looks over to it. He reaches to the floor for that discarded condom, picks it up, and walks it over to the receptacle.

The door suddenly bursts open, and "oh, shit," exclaims a startled voice. It was the Latina from the stage. She stood in the doorway with a look that was more interested than surprised. Kevin stare at her with the wet condom dangling from his right hand and his still-half-hard dick dangling from under his shirt. He thought he should say something, but he could not find the words. They stare at each other for a moment as the music and light seeped in around her. A guy was walking hurriedly past her with his head down and heading for the exit.

"You need some help, boo?" Her solicitous question reminded him he was still hungry. His dick jumped as she stepped partly into the room. Her face and body are as beautiful and motivating as any of the others, except the Riddler; she's special. This day's discoveries have been taxing, though, and he thinks it a better idea to go home.

"Umm, no," he hums, then smiles as he turns away from her and moves toward the bed.

"Twenty dollars, boo, and I'll deflate it for you," she says as she steps farther into the room but still with a hand outside the door.

"I don't have any more money," he admits while pulling on his boxers.

"Pss, well" was the last thing she uttered before he heard the door shut.

What the fuck am I still doing here? he thinks while standing with some frustration on his brow.

He dresses, arranges, and checks himself, making certain he is leaving with everything he came with, though one hundred-plus dollars light. He moves from the room and up the hall to the door that leads to the barroom. A hand kept the door partially open as he approached. He pulls on it and startles the waitress to whom the hand belonged. He opened it and stood in the doorway against a peach backdrop. Before him was the Latina, Shorty, and another dancer he had not seen before. They went silent. He wanted to laugh to keep from crying, but he does not know if his tears would be from embarrassment or disappointment. He did not see the Riddler anywhere in the room. Any tears now would certainly be from disappointment; he wanted to see her again. He walked past them, politely excusing himself, and headed for the door.

The outside air greeted him in as fresh a manner as New York City air can. At any rate, it was a lot more refreshing than the cigarette, alcohol, and ass-heavy air of the bar. He turned to his left and headed up Tenth Avenue toward One Hundred Thirty-Third Street. Some pedestrian and vehicle traffic were out and about. Then there were those lingerers who were like multicolored bottles cast to the curbs. These broken shards of people lay wasted in stoops, poised against cars, or gathered before twenty-four-hour stores, and they all looked ready to cut the too bold or too careless. Kevin's thoughts follow him like a mentor's teachings and whisper their intentions in his head. He cannot escape the "mother" issue. He ignores those thoughts and proceeds on his way.

His car is wedged between two buckets. The first is an early eighties white Honda Civic with one blue door and a cracked back window, and the other is a brown seventies Lincoln Continental with one hubcap and fuzzy dice hanging from the rearview mirror. Both are rusted and dented. His car is a burgundy 1994 Honda Accord. He steps between the front bumper of his car and the rear of the Lincoln and into the street. A car passes him then stops at the corner. After a moment, it turns down Tenth Avenue toward the bar. The sound of glass shattering then skipping across the pavement comes lightly to his ears from somewhere up the block. He climbs in his car, starts it, and pulls out onto the road.

His mind has drifted away to his fantasy place. His body is driving the car on reflex memory. He sees himself seated in the room with his dick in hand. He visualizes her, the Riddler. He was licking her pussy, sucking her clean asshole, and French-kissing her feet. She was verbally abusing him, but not in the whispered manner she had in reality, now her voice is hard and barking at him. She soundly smacks his face after every fourth tongue stroke, and he does not pause or skip a stroke.

She makes him lie on the floor. She stands over him with a foot planted on each side of his upper torso and his arms to the outside of her feet. She squats over his face while firmly holding his erection in a tight right-handed grip to keep her balance. Her ass is stretched before his eyes like a great taut dark fleshy canvass, and her pussy hovers just above his nose. With her free hand, she pulls a cheek apart. At her command, he licked the smooth dark skin of her left cheek then allowed his tongue to venture boldly into the darker crack of her ass.

The glorious essence of ready ass and pussy pushed its way into his nostrils and filled his mind with gratitude for her gift. She swayed that dark treasure over his face, periodically resting her asshole on his mouth to allow it to be properly sucked. She slides her treasure up to his nose and over his eyes. The tightly stretched skin of her wrinkled sphincter teases his eyes while his tongue strains to get a taste of the pussy that is covering his nose. Her sphincter rides a slick easy course from his eyes, down the ridge of his nose to its wide puffy bulb of an end, over his anxious mouth, and to his stubble-covered chin where it rests. He felt her weight as her huge ass rested against his face. When she spread her cheeks, he could feel the soft wrinkly ridges of her brown eye riding his face all the way back up to his nose. She is using him for her selfish pleasures, and she should.

There was a pause just long enough for him to see her sphincter twitch before spreading open. Her waste falls to his nose and mouth then rolls down his neck in thin warm brown logs. When she is through squeezing them out, she drops to her knees and pulls his legs back like one would a baby when changing it. She leans forward and engulfs his long brown dick. When she leaned forward, her ass spread over his face like a dark fleshy parachute. The crack was still warm from the discharge. He wedged his face into her chasm, where her twitching anus, still glorious with the scent of fresh feces, opened to accept his slavish tongue and face.

These images take him down the West Side Highway to Bowling Green and around to the Brooklyn Bridge. These images plagued him through Brooklyn and over the Verrazano Bridge. These images enticed him down Bay Street, to Clinton Street, to Brewster Street, where they finally swayed him to satisfy them.

He parks, exits the car, and locks it. He walks up three concrete yard steps, then six wooden porch steps. He moved quickly through two wooden doors and up two flights of stairs to the attic.

This is his parents' house. It is a two-family dwelling in the suburbia called Staten Island. Staten Island is as far south as one can go and still be in New York City. His bedroom suite is the entire attic space. He inherited it from his elder brother Herbert, who is now married with children and living in Winslow, Canada.

The middle room is equipped with a three-quarter bathroom, a small kitchen area, and all built and installed by his brother and their father, John. His bedroom is in the back portion of the space and has a full view of the kitchen and bathroom and living room. Then there is the study and guest bedroom. The front stairs open into this room. It has one oak desk with a computer and various papers and other related paraphernalia scattered about. That whole unit sits against the wall nearest the front window. Along the length of the wall, to the right of the computer desk, is a drafting table, a chair, and a six-foot-high wood cabinet. The length of the wall across from this is taken up by a large bookshelf. It is mostly full of books, but there are a couple of bowls—terra-cotta and crystal—two candles on stands, and a small stereo system. Above the shelves are four of his sketches that have been framed and mounted. Under each of them is either a ribbon or a certificate that shows what place his work won in local or national contests.

His clothes begin falling off by the time he enters the room. Blue neon screams at him from his right. It is a digital wall clock framed with neon tubing chanting 3:53 a.m. Below this is a window at the front of the house. He turns to the left, leaving a trail of clothes from the living room entrance and across the dining room. The only other source of light is from the moon shining through the skylight above his bed a room ahead. In his desperate condition, his erection is a better guide than his eyes in the dark. His imagination is master, and he desperately wants to serve the master. He stumbles over something at the foot of his bed. As he bends to pick it up, his eyes have adjusted enough to allow him to see a figure huddled in his bed and under the sheets. He holds the object and recognizes it as a woman's sneaker. The figure stirs and turns to him. The shoe falls to the floor, and he stands erect with his penis.

"Hi, baby," says the voice.

"Hey," Kevin responds, trying not to sound too surprised or disappointed.

"Where were you? I waited all night," the voice questions while peering at him with an open right eye. The left side of her face is pressed into a pillow and the sheet.

"Well, I didn't know you were coming over, Lauren," he responds while removing what clothing was left. His T-shirt and socks fall to the floor.

"I know. I wanted to surprise you," she affirms softly.

He sets the sheets back as they speak and her skin is bathed in moonlight. She is an athlete, and she has an athlete's body. She is tall and lean. Her beauty electrifies him. It always has. She has been his inspiration since middle school, and there are few who have ever been her match in his mind. She is two shades darker than him, and she has always carried herself with an annoying femininity. He seems to think there are times when she could be more assertive without breaching any rules of gender etiquette, and he has told her so.

He climbs in next to her and settles into position. She turns and repositions herself, resting her left leg over his right. Her body is nestled snugly to his, and her left hand probes his bare chest and stomach. Ordinarily, he enjoys the affection, and especially her touch, but that image that drove him home was fading.

"So?" she questions.

"So?" he comes back

"Where were you?" she inquires without looking him in his face. She seems occupied with his chest and continues to caress it tenderly.

"Chillin'." And the erection starts to fade to white.

"By yourself?" she asks between soft kisses to his stomach.

"Nah!" he states bluntly and rolls to his back to give her clearer access to his parts.

"With who?" she continues, and her kisses move up to his chest.

"Just some heads. A guy from school and a couple of his friends," he responds, as he notices her hand finding its way to his joy, still stiff enough to draw attention.

"What's this?" she inquires with feigned innocence as she gently strokes his penis with her fingers.

"Why do you ask?" he retorts as his mind empties of those images of that bar, except the Riddler, and their influence, except hers, and fills with thoughts of his life love.

"Can I kiss it?" she asks playfully with her mouth already kissing down his abdomen.

"No! Leave it alone!" he says teasingly. No matter, her nose has caught his scent, and her lips are on the trail.

Those damned voices, the ones that drove him away from that bar tonight. They never seem to have said enough:

> *I wonder if Ms. Riddler had anything?* I wore a condom. *What if she had crabs?* But she didn't have any pubic hairs. What if she was tainted and her juice wet your balls? I used the baby wipes. *You seem to have all of the answers, don't you?* Yes. *Well, if you think you're sure.*

He pulls Lauren up from her course and thinks to kiss her, but then remembers the taste of whiskey in the Riddler's mouth. He remembers looking between his legs and seeing painted lips and studded tongue work their charms. Her method tortured him from the balls, up the shaft, and to the head. Sperm leaked from the corners of her mouth; sperm dotted her face and clean-shaven head, leaving a thick clear coat glistening on her cheek and chin; and, sperm oozed down her throat as her tongue hungrily lapped up his cream from his belly and her fingers. Lastly, he remembers her painted lips. He can imagine his genitals, thighs, and belly stained in her shade.

He kisses Lauren on the forehead and slides out of the bed. "I should take a shower," he throws at her as he moves through the dim room to the bathroom, betting hard against himself that he would not look back at her through the moonlight and darkness. He lost and peeked back at her. She met his gaze, though he will never know it. These melanin ethers between them can keep a secret.

He showered his mind blank. What grimy thoughts he had left melted with the water, rolled from his hair and down his body, and disappeared through the drain. He still struggled with the question of his actions. His conflict is he is not convinced his actions were questionable. He does not want to think now though. He does not want to hear any more questions or give any more answers. He does not want to hear any more voices.

He exits the shower and walks dry and naked back to bed. Lauren was curled into that comfortable fetal position a person assumes when the

230

intent for a peaceful rest is strong. She appears to be asleep. He slides in under the sheets and still she does not move. He enjoys the silence.

In the grip of slumber, there is order, but as the grip fails, chaos. He hears her moving about the room. The early morning light is warm on his body and bright in his eyes. He keeps them closed and clings to the thread of sleep left hanging in his darkness. It is Sunday morning. She is going to church. She probably has to go home first unless she carried some clothes with her. He thought he saw 7:37 a.m. blinking on the alarm clock on the stand next to the bed. *That would make sense,* he thinks, *it's a nine o'clock service.*

Within minutes, she is showered, dressed, and out of the door. He listens to her move lightly down the stairs to the second floor, the first floor, the front door, and gone. And all without a good-bye kiss or word.

What a break, he thinks. His reliance on his fantasy world and his hands sometimes cause his great misplacement of his energies. His eyes pop open, and the sheets jump from his body. He walks across the floor to a footlocker under the window and to the right of his bed. The room is clean. He opens the locker and fishes through stacks of magazines: *Blacktail, Big Butt, Tailends, Black and Beautiful,* and an assortment of others. He selects a mixed stack and places them on the bed. There is not an article of clothing anywhere on the floor where he left them. Already he is erect. His right hand strokes along the sides of his penis as if a genie would soon pop out. In the bathroom he finds a large towel and removes it from the shelf. Under the shelf is the dirty clothes basket. On the basket lay his lipstick-stained white silk boxers with a small piece of paper pinned at the crotch. It had some writing on it done in that bronze shade of lipstick Lauren likes to wear, and it read "FUCK YOU!"

August 7, 1994: The Good Friend
Unhappiness is not knowing what one wants in life, but working a lifetime to gain it.

—Unknown

Warm summer evenings in Greenwich Village are static enough to raise even dead spirits, and then especially on a Monday. It is seven forty-five in the evening. Words that are black and positively charged from being brewed in the selfless mind come pouring out from in between tar-stained teeth and into the ears of those surrounding, walking, or riding within the vicinities of the makers. They smile and laugh, traversing city streets however they might, all en route to one spot or another, and all with the misguided look of happiness on their faces.

The hot zone comprises streets running along Seventh Avenue, Sixth Avenue, and Broadway. On Bleecker Street, near Sullivan Street, is the bar titled Mondo Perso. The sun sets, and the sky turns a drowsy blue with Pegasus climbing overhead. Through the door, this place is like any other place. The tables are small, and small chairs crowd them. That is what efficiency insists is cozy. Young waitress bodies move like running water around idle, stone-faced crowds at the bar. The drinks appear on the tables with a smile. There is a band called——, and they are playing through whirlpooled conversations that draw each other's attentions and their own demons. There are enough tables for smokers to be happy. The crowd is mixed; there are more women than men and some couples.

Kevin sits at a table aside the path from the bar to the bathroom and in front of the stage. He wears a black T-shirt under an oversized beige cotton casual dress shirt, brown denim jeans, and sand-colored casual shoes. He is sipping from a glass of water with ice and a twist of lemon. There are voices around him that are as amusing as most of their faces. The guy behind him sounds gay. The dark-haired woman sitting in a group of four in a booth to his left reminds him of a woman at the Forty-Seventh Street playhouse that he had paid to give another woman in the booth oral. The girl in front of him, giggling with her guy, resembles the one he dildoed through the booth window at a show house on the Deuce. Finally, one of the barmaids is the clone of a chick he convinced into a three-way with him and another dancer in an Elizabeth, New Jersey, show house.

From the first to the last, there is no question in his mind he has become sadly addicted to this type of stimulation. He is a debaucher. He fiends for the interaction despite the health risk, and those are substantial. He has missed class and has sacrificed eating to pursue this stimulus.

He has lately, though, slowed his support of the erotic entertainment world down to a trickle. He came to a point where his grades began to suffer. Lauren refuses to speak with him despite his many attempts at asking her forgiveness. Betrayal is difficult to forgive. His bank account has dwindled to an unimpressive level. And his parents are wondering what he is doing with his time. In fact, he has wondered what he has done with the last five months. What began as the curious and energetic exploration of a new world has evolved into a debilitating habit. He has become so hampered by this crutch that he was forced to finally ask, what does it do for me? It is a query that females have posed to males because of the very same category of interaction, and that for too many generations; they still feel as though they have not received a satisfactory reply. He has found that other than a single ray of sunshine, he has greatly wasted time and resource in the pursuit of the fantastic things that world can tempt the weak mind with. However, that one bright spot seems to make all that he has done and endured worth the effort. There really is a good reason to go to hell and back.

He spies his sunshine maneuvering through the crowd and to the table where he sits. She is Claire. She is the dreadlock girl from that bar two months ago. Her hair is pulled back and tied with a kente scarf. She wears earrings, a necklace, and a ring that are part of a matching set. They seem to be a Native American design. She wears a very appropriate sundress, clay-colored, with some African symbols dyed into it. Her feet are in some brown strap sandals, and she sports silver toe rings on the index toes of both feet.

"Hey," he starts with a smile.

"Hey, yourself," she continues while matching his smile. He stands, and they embrace. "Sorry I'm late," she adds as he pulls out the chair and prompts her to sit. She places her bag on the table and sits. Kevin moves around to his chair and eases into it. "You were about to leave, weren't you?" Her face seems rather certain despite the question.

233

"As soon as I finished this water." And he takes a sip.

"You know, that can get on somebody's nerves. People are late sometimes, ya know," she says it with no particular type of attitude and while waving down a waitress.

"Late sometimes is one thing. When it becomes a character trait, ya lost me." He suddenly stares blankly at the band as if someone in its ranks whispered his name then, just as quickly, turns back to his date.

"You're ready to order?" the waitress says, looking from his face to hers with the pen poised on the pad.

"Whiskey sour," says Kevin.

"Bailey's," follows Claire.

The waitress is a wispy white girl of average height and looks with blonde hair via Revlon, cut into a punk style. She leaves as the band finishes a song and pauses for consideration. Kevin looks at Claire, who is talking, then to the faces behind her being very distracting despite his disinterest. She continues to speak.

He does not notice her voice immediately but the movement of her lips. He studies her face for the millionth time and is again genuinely impressed by her ability to move him without a word. Her skin is the color of the face of the Sahara Desert. It is a place where males who want to be men have their metal tested. She has light brown eyes, a thin but fleshy nose, and a wide mouth with thick lips that are strong enough to support the wisdom of her heritage. Add to this an uncensored mind, and she is a highly desirable female. He believes she is more beautiful today than yesterday, and certainly exceeds her charms of that first sight that night in that Harlem bar. They became friendly upon his second excursion to that uptown watering hole that was the scene of some learning for him. He went back the following Saturday night after Lauren discovered his indiscretion. She remembered him from that first time as well. She thought he tipped well for water. So when he returned and made a friendly gesture toward her, they spoke and eventually began dating.

"What?" he exclaims as the band begins playing again.

"Do you ever listen?" Her face is a smile.

"Yeah, I was just . . . nothin'. What did you say?" he insists.

"I was telling you about Michelle," Claire offers this and settles into her seat for what Kevin predicts will be a long story. His face settles into an "OK" type of look.

She continues, "She broke this dude off the other night at the club. He was talkin' all of this stuff about what he wanted to do to her, and this is while she was onstage. She finished her set then took him to the back room. Ten minutes later, my god! She waves us free hands down, and four of us follow her back, but we don't know what to expect because we know Michelle, but we don't know this situation. So we get back to the room, and she got this motherfucker shackled facedown on the mattress and ass in air. She straps her harness on with like this twelve-inch dildo and walks up on him like *what!* She grabs a tube and squeezes some lube on his asshole then squeezes some on the dildo and rubs it around the head and shaft. She starts rubbing the head of the dildo along the guy's asshole, and he's feeling it. Slowly she's pushing into him, then more rubbing. Finally, she just plows it into his ass. He lets go this bark of a squeal. She doesn't even pause. She starts workin' him like a porno pro, smackin' his ass, spittin' on it. He's squealin' and moanin' and pantin' and shit, but his dick was the hardest I've ever seen a dick."

Kevin injects with "and you've seen plenty!" Then he smiles.

She continues with "fuck you, but yes, I have, so I should know. Next thing ya know—"

The waitress returns with the drinks, forcing Claire's pause. She places the drinks and walks away.

Claire stares the waitress past, then continues, "The next thing ya know, after like ten minutes of this, she got this man begging all of us to fuck him in his ass."

"And you?" Kevin asks, breaking her confession.

"And us not being the types to let a good man beggin' go to waste, well, what's a woman suppose to do?" And she meant it. He could see it in her face. "Michelle started giving it to him harder, and he just wanted more.

"Watching you guys fuck is one thing, but this was something else. Michelle told a girl to hook him up with one of the dildos while she pulled out of him and removed the harness. She passed it to me, and when I strapped that dick on, I felt something. I lifted that thick brown dick up to his twitching hole and pushed into him. I heard him exhale as the inches disappeared into his ass. I heard him feel the joy of surrender. That's when I knew what that feeling was, Kevin, it was power. I felt powerful, and it was real power, not the delusions you guys suffer through."

He floats a smile and a mock chuckle across the table and into her eyes.

She continues, "When most guys have sex, it is just fucking. It is a moment they reserve for the sake of the nut. The pleasure involved is as fleeting as it is incidental, and that's because most guys have learned not to feel anything real for themselves, and so they cannot feel anything real for a female. It's all physical because that's what y'all are stuck on. Each of you has a different recipe for your ejaculation, but it's all the same ingredients: you and someone to surrender to your wants. Ultimately, it seems to come down to a seemingly inextinguishable desire to control flesh. How utterly unevolved."

"Unevolved?" he lightly injects as she politely ignores him and continues. The band is in such a hard groove, even pedestrian traffic pauses to listen for a moment. The drinks are flying, and people are laughing and having a good time.

"But what a concept. And in an attempt to assure control for all time, those more unevolved males have created religions and governments and other institutions to reinforce the idea of controlling flesh. They created armies and police forces to brutalize those who refuse to submit to their control. It's all bullshit, baby."

"It is bullshit," he quickly adds. She goes on these types of rants frequently. Very often, like tonight, she makes some interesting points. Sometimes, though, he does not see her point until much later. He usually adds his thoughts to hers nonetheless, and they talk for hours about things that most would rather not talk about. Some may avoid these conversations because they seem to lack relevance. Even if any of it is true, what can one do about their end of it this moment. But their partaking of seemingly irrelevant conversations has led to a revealing of themselves to each other. Within that supposed irrelevance was a disclosure of the mind-set that created the idea that birthed the thought that motivates the action of that person you have chosen to share time with becomes the object of his scorn and contempt. She smiles like a champion on the podium.

"Self-abusive, self-negating behavior?" he adds and looks to her for verification.

"Yes, and all because you all are so unevolved from basic animals. If that wasn't bad enough, you have the power of an undisciplined spirit to help you commit the evil that men do." She picks up her beverage and takes a swallow. He takes a mouthful of his and checks out the room. Everyone is just where he remembered them. She smiles then continues, "The ultimate logic of flesh is the sacrifice of flesh. Flesh is transient. That's why the safest option is to never become consumed by the idea of possessing or conquering flesh. But you all are so deeply dedicated toward that end that you don't even listen to your own conscience when it's trying to help you. That's why you all have a need and a desire to be saved."

"By a woman with a dick?" he questions for a good reason. He realizes she knows they are on the same page. Some males not only desire to be like the alpha male model but to be touched by the alpha male model in some effort to legitimize their existence. Sometimes the course of legitimizing oneself makes one the alpha male and, is that position ever as fulfilling until other males show their recognition of the achievement?

She continues, "And that male knew it, understood it, and embraced it. Kevin, I came. Standing right there in midthrust. I had an orgasm and nearly collapsed it hit me so hard.

The pointer finger of his right hand flies up, and an "excuse me" follows. She pauses as he squeezes his voice in the conversation. "And your telling me this because?" he questions.

She smiles slyly while leaning back in her chair and laughing. All she needed was a furry white cat and a monocle, and he would have thought himself in some serious shit. "Well, Kevin," she starts, "we've been going out for a time, and I don't think we should hold out on each other. I think spiritually, mentally, and physically, you are so much stronger and so much more in tune with yourself than the common male. Let me be your completion. I want to do it again. I want to do it with you."

A smug picture paints across his face. "Well! I certainly appreciate ah . . . , being considered, but . . . ."

"Don't play with me, Kevin. I'm serious," she says as she lightly kicks his shin and paints her face an authoritative mood. "You don't have to be gay to let me make love to you."

"Make love, what? And who said anything about being gay?" His best maneuver when trying to avoid an issue, play dumb, then confuse the situation with not-so-unrelated issues of the opponent's prompting. She does not seem to be having it.

"Let me fuck you," she whispers in her true aggressive dominant fashion.

Kevin lies back in his chair, slowly shaking his head side to side as if pitying the moment. His face is working on being some shade of disappointed, and his hands rest in his lap. "So this was it, huh? That was your rap?" he says as she sits back in her chair with her drink cupped in both hands and in her lap. There was a "pleased as punch" attitude sweetening her entire posture. "You went through all of dat bullshit just to come ta, 'Let me fuck you'?" It is when he threw on that smug as hell mask he wears she hates that pushed her.

"Let me fuck you!" she says suddenly, jumping at him in an aggressive speaking voice and loud enough for those closest around them to hear. Her intent shone through the intensity of her eyes and in every muscle tightening her mouth. In the event, this was not clear enough; she issued another light but effective kick to his shin.

"You ain't fuckin' me," he barks in a low voice while reaching with his right hand to comfort the wounded area.

He can feel the people around them trying to listen harder. The gay guy, the couple sitting in the booth to her right, the band, everyone. He thinks perhaps his objection was just a little louder than he would have wanted.

"How do you expect us to build on a relationship with these types of limitations?" she says with the most serious face she can manufacture.

"You are not fuckin' me," he ejaculates in all seriousness, and growing louder.

"You was gonna let Michelle fuck you," she throws it on the table with that very matter-of-fact tone of voice that makes the accusation seem a lot less like mere speculation. She is to be respected for her use of information.

"Get the fuck outta here!" And Kevin kicks back in his chair. And there's that damn smug look again. He melts into a posture, confident that her suggestion would remain on the outer limits of ludicrous where he subtly insists it was conceived.

"Kevin baby, please." Her hand motions across her throat like a blade. It is the universal sign for "don't make me pull your card." She proudly continues, "Michelle is a professional. Did you know that?" And he mockingly shakes his head no. "She has a gift. She can know what you want and how you want it just from listening and looking. So when she picked you, I knew that you had some kind of potential. I knew you could be one of her special friends, like that guy we did that night. Maybe you don't realize it, but she could see it. You would go there, and you would like it. She has broken bigger and badder guys than you, and every one of them will drop to their knees and kiss her ass if they think she might want her ass kissed. OK. So when she says that she could have fucked you that night, that shit is the truth."

He does not have to think hard to recall that scene. That woman's image has been etched into his mind like the sweet smell of green in a tropical forest. He settles into the chair with a posture adjustment. He is not about to argue that point any further. To think about her and especially now that he has this new information about her special friendships, he knows he wanted to be her friend. However, not quite that friendly. That is why he went back to that bar the following week, he wanted to see her. She was not working that night, though, so he settled in for a drink and some sights, and that is when he and Claire began to talk and hit it off. He does not regret not seeing Michelle that night, in fact, he has privately celebrated that night he and Claire discovered each other.

"She told us she could've had you, and you would have loved it. Ya know why she didn't?" She pauses a look at Kevin's nearly subdued stature.

"No," he says plainly.

"Because of me," she retorts.

"You?" he questions.

"Yes, me. So she let you off. You would have followed her anywhere. She had your mind, my love, and for you, there was no escape. Tell me

I'm lying." She comes to an end, looking every bit as certain as she sounded.

He stares at her, then away, and grins. He wishes that he could deny every part of this, but this is so delicious an image that even his maleness is enticed. Besides, some of it was true.

"Ya know, she always says that most guys are at least bisexual. They just need someone strong enough to show them." She pauses with a grin. With so many tools at her disposal, none are so crucial to the desired effect as the art of knowing when to employ them. This one is a look of earnest so powerful that its suggestion, no matter how unsavory or unfounded, must be given consideration.

"I'm not bisexual," he says plainly.

He has never considered males in any sexual manner. He tries to picture some dicks but can only come up with his own treasure. Besides that, images of women cause his blood to rush. He believes that nothing is better than the company of a right female, spiritually and intellectually speaking, and physically his hands are running tie for third where his pleasure is concerned.

"I don't believe that shit though," she starts. "At least, not about you." She then pauses for another sip from her cup. "She still wants you, ya know," she exclaims with an easy force as she relaxes the assault to allow the situation an exhale.

"Who?" He was not confused enough to miss the obvious, he only needed to hear it again.

"Michelle," Claire repeats, almost sounding annoyed that she had to.

Hearing her name the second time causes his mind to sparkle, ignited by the possibilities he imagined for him and her. And he cannot believe she has such a grip on him. He cannot believe he still thinks about her.

"You're the one that got away, and she's finding it difficult to live with that. She wanted me to set you up so she could get it," she tells as images of Michelle in his arms again raise his pulse. Then he realized how she meant, and all motion of thought paused. "But I decided to do it myself," Claire injects into his contemplative countenance.

"Well, I am not swingin'," he says calmly but sternly. His posture and eyes show exactly the amount of certainty necessary to be convincing, and the words oozed from his lips like a Pao Pao lava flow.

"Baby, you don't have ta tell me. I've been with you, and there is nothing suspect about you. All I'm saying is I want to be you for a night," and she pauses.

The waitress zooms by, checking their drinks and smiling her way past. The band is playing louder to compensate for the crowd that has grown louder.

She continues, "I want you to come home to candlelight. I want to greet you at the door naked and slowly undress you all the way to the bathroom. I'll put you in the shower, and as I stand behind you planting soft kisses on your back, shoulders and neck, my terry cloth hands and ivory soap will scrub all the people's dirty minds off of you. This is what you do for me, Kevin. I want to lay you down like you do me, and give you foot-to-head oral devotion like you do me. You make me feel like I'm the only woman on earth. Let me make you feel like the only man." She is as light as air, and she is dark; the sun is but a boil spoiling her divine cover.

By this time, her hands had his left hand in a firm grasp. He was silent. They stare into each other's eyes as she laid the proposition. When she finished, only their eyes and the whirlpool of thoughts remained.

"Get the fuck out of here!" And he motions for the waitress.

Claire smiles.

The waitress is at another table but acknowledges him. Kevin turns to Claire and notices her beaming and smiles back. They say nothing until the waitress arrives.

"Check please," Kevin sounds.

The waitress scribbles out the bill, rips the sheet loose, placing it between Claire and Kevin, and strays off.

"Late people should pay," Kevin follows the words with his big eyes and easy smile.

"Oh, I don't mind paying for a piece of ass," she says, reaching into her purse. She lays twenty on the table.

"You are not fucking me," he repeats while standing up with her.

She steps to him. At five foot ten, she fits snugly under his six foot five. They kiss lightly with just lips. She whispers, "I'm gonna make you moan like a little whore tonight." Then she lets go a most disturbing laugh and leads him through the crowd and out into the night.

(Later)
What can it be compared to? A necessary natural function like breathing? In his eyes, to please her is the greater obligation. So then, what to compare it to? A summer's day, a favorite food, a fond memory. They are all fond memories, but these are the ones that make your body smile when it remembers. It is what it is. It is a thing as unfathomable as the name of God and as abstract as the idea of a needle in a haystack. Some call it making love, and others say it is fucking, but it's all not just sex.

He is everything she says he is. He is as giving a lover to her as Jesus was a sacrifice for the sins of Christians. His hands are slow and gentle, and his mouth is as unpredictable and wise as nature. His eyes know when to look deeply into hers and when to close and embrace the sweet blackness. His voice knows when to comfort and excite her ears, and his body knows when to press firmly to hers. In knowing, there is awareness; additionally, how he applies the knowing is intelligence. His applications reek of intelligence. To think, after all of his efforts to be a beast desired for his sex, he is adored for his mind.

It is amazing what one thinks about during sex. Past conversations whisper through her mind, hushing those animal sounds they make in pleasure and move her thoughts.

She knows his parents were not happy about the Lauren situation. They became more disappointed when they were told what type of dance she did for a living. Kevin warned her, "Being the good Christians they are, my parents won't resist judging and casting stones. I wonder how many of those stones would carry my name if they knew I frequented Forty-Second Street peep shows with my face wedged in the cracks of strange women's asses."

She wonders what he thinks of when they are intimately together. She will never know for certain, though she can hear him, feel him, and smell him. His scent is on her. His mind is on her. When she moves, he moves and adjusts the treatment to her slightest sound as if a Pavlovian command.

She knows he has worked hard for his parents' approval and to maintain the relationship with Lauren. He worked hard to determine if that was the path he should follow.

Two minds touch in the wake of an awakening. They will embrace this wave of energy until it fades from the truth of the moment. The truth is in the conscious and will of the elements. The wave gives way to a faint pulse that grows until it becomes the beat of their hearts singing in unison. A single rhythm beating becomes two, and the rush of blood makes their minds aware of their bodies. They are people again.

"How's your ma?" she starts.

"Everybody's fine. I don't think they're trippin' anymore." His head rests on her stomach. His left side is pressed onto the mattress, and his right limbs rest on her. She caresses his head and neck. There is a pause so dark and peaceful it reminds them of that wave. They sigh together.

"Did you get your grades yet?" It was a question out of the blue, but not really. She has been wanting to ask him about his progress all summer. He had some damage to repair from that spring semester. His parents made a major issue of it. He had already stated his intention to satisfy his expectations of his capabilities though. She did not know how sensitive he might still be on the subject.

"Yeah," he responds in that prompting tone that begs further inquiry.

"How'd ya do?" she asks after a decent pause.

"3.79 GPA," he returns, sounding both pleased and disappointed.

"You slipped some. Maybe they were right." She had to throw it out there because it's been on her mind.

"It's not you. I just need to focus. I've been a little distracted. I'll be back up soon." He is so sweet to believe it so strongly as to try to convince her of it.

"Is it her?" she asks almost rhetorically. Claire knew she was the least part of what has taken his attention away from classes, but for the most part, she felt it was the memory of Lauren.

"Is what who?" he spouts.

"Is Lauren the name you are so preoccupied with?" she asks and waits through a pause.

"Yes." And with that, he shifts his body closer to hers.

Through experience, she has an idea about her part, but where Lauren is concerned, she has only speculation. He has come to this point in the conversation before, and each time, he stops before he says too much. What too much could be she does not know, but it has been obvious he needs to let it out. She supposes that anyone who was in a relationship for ten years then suddenly breaks up under any conditions would have at least some personal questions to answer. She opens the door.

"So what about her?" she prompts. Kevin's face started to look as if it wanted to seem confused by the question, but that is when his mouth volunteered the information.

He begins softly, "Ya know, she never knew there was anything wrong. She had no reason to. Our relationship was so perfect it was like a dream. I mean, she and I were friends since junior high school and dating from the tenth grade, ya know. We went to the same schools, and we ran track together. We even took a dance class together—ballet. Come on now, ballet. But that's how it was with us. We would do things for each other that probably no other person on the planet would volunteer for. I got sick once—fever, vomiting, and diarrhea. She stayed over the house for three days, cleaning soiled pajamas and sheets, and me. At the time, I thought she did it to give my mother a break. They're close. But that's not why she did it.

"My parents have a certain understanding of things, as all parents do. My parents had been training me to the extent of their understanding of things, and though my training was not nearly complete, I developed a need for a different perspective. I developed the need for a perspective that was not theirs, mine, or Lauren's. I required a proof that none of our perspectives could offer. So I stepped out into the world according to other minds with other understandings of things. I now see that my parents had a good perspective of the world and some of those things in it, but then, they were mistaken about some things as well.

"None of that matters though. What does matter is that I have remained open to whatever moments would serve as instructor in my quest to know.

There is great wisdom in those circumstances that insist a response from us as they form, step-by-step, the path we walk. Those circumstances are as much a foretelling of our greater potential as they are a reflection of who we are presently. They are the story of us, each of us, and they all have the potential to have happy endings because we all have the potential to choose to accept the wisdom of our moments, understand the greater lesson within it, and then conduct ourselves according to a more-complete understanding of ourselves.

"This was not my goal when I took this step. The life was new, bright and shiny, and I wanted to play with it. So I did. For me, fortunately, I did not have to spend a great deal of my life involved with this or that activity to learn that it is mostly a great waste of my time. And then it is a waste only to the extent that it is not conducive to who I believe I am or am to be. Thus, it is a distraction. Besides that, it was necessary to my learning what I needed and purging what I didn't. So while a distraction, it was instrumental to my enlightenment.

"I had to learn this in my time and in my way. It wouldn't have mattered if I were a prince with incredible means or a pauper with none, I still had to find my truth. Now I possess a more-complete understanding of myself than I previously had. I am concerned, though, that Lauren and others may feel that I had no reason," he ends as softly as he began.

"And you feel as though you had a reason?" she questions on cue.

"I didn't feel I needed a reason. My actions were involuntary like breathing. I was performing a reflex function necessary to a level of existence," he states.

"Breathing, huh? Did you love her?" Claire asks.

"Yes," Kevin answers.

"Did you want to lose her?" she adds.

"No, but—," and he starts to add that antilogical fluff that can only more deeply complicate the simple.

She quickly cuts him off with an insistent "daaat, did you want to lose her?"

"No," he says plainly and in reflection of him and Lauren.

"Maybe there was a part there where you should have held your breath." She makes the simple easier to take with the caress of her hands about his head and neck.

The moon is only a sliver this night. It is at the end of its waning period. Only darkness moves, and the trees outside peer through the windows at their naked bodies on his bed.

"Why don't you stop stripping?" If she asks him why he asked, he'd claim that he doesn't know why he asked. He has always felt he could not ask, or should not. The reasons to strip or not to strip, and in fact, to do or not do anything are much too numerous and diverse to debate their validity. Everyone to their path. We must walk it as we see fit.

"Why did you ask that?" Her fingers pause. She is sure that he will not be truthful. She suspects something greater than parental pressure. He suspects that his parents have gotten to him.

"I care for you. I wish you were not working the shows. Was it a stupid question?" And he raises his face to hers and softly kisses her nose. His lips ride to her lips and place another soft kiss and a stroke of his tongue upon them. She smiles. He settles down next to her with his left side pressed to the bed and his right leg and left arm bent into a triangles that he rests on. He stares her in the eyes and carefully takes her right hand with his and places it on his genitalia. She laughs as her hand instinctually begins to softly caress his package.

"Maybe not so stupid," she injects between a mouth still nervous with laughter and that smile.

"Well, nonetheless, I don't know how much privilege I have in that area. I do know that it does bother me knowing what goes on and knowing you're a part of it." He is still, but contemplation ebbs through him disguised as calm.

"You're part of it," she chimes. "Does this mean that you will no longer attend strip bars and peep shows?" she says it and leaves a pause. It is the type of pause that is full of some expectation. He leaves it empty and momentarily dissatisfied. She continues, "Yeah, well. When you can stop going, I can stop going." And her fingers resume their course about his head and neck.

"I did try once. When you and I first started going out, I didn't even think about it for nearly a month. And you know what, I didn't feel it at all. Then little by little, I crept back into the life." His contemplations move his hand slowly along her belly. His fingers walk from the right side to the left and occasionally pause to circle her belly button or to play in the rough of her pubes.

"Crept in, you say," she puts plainly. Her hand has grown very interested in his length and follows it with two gentle fingers from head to sack.

"Crept in, lover!" he exclaims. "When I got back in, it wasn't the same, and it hasn't been the same. I think I like that. I wasn't the same guy, and that disallowed me from being able to do those same things I had previously. I had feelings, which is not to suggest that I previously had none, but that before I didn't know myself or those women." His hand becomes as busy as his speech and finds its way to her lounging breast.

"And now you think you do?" she interrupts.

"And now I do feel differently about me," he adds.

"Ain't that a blip!" she states, smiling, and her light sarcasm is felt. He smiles with her. Their eyes rarely leave the gaze of each other. They enjoy what they see in each other. It is a fonder recollection than two who have just met. It is the connection of kindred spirits. They enjoy the other's smile and know each was a part of creating it. They enjoy each other.

He continues, "The dilemma then became a personal issue and possibly a cultural issue. How could I continue to regard anyone in a manner that disrespects the name of that person? In fact, the name of that other person was not the issue. The only real issue was how I could continue to regard anyone in a manner that was contrary to how I desired to be considered. I am more than my name. I am more than the son of Teresa and John Scott. I am me, and *we*." She enjoys listening to him speak, and then especially when he has found a bright idea worth pursuing. It makes him shine.

"Who are *we*?" she injects.

"*We* are you and I. *We* are us and them. *We* are I and all of you. I have a responsibility to maintain the highest level of respect, compassion, and love to *we* regardless of the fact that *we* may not be aware of or care for their responsibility to I." And he is all smiles as he allows his brain an unencumbered use of his mouth.

"I don't even know what the hell you just said," she says with a face suddenly masked in a questioning gaze of obvious deception. She continues though, "So you're reformed now?" Her hands caress, and her face pauses in eager expectation of his response.

"Yeah! Well, no. Yes. Yes, I am trying, and it gets easier every day. I saw a doctor, and he gave me a patch. Something called Dik-a-derm. It's only available through prescription." He does not laugh, and that is the point. That is one of his skills she most enjoys. He does not mind being dim or bright, corny or cool, and for his pleasure or hers. His flexibility is a great comfort to her. When she is with him, she feels she can relax and be who she is rather than having to extend the play of the role she is in at the bars and clubs or within those circles outside of him.

"You are so silly." She has said that many times before and with that same contented smile. "That's why she misses you." And she is not surprised she said that.

"Who?" Kevin questions with more sincerity than she expected. He then licks and lightly sucks her right nipple.

"Lauren," Claire answers.

"I don't think so," he returns, then begins to run his fingernails lightly through her pubes.

Claire suddenly starts, "Look, I don't mean to pry, but I have to know what it was that made you give up a person like Lauren. I mean, I am where you are, I enjoy *we*, but my perspective is totally different from yours. When I first started working, I was dumbfounded at the amounts of money people spent at the shows, and there are as many females as males paying for our company.

"What we do, we do for survival, convenience, or entertainment. Don't make the mistake of believing that they all get involved to the extent that some do and, in fact, that I have. The majority will not go beyond being felt up or kissed on. Those who will, do so for their own reasons.

"What we do has as strong an influence on the image and posture of a society as any business. We carry a following of devoted fans from all walks of life, which includes every people, religion, and political orientation. Some can afford to come and have a drink and watch bodies float by. Others will drop a hundred or two, and some come in with their lottery winnings or pension checks. Then there are those who come and spend the rent money or the car payment. And when I first started, I couldn't believe what I was seeing, but a girl's gotta eat. So I went and got that money.

"And back then, I didn't care where the money came from. Now, though, I have seen some things. I have seen how males look at females, and how females look at males. At the shows, you might accept that there is a level of expectation on the faces of the customers, but on the street? It seems that this thing has to some degree artificially turned every female into some sex worker who can be lewdly approached and propositioned to perform some sex act for a fucking dollar. There are times at school or on the street that I have been approached by dumb-ass niggers who recognize me from wherever, and the shit they say, Kevin," she pauses. She is fighting against a rush of emotion that is fighting to come out. They stalemate, but a tear leaks through and runs from her left eye and down her cheek. His eyes are on hers.

"But it's my fault. I volunteered to play that role, so I certainly cannot complain if the critics and audience's judgment follow me offstage. I volunteered for that shit. I volunteered to learn to see people as a source of revenue and my body as the means of productions. I volunteered to become the supply for the lascivious demands of the unenlightened mob. I can volunteer myself back out, though, as can anyone. And I believe I have seen enough to convince me it's time to move on.

"So what I want to know is, why did you volunteer to betray a female who had your confidence and respect? Who did not see you or herself as whore or whoremonger? And who probably only saw a beautiful future for you and she? Why did you volunteer to become a part of the mob?" They are both almost stone. They are so still. The dim of the room falls softly on them like dusk on a range of obsidian mountains.

Kevin takes in a deep breath, then says, "Because I didn't know. I didn't know what I had in her. Perhaps because I had nothing to compare our relationship to. Because it was new. Because it was exciting. Because it gave me something I thought I was missing. Because there was a part of me that was weak, and it made itself known in the only manner it could. It urged the type of behavior that is damaging to person and community, and I was too weak to stop it. Because we live to learn, and experience is our teacher. I have learned a great deal. That part is no longer weak. And I am no longer subject to the damaging urges of any source, especially the mob."

"Do you still love her?" Claire asks.

"Yes," Kevin confidently responds.

"You should probably tell her. Preferably before it's too late. She's not going to wait forever," she adds as she turns her body to his.

He knows she means every word. This is their relationship. There are words that neither can say, but that they both feel with matching intensity. They love each other, and they have known it from the start.

Theirs is like a story of the reunion of kindred spirits. Each has their destiny, and they pursue it studiously. It is like their paths have crossed through innumerable lifetimes and always at the scripted point—scripted because all energy flows in predictable patterns and, like energies, will intersect at predictable places. This point is that part of their story where both were in need of the change of perspective that would set them right again. They both needed saving.

This night is a celebration. This night recognizes yet another section of their puzzle completed and those sections that are begun. They will celebrate each other as the necessary element to their growth in being and whatever awareness is attached to it. Tonight, they will celebrate love.

October 29, 1994: Passion

"Hi," his voice is heavy and full of hope.

"Hello," her voice is light and not immediately offering any hope.

Her hair is dark and long. She has it relaxed, and it hangs about her shoulders. Her skin is as dark as her hair, blemish-free, and has a natural healthy glow. She sports big bright dark eyes that show as much as they see, and she can always see through him. She is six feet two inches tall, thin, athletic, but deceptively strong and muscular. She is usually never caught without her smile or compassion for people.

"I love you," Kevin says it as Lauren removes her jacket. His face is as blank as a career politician's and assumes nothing. Hers is full of response.

"Don't come to me with that shit, please!" she says it as she places her jacket in the seat and sits. She is not in a rage, and neither is she wild. She is calm, quiet, and very selective with how she arranges the pieces of her pleasant countenance and how she conducts those words. She did not raise her voice above the level of intimate conversation. The people in the booth behind them probably could not hear her response.

Kevin slowly nods his head affirmatively, then "all right" leaks from his lips. He studies her face. He remembers every square inch. He so much identifies with those parts in his definition of his lifelong being he feels he is looking into a mirror. The image gazing back, though, has not yet admitted any kinship.

"What do you want?" she asks with an unwavering posture set on stern.

He understands this moment is much too tense to jump into the reason he asked her to meet him here. He picks up a menu and diverts her attention to the obvious. "Breakfast," he says with as plain a face as bacon and eggs make on a plate.

"Are you buying?" she questions, smiling slightly and sounding genuinely interested. He remembers that smile. He has thought about and dearly missed that smile.

"Naturally," he comes back and so eagerly he thought he may have rushed the response and tipped his hand. He does not want to appear as anything but her equal at this moment. However, he understands that in the most relevant way, he is not. She controls the board. But he is desperate because his situation has become desperate. So even if he had given some indication of his condition, he intends to leave this table with all or nothing.

She picks up the menu as he drops one to the table. It is the kind of uncomfortable desynchronized movement that the unpracticed suffer. However, they have had years of practice. This is not their first meal together. It is their first meal together after a time of not being together, and the weight of the reason why confounded their natural ease of interaction and made it clumsy.

"Well, I know what I want," Kevin states as he shoots a gaze across the table and into her eyes. She purposely lowers her head. She can feel him as the obvious intent of that comment penetrates that simple defense. Her eyes study the area the words of the menu occupy, but she can only see those beautiful moments they shared. She can see the words, but they blur into the shape of all of the *I love you's* her lips have ever directed toward him. She can see the words, and she knows what she wants, just a few more seconds.

"I want you to want me back," he says the instant she raises her head and her eyes touch his. His voice was not certain how hers would respond, so it lacked a percentage of spine.

"No, you don't," she responds, seeming as though she had to force the words from her throat.

"I'm sorry," Kevin says plainly, and he reaches for her hand. She spots his effort at affection and influence and pulls her hand away.

"To avoid being sorry," she starts, "you should have been more careful and more respectful. You should have—," and she pauses. His words incited her. She is suddenly aflame with every image of what he may have done to betray them, she has learned to forget. She is burning too intensely and too quickly though. With just a few words, she has used most of the oxygen in her space. She chokes on those last words because it was best for both of them. Those words represented the worst of that imagery, and as such, they represent a cancer to her spirit. So to not feel that pain again, she has allowed them to fade into remission, and that is where they will remain.

"I need to be forgiven, and I need to be allowed to save myself." When this scene began, he was searching for a confident, or something like a confident, posture to represent his will. He wanted to appear strong so she would not get an idea about his pain. His voice no longer seems to be concerned how she will perceive him. It confesses his remorse for his betrayal.

She can see it all in his face. He has not learned how to discipline that carcinogenic energy away, and his life is in danger. She refuses to allow him this moment though. "I thought you were ordering breakfast?" she says it in as nice a segue as he has ever experienced.

"I am," he retorts, having quickly composed himself. He waves down a waitress who responds immediately.

The waitress is an older Hispanic woman, probably in her forties. She is Grandma fat; that comfort fluff that makes those big hugs so memorable you call her every weekend just to say, "Hello, I love you." Her eyes are very light, almost green. Her hair is very dark, pulled into a ponytail, and pinned up at the back of her head. She has great legs for a woman of any age, and her black sneakers are worn at the heels. "You're ready to order," she says to the table.

Kevin digresses to Lauren with a nod of his head. "I will have the oatmeal with cinnamon on the side and half a banana, the fruit cup, and a glass of water, please," Lauren says. The waitress smiles, then takes her menu. The waitress then turns her expectant gaze to Kevin.

"The same," Kevin says, then offers his menu. The waitress takes it and leaves.

An awkward silence comes from parts unknown and walks over to their table to replace the waitress's presence as buffer between these two.

256

What do you say to someone whom you are in love with but have hurt significantly?

"I miss you," he whispers. After it is said, why are those words an insult worse than the original injury?

If you placed a wax statue in a very hot room, eventually its face would look like hers. From her brow to her now-gaping mouth, her intense indignation was like the sun rising on some helpless Nosferatu. That stunning response pushed him back into his seat.

Then finally, "You what? Well, if I knew I was coming here to listen to this nonsense"—and she begins to gather her things—"I would have stayed home. And you need to stop sending me flowers. It doesn't look right." She grabs her coat and starts to slide across the seat to exit the booth. He immediately steps out of his seat and quickly blocks her exit. He uses his weight to prompt her back into the seat, and she reluctantly complies. He then slides in next to her.

He had been sending her a variety of flowers to either her home or to school once a day for over two months. Each had a card attached with a poem or verse he had written, and each became more desperate in asking her to contact him. He did this knowing her address, phone number, and they do attend the same school, New York University, but also knowing his offense, and that because of it, he needed to submit to her desire to be contacted. She finally did, and here they sit in a Staten Island diner, having breakfast at three forty-three on a Thursday afternoon. And now that she is here, he will be straight damned if she leaves before the matter is settled.

His second source of confidence for such a bold move is that it is the end of October 1994, and she is still here. They both applied and were accepted to graduate school at U.C. Berkeley. She graduated in June of this year, and he not until June of '95. Berkeley was their idea. In the summer of his junior year, they went on vacation together. It was a fantasy trip he had told her about the year before. He called it the California Excursion.

They flew into San Diego, rented a car, and spent the next three weeks touring the state. They visited points mostly along the PCH (Pacific Coast Highway). They spent at least a few days in San Diego, Los Angeles, San Jose, San Francisco, and Oakland. They lay on every beach, met or exceeded every friendly gaze and conversation from locals and other tourists, and saw every desired attraction, including the Dodgers. The best few days, though, were spent in a bed-and-breakfast in San Francisco's South Bay. They decided then that if it were possible, they would pursue their further schooling together at Berkeley. And she is still here.

His primary source of confidence is that he refuses to walk out of these doors of this diner without her.

Additionally, she lies. She agreed to see him at the least to achieve closure to that chapter of her life. He remains hopeful there is more to it than that.

The waitress returns with two glasses of water. She stares at the pair sitting quietly. She places the glasses on the table, adjusts the settings for their new arrangement, replaces the glasses on the settings, then jets off to an adjacent table where an old couple smiles.

He takes her left hand into both of his, turns to her, and says, "I love you."

They see each other in a flood of memories that shock their minds and cause their bodies to tremble. Those memories remind them of who they were supposed to be.

"No," she says into his eyes. His eyes once spoke in a voice for her heart only. They are wounded now and crying for hope of healing. He will not leave without her, so he persists despite her denial.

"I was everything a person should never be, and I will never be any of those things again. I have been everything we have both needed me to be, and I can be that again." He does not attempt to deny or wipe away the tears rolling from his eyes. They are flooded. He is exposed, and he makes no further attempt to defend himself.

"No," she repeats in a slightly louder harsher tone. This is not meant so much for his dismissal as it is to ward off her own emotions. It does not work. Tears begin to cascade down her face.

Then, "You bastard." And she rips her hand from his. "You fuck!" She tries to push him from the seat, but he does not move. A pair of eyes two booths in front notices their action. She punches his shoulder.

"I love you," he repeats in so heavy a tone it fell from his mouth and had to crawl along the table and up her left side to enter her ear. His eyes are glassy and turning pink. His hands are folded on top of the table. His head is lowered, and his tears dot the tabletop. He is helpless, and he will not leave this place without her.

She draws back her right hand and punches him hard on the right side of his face. The mouth below the peering eyes two booths up fall open, and the back of the head in front of those eyes turns to see what caused that response.

Kevin does not move. Lauren is turned in her seat and faces him as his tears fall. She watches. Grief, like laughter, can become contagious. She leans to him and kisses the spot on his jaw where she punched him and chuckles lightly. A tear streaking down her cheek mingles with his on the spot where their cheeks press together. She pulls away and kisses him again. He turns his face slowly to hers. She kisses his nose. He kisses her chin. They hug. They dot each other's faces with kisses until their lips meet. And then, their eyes meet. Passion, it is submission to the kiss when loving spirits mingle.

.

July 2, 1995: The Good-bye When We Met
Step for step they stride along the path keeping runners' rhythm; that synchronizing of pace of mind and body that is in itself telling of the efficiency of form. They are pushing hard now and have been for several minutes. Their mark is just a few meters away. Their eyes are full, and their hearts are into the work. The end comes quickly.

The run breaks down to a trot. A pause that trailed them moves up easily now and passively takes position between them. It imposes no more than the temporary separation of their persons, and the trot warms down to a brisk-paced walk.

"Well, you turned out to be something after all," El starts.

"Yes, it would seem I have. But I'm not done yet. And I suspect neither are you," Kevin responds.

El smiles, then, "Indeed, I am not."

Kevin shoots him an earnest glare, saying, "I don't mean with the whorin'."

Ellis bends his face into a chuckle as they stroll then suddenly straightens it to more serious. "I know, but I'm not done with that either," he admits.

Some birds chirp excitedly at the wind in the distance up the hill as a female runner cruises by them. She is Caucasian with more hips than legs, a flat well-defined abdomen, and a very pretty face.

They take some steps and admire the scenery. It has always been a beautiful thing this bit of nature. They have always appreciated it, and especially now.

"Did I tell you an advertising agency bought some of my winter tree sketches?" Kevin suddenly offers.

El gives the information the required look of both surprise and delight, then, "Actually, no. No, you didn't. But I haven't seen you damn near all year. And why do you bother with leafless trees?"

Kevin's face became a pallet crowded with the variety of colors necessary to paint so uncomplicated a response as "because there is so much life in them."

"Uh-huh. And you just graduated with what?" Ellis pauses.

"A bachelor in accounting science," Kevin chimes.

"And you're going to graduate school for?" and again Ellis pauses and eagerly awaits his friend's retort.

"A master's in education administration with a concentration in English writing," Kevin sings as more runners flash by. These are young guys wearing a variety of high school T-shirts: Curtis, McKee, New Dorp, and Wagner.

"Your parents must be scratching their heads," El says as they wind easily down a slope along the path.

"Why?" Kevin inquires.

"Because you have no idea what you want to be," El offers this in as inoffensive a manner as he can manage.

Kevin seemed ready for the comment. He smiles, then responds, "Not entirely true. But thanks to my parents' patience, guidance, and support, I have a list of things I could be until I decide what I am."

His logic and reasoning is personal to them both; they have benefitted greatly with the support systems they have. Ellis can only come up with one response for Kevin's answer. "Amen, brother."

Their brisk pace cools down to an easy walk. A couple of bicyclists on hybrids approach them quickly and pass. The left side of the path is a steep sloping hill crowded with a variety of low-growing vegetation. The right side sports thick brush and flowery growth with clearings every one hundred yards or so. At the edge of the growth and the clearings is a body of water belonging to the Clove Lakes system. The larger lake begins to funnel into a fall at this point. It then streams until it again opens into a smaller lake. The path itself is about ten feet wide and made of asphalt. They like to run in the grass that runs along the waterside of the path.

This park has been a part of their lives since childhood. They are both younger brothers, and their elder brothers and families were very close. This is one of the locations the families would picnic, hold birthday parties, or come for a day out among the trees and running water.

Kevin's first memory of Ellis saw him fall face-first into the ankle-deep portion of water along the bank of the smaller lake. Kevin was eight, and Ellis twelve. They were copying the actions of their elder brothers and some cousins who were all at least two years older than Ellis and who were busy trying to corral crawfish and tadpoles. Ellis was on the trail of a formidable crustacean when he stumbled on some rocky debris and got wet. Everyone laughed, of course, but Kevin, being the smallest in the group, caught Ellis's emotional response. He pushed Kevin with a face and force that was embarrassed for lack of a better answer. Kevin fell ass-first into the dark water and mud, and there he sat. And he sat until the shock of the moment faded, then he began to cry. The entire area paused, of course. All minds contemplated the reason for the chain of events and found this result unreasonable. Even the crawfish had to respond; its head was just above the water, and it wore pitying eyes while its head shook slowly and disapprovingly from side to side; it then sunk slowly beneath the water's surface and disappeared from mind.

Divine wisdom created the law that created the word that created things and the product of things. One of the tools the conscious being inherits is remorse and another is forgiveness. But like any attribute, they must be practiced to be effective tools for survival and evolution.

All concerned eyes saw that Ellis felt remorse of his reaction. The pause in him showed it. His countenance was stretched by it. He walked to Kevin, who was still seated and crying. He took position next to him and dropped himself on his seat into the water. Kevin's tears ceased as he and Ellis stare at each other. Ellis then says, "I'm sorry. I was angry, but that is no reason, and I won't do that again." They both then smiled and laughed, rose to their feet, and they continued their search for aquatic life-forms. All they managed to catch that day were three tadpoles, two crickets, and a garden snake. And they have been brothers ever since.

Their cooldown carries them to an area more familiar than the others. The path meanders until it curves right and into a public sidewalk. The sidewalk ran along——Street. Across the street, the path they were on continued into the other half of the park. To the left on the sidewalk took one toward the Armory and Reserve Base. To the right led to the south side of the park path and farther along that street ended at the Staten Island Zoo. There are some cars parked along both sides. At the point they stood was a bridge that connected the sides of the lake. The bridge is made of large gray cobblestone and mortar. At the base of this bridge, on the bank of this lake, is where they met.

They walk a few feet onto its surface and slow to a standstill. The wall of the bridge is about four feet high. They step to it and lean their forearms and weight upon it. Their eyes start at the top of the tree line in the distance. That green has never been so green as it is today. It is a magnificent contrast to that blue in the sky above. Green is probably the only other color expression in nature, that is other than brown, that has produced so many brilliant shades of itself. Their eyes continue to fall slowly to the point the water appears. It is calm. Their eyes float like fallen leaves on its surface motivated from bank to bank by the crisp images of the memory of parenting trees and the comfort of their high branches the water reflects. They are not disappointed, though, to discover the illusion. The water too is comforting as it is within that circle of inevitability of things that is the natural order of God's world.

Their eyes finally find the bank on the side that they stand. There is a thicket of reeds and cattails growing out of the mud and hovering over the water, as if supported by their own reflection. And the dark water is still.

The water remembers them as much as it remembers any life it has bore. It tells the story of their lives according to its best recollection. Their memories play on its surface like the fables an elder tribesperson would relate to the young, so they don't forget the path of circumstances that have brought them to the present and fell into the sin of disrepute.

Ellis is always eager to speak. "So ya' know we were doomed to this from the start," he offers as the water seems to agitate itself into an infectious wave of ripples that play like applause, and that brings the storyteller back to the moment. The trees and sky again begin to record their moments.

Kevin paused for a moment, then, "I realized it was inevitable. We would eventually have to say good-bye to each other someday and for some reason."

"Growing up, I think, is a good reason," Ellis responds, still with his eyes caressing the memories of the dark water.

"The goodest," Kevin inserts, and they chuckle. There was a time when they developed and used their own language. Nothing serious of course, just plays on phonetics and word tools that only their intimate circle of people would derive any amusement from. Then, "What's next for you?"

"Well," Ellis starts, "you inspired me. I've decided to turn my hobby of Spanish studies into actual studies. I'll do a year of certification starting . . . ," and he pauses to think for a moment, then, "next week, actually. Then two years on a teacher exchange program in Spain. When it's all done, I will be a certified foreign language instructor. I believe it will help me to achieve my goal of being the very finest special education teacher on the planet and give me the credentials for the mobility I desire."

"Ah, so your puttin' your ramblin' legs on?" Kevin questions.

"Well, yeah." And he looks to his friend. "There are some places I'd like to see and some things I'd like to do before I settle on settling. Ya know?"

Every part of Ellis is sure about what he is saying, as sure as any chick when it is about to jump out of the nest. He has had his own apartment for years; in fact, it is only about a mile and a half from this park, so he ran here for this meeting. However, it is still on Staten Island, and Staten Island is still in New York; he is still in the nest.

"Yeah," Kevin begins, "I know that feeling exactly." They have shared a mind for so long one is the other, and to every appreciable extent.

"How's your baby?" Ellis suddenly says.

Kevin laughs and smiles, then adjusts himself as the vision of Lauren grows within him. She is always there, but the verbal prompt from Ellis gave her image and all that is attached to it reason to assert itself on his conscious.

"She's probably at home figuring out more shit we need to take with us," he responds.

"But they do that!" Ellis quickly adds.

"I know!" Kevin says, raising his voice to a low shout.

That pause finally moves from between them, climbs upon the bridge wall, and hops into the water where it belongs. They turn to each other, step close, and embrace.

"You probably better not keep her waiting then," the words stumble out of El's mouth as if mortally wounded but determined to live to fight another day. They are accompanied by streams of tears that wet both of their faces. Those drops run down their faces, fall off their chins, and splash onto the dark asphalt. They will eventually find their way to the waters of the lake and add more love to the portfolio of their memories.

"I know, brother. Until the next time."

The Day I Died

It was morning, so the sun rose.
It had to push its way through despair
And the multitude of perversions of God committed overnight.
The mass of it had gelled and hardened
like a skin on some funky ass pudding
containing nothing you'd want to eat.
Sin has no nutritional value.
Just look at anyone who was raised on a diet of self-hate,
and you will see their growth was stunted.
You can't be a shadow of what you could have been.

With the light came the heat,
and what the light didn't move, the heat did.
I opened my mind to the possibilities
of the next few moments and decided I needed help.
So I said a prayer, "Jah's will,"
I thought in as humble a manner I could
—eyes closed and on my back.
My eyes then opened like a string was pulled,
and what pulled the string was aware of me,
although I was not aware of we.
I always believed I was singular.

I tried not to think of another thing for the next few moments;
that is, not a thing in the way of expectation.
This as the reality that I was not dead yet began to weigh on me.
That realization was supported by those cravings
for those things I thought I didn't have, and they got the best of me.
So I yearned for more understanding because maybe I could get it right
today, and
I had not yet realized inner peace would have been a better goal—

that answer is inside me waiting to be discovered.
Nonetheless, I would occupy myself by gathering
more information because knowledge is power.
The same people who taught me to be singular convinced me
the more shit I knew, the better off I'd be.
I am now many years into waking to a day
armed with the tools of my eventual demise.
Not that information, it's harmless.
The mind that wields it, though, is in distress.
I was in danger, and I promise you,
I did not know I was my worst enemy.

Finally, the day began and ended exactly as it always did.
It was a blur of detachment, like how cravings can
cause a body to feel out of species.
Then other people seemed no more than a means to an end,
and we used each other that way.
Or like lack of sleep can cause a mind to feel outside itself.
The chaos of separation translates to the body.
The person becomes sick with a virus that can't be cured with no pharmaceutical—
they are too far removed from the truth of the natural order of life to be an answer.
I was sick with fear of what might become of *we* if I died.

I remained all day intoxicated on the possibility of all things.
I was out of position to achieve, except by Jah's will.
And I was not helping my cause.
Things are an anchor to a familiar reality;
that of possession of the next thought,
the next breath, the next experience.
They had all become the basis of comfort to me.
I was sick.

It was then I realized the truth. There is none but Jah.
The answer to the dilemma, the I in me must die so the Jah in we can live.

There was no other way. The best proof available
to support the conclusion was the sad condition I led this being to.
There were attempts at every way but that natural order.
That path called, and I ignored it.
I chose away from that blessing of divine being
to become a perjury of being as Babylon was entrenched in mind.
I confessed allegiance to it when I did not denounce it.

What has been in error can be corrected.

Stop. Take a deep breath. Be still enough to feel the heart beat.
Feel the inhale and know the will. Feel the exhale
and know the will. Be so still that quiet becomes like your soul,
at perfect peace and unity with we who are eternal.

I have razed dreams and relationships en route to this moment.
This is not the destruction, but the correction of self-negating ideas.
They were all in the forms of people who insist I disgrace myself
in some hell of disobedience to the divine way.
That is what the figures of Lucifer and Satan represent,
those levels of absurd contradiction to divine order.
The will can level that place
and those ideas that have never been a convincing reproduction of we.
I must die because I am rooted in that very same type of arrogance
that led the Morning Star astray. The difference is I am not so far gone
I cannot admit I have been wrong. It can be corrected.

It is dark now, and the moon full and bright. There is a calm
as that dark moves from me and washes over the perceptions of being. Focus
on the word. Focus on the truth in being everything and nothing, now.
What can't be done? If we are the truth, what can't be done?

With being in right alignment, the words "Jah's will"
carry I to the final resting place of all transient things, the
mind. In the spirit and form of the all creator be we.
There is no place here for fear, we live.

What If?
(more good questions)

What if my life is not my own?

What if I occupy this space for the express purpose of allowing Amen (God) to experience being on the material plane?

What if being all things (life) in itself is the requisite manner in which a supreme being can come to understand its own existence?

What if those experiences that a life must endure are the necessary motivation to inspire a being to remove whatever impurities may retard its abilities at realizing its potential as divinity?

What if we possess the ability to deprogram those learned inclinations that support our physical and intellectual retardation and program in those that support our physical and intellectual evolution?

What if those who engage in poetry and prose, song and story are unconsciously leaving themselves messages for use in a future lifetime?

- As an update on what and who they were and how much was accomplished in some previous life? Or ultimately, as a guide for progress as the cultivation and maintenance of pure qualities will be encouraged as will the continued elimination of those impure qualities?

What if the greatest power we possess is the ability to realize our greatest potential as representatives of God on earth and reflect that divinity through our being? What would we and the world be then?

What if our physical realities are the direct result of the power of our intellect?

What if our intellect and what it is capable of is determined by what discipline of control we have achieved through our spirit?

- And if our spirit's capabilities are currently on the relative level of an animal, what would we and the world be?

What if there is no God?

- What if that would better explain the inclinations of people to integrate with one another, even violently, than a theory such as survival of the fittest.

What if there is a god, and God is exactly how one of the world's beliefs, systems, or religious orders have described?

What if those various belief systems and religions are all wrong?

What if the origins of the various images and fundamental attributes of God we the people of the world have been assaulted with were created by barbarians?

What if the current ideals, practices, and philosophies of those very same belief systems followed those same animalistic motives?

- What would the world be then?

What if not only the potential of God but the greatest potential of people cannot be captured by thought, expressed in word, and trapped within the covers of any book?

What if this same high potential can only be expressed through the quality of life a person lives, and additionally, through the quality of the societies that people create?

What if the only true word of God is that which underlines the natural order of life that dominates all of known creation?

What if the quality of the person's life is the only true measure of how powerful their belief in their self and their god was?

What if the greatest social development a people can achieve is not in its technological advancements, but is to become a responsible and adult society?

- The nature of one's technology will follow the level of social maturity.

What if the only way to achieve a responsible and adult society is for the people to have and maintain complete control over those social systems that represent the will of the people?

What if the only duty we owe to our many and varied beliefs in some higher power is to come to a full comprehension of the fundamental laws that govern all life?

- It would seem a disappointment to dedicate one's life to the study of a god and belief system only to find one day that the journey began at the wrong place and created a path in contradiction to God's will.

What if Church and State cannot be trusted?
What if the ranks of government and religion are composed of the very same variety and quality of persons as we commoners?

- Are they not then just as susceptible to those ill motivations that lead to the type of personal corruption that common people are jailed for?

What if these elected officials and public figures are motivated by the basest of passions that plague the common person?

- Then are they not just as unqualified to hold the public trust as an unqualified common person?

What if there is no distinction between Republican and Democrat?

What if the core of every elected official's political life and the survival of the system that provides those positions demands an us (politicians/ elected officials) vs. them (we the people/mob) scenario?

What if the people have never had control over their government and country?

What if the practice of democracy allowed the people to choose who they have calculated to be the best choice for some position, rather than having candidate choices placed before them?

What if the people have merely been enjoying the illusion of power and control through a system of checks and balances that has always been outside the control of the people?

What if misery, fear, and the threat of death are a big and profitable business, not only through the industries whose technology makes it all easier, but also through the variety of industries and agencies whose existence is dependent upon them?

What if the goal of the business of government is to be profitable through the efficient management of its primary asset, land, and not the care and safety of its secondary asset, people?

- Land is the primary asset of government because it is less easily replaced.

What if opposites really don't attract, but have developed some perverse fascination with repulsion?

What if some people who commit suicide only do so to keep from killing others?

- Would it then be considered a noble act?

What if those entities that are currently in body but unlearned on the dynamics of existence within and without the physical body refrained from creating and enforcing laws that attempt to deny the person the right to live and die as they choose?

- Would not that be a better reflection of an entity's comprehension of the highest spiritual attribute of God inherited by people, choice through free will?

What if we people, being a conglomerate of energies and thus subject to those laws that govern energy, are in actuality not subject to time and space?

What if the idea of death is just another illusion used to instill fear into the perspective of a person to make them more compliant to another's will?

What if the prospect of death were truly viewed as the transition of the being's intellectual and spiritual energies rather than the finality of life, would there still be a reason to mourn?

What if it is on earth as it is in heaven? Would that explain why the doggone could see the effects of celestial events occur on the face of this planet?

What if, though, their ability is more a people's great comprehension of the unity and symmetry of all things found within the science of divine creation?

What if I chose to not believe in anything other than the satisfying of my sensual pursuits?

What if destiny is real, is there any point in dreaming?

What if every moment of every person's life is a reflection of their self-image?

What if what we consume as food has little or no nutritional value?

What if despite what little nutritional value the common meal contains, its effects on the body makes it no more than a poison?

What if the body has only a limited amount of energy available for use throughout its systems at any point throughout life?

What if the consumption of those commonly accepted poisons such as dairy, meat, and other stressors diminishes the body's ability to positively affect all of its systems through the even and efficient distribution of energies in the divine manner that the body was designed?

What if after a short lifetime of abuse through food poisoning, the body becomes so encumbered from fighting off the ill effects of incompatible proteins, harmful bacteria, and chemical additives that it begins to gradually shut some systems down in an attempt to maintain life?

What if there is a good reason why even cows do not drink cow's milk after reaching some months in age?

What if it really is a great idea to give one's body a break from having to defend itself from the daily poisons and at such a high and constant level by simply not consuming those stressors and fasting several times per month?

What if people are constantly being misled or lied to about what good nutrition is for the body?

What if there is a dietary reason for the high incident of diabetes and colon and prostate cancer in African American males?

- Do other descendants of Africans and Africans living in America or elsewhere suffer the same unreasonably high susceptibility to those ailments? And what composes their diet?

What if there is an inseparable link between how we treat our bodies and minds and the quality of life we live?

What if there is an inseparable link between the evolution of our person (body and mind), ourself (spirit), and the evolution of our being?

What if it is never a good idea to discount or abandon those genetic qualities that make a person and people unique for the purpose of being assimilated into any system of culture?

What if it were true that the only difference between good and bad actions from people is circumstances?

What if after all the marching, picketing, rallies, violence, death, ignorance, supreme court judgments and amendments, the formerly righteous and abused have developed into the new righteous abuser who is poised and ready to continue that tradition of ignorance on the next minority victim?

What if there really is no good reason why some African Americans in positions of authority seem compelled to engage in behavior that would deter or cripple other African Americans from the pursuit of happiness while giving every possible consideration to non-African Americans?

What if both MCK and Malcolm X were right?

What if not enough people have learned a positive lesson from the disgraces life has suffered throughout the history of people?

What if everyone has lost their minds to man-made fear?

What if African American culture had gained complete control of the greater of its assets and products, would any peoples still be throwing the word *nigger* around so easily and with such bliss?

What if our African ancestors could see us now?

What if the better is yet to come from us decedents of those ancient peoples?

Reservations about Religion
(a healthy regurgitation)

I feel obligated to state I respect every person in their choice of belief. I state this knowing that I may write some things that may be hard to read for a person zealously anchored to a single belief; and as much in knowing whatever my opinion it may be taken as every way but the constructive cogitations of a person in search of some personal truth.

The obligation is not generated by my desire to not cause insult exclusively, but additionally by what has been experienced in this lifetime and the wisdom with which it allows me to conduct the rest of this life. It could be a wise choice to not say anything. I believe, though, there has been too much that has gone not said that should have been; too much that should have been debated and resolved by now; and much too much negativity created by the cumulative friction of all that has not been addressed.

That latter statement, though, is admittedly an opinion from a limited perspective. It assumes fault and error on the part of a system created by an infinite intelligence. That same system has transformed cosmic elements like gases and other forms of energy into the various expressions of life. All life is then subject to the divine law that is its matrix. Some of that life can choose to be in or out of compliance to the divine order that is the genesis of its existence. For we people, that genesis expresses itself through earth.

However, no matter the decision, life cannot choose wrong. Life is submissive to the rules that govern the forces that created it. The truth may be that everything has occurred in its proper place and time, and with the proper elements. There is nothing wrong with the world or anything that has occurred since the beginning of the beginning. With that in mind, let whoever may read this take it as just another well-placed event in the history of life.

Though I have some issue with the many systems of organized belief and government, I will concentrate these comments on belief and then specifically on Christianity. I was raised in the Christian system. This country was created in the Christian system, and despite the existence of other ideas, it has been the Christian system that has dominated as the guiding religious force in this country.

Religious systems have been made synonymous with morality by attachment to the god it hails as its motivation. It is actually that deity and its attributes and qualities that are made the foundation of the guiding principles of some religious institution or another. Because of Christianity's dominance in the establishment and growth of this country's self-image, all that follows from this country's self-image is thus a product of those forces at its roots. A country's domestic and foreign policies, as well as its economic and social systems, are all a product of that entity's self-identity.

If those forces that shape an entity's self-identity are in contradiction to the divine order that is the will of the god at the center of all things, then is not the product of that entity likewise in contradiction to God?

It seems to me it should be. This writing is an attempt to try to explain why I believe it to be so. Additionally, I hope to express some other issues I have with the major belief systems as well as some specific points.

What is critical to me in a belief system is how it chooses to express its philosophies and doctrines concerning its belief in some deity. Those philosophies and doctrines not only tell the story of that people's belief in their theological system but also in their belief in themselves through the history of their social system. The two are linked. They are a marker that indicates that at a particular time and space, we believed this about our world. The social history of the people becomes the evidence that can be used to support how and why they developed and maintained such beliefs that became or have become the foundation for behavior both within and without that society.

That being said, I will proceed with the issues I have with the business of religion. The first will be more personal, but all that follows is my opinion.

Prayer

Many people pray. Many who are attached to a belief system pray as well as those who are not formally attached to any system. People pray for many reasons. There are those prayers that are for the single purpose of communing with God. They are performed in a state of trance or near trance, and I like it more as legitimate meditation than prayer. In this state of trance, the person is attempting to connect with their self (spiritual being) that is at perfect peace and unity with all things as the essence of God. The goal in meditation is the unifying of being through right alignment with the divine creator. The goal in the most common form of prayer is the satisfying of sensual delight.

I have listened to the descriptions of the prayers of many, and I have heard as many prayers as descriptions. Despite what belief system they are attached, people's prayers seem to have at least two things in common: Two, prayer lends the actor a sense of community with others who pray or share a common belief; and one, prayer lends the actor a sense of immediate satisfaction of some dilemma within their perception.

There was a time when I prayed. It was a simple prayer consisting of two words, "God's will." I felt those two words better reflected my intent toward my god than any other words I could manufacture. Those two words represented my willingness to accept whatever conditions the moment would insist upon me and to conduct myself as a traveler on the path. Those words represented my commitment to realizing myself as the greatest representation of my god I could possibly be at any moment. I said those words until one day I realized that even those simple words were an imposition on the relationship that is person and God.

The words represent the recognition of the idea that "God's will" dominates my world.

Intellectual and physical realities and my perception of them are constructs of the divine will. There is not an event or action that has or will take place that has not been accounted for by that will. There has been joy, and there has been sorrow, and there shall yet be. There has been feast, and there has been famine, and there again shall yet be. At no point was I able to avoid these things because at no point did I possess the active and conscious attribute of *all-knowing* that the source of all possesses.

I believe that every thing that is and that is not is a reflection of the existence of a divine intelligence. I believe the natural order of life whose foundation is the equilibrium of all is a reflection of the divine wisdom that guides that intelligence. Finally, I believe both of these proceed because of the very existence of the vessel of consciousness and awareness—God. Therefore, there is nothing material or immaterial that is not God's will.

There have been such contrasts in the moments of this life I live I have determined them not to be random, but specific and escalating spirally. They are specific because they seek to teach me something about myself: what I am and what I could be. They are escalating spirally because they occur along the course of lineal existence that things belong. They occur along with those things created (ideas equals action) by the very fact of existence of a thing, and they are all in the same constant state of evolution.

No matter what may occur at any point in the history of a thing, and then especially people, it is for the ultimate good of all life. The moments of a life are for the purpose of evolving that thing from what it is to what it will ultimately be. What a thing is and what it will be are always in compliance to the divine wisdom that regulates the natural order of life.

A cup is a simple item. There was a point, though, where a cup did not exist. There was also a point where someone had an idea about how to perform a specific task. That idea motivated the action that created the cup. The cup I use today is as artistically dissimilar to that first cup as it will be to that used many centuries from now. Still, though, a cup is a cup, and it performs a basic function. The basic function of the cup has remained the same since its inception. A cup is a vessel for holding and transporting a variety of information. The cup does this in the variety of forms that the perceptive mind can imagine. The cup will continue to do this for as long as the perception of the need persists.

Essentially, the phrase "God's will" is an expression of the ultimate inevitability of completion of a thing's evolutionary process as it moves from what it is—incomplete, to what it shall be—complete. This would have to be true if God is everything I believe God is: loving and munificent as some qualities; all-knowing, present, and capable as attributes; wise by nature; and most relevant, the all-parent from which I draw my potential of being. Therefore, whether I could see beyond the present and into what would be for me or not, I would not choose to avoid or change my future/ destiny or choose to believe I could or should with a prayer. I am a cup today, but I won't be the same cup tomorrow.

Because I found this to be accurate in respect to the course this life I live has taken, I then determined it was inappropriate to state the words "God's will." It not only restates a previously established ultimate and obvious certainty, but it also begins to function as a crutch against personal responsibility for the path and how it is managed. I may not be capable of seeing what is going to happen in the next moment, but I certainly can have and maintain a perspective of myself and my god that will guide how I conduct my person and self through any moment. That conduct becomes the proof of standing along the grand dynamic of the evolutionary scale of living things.

"God's will" used as a prayer is a statement of doubt despite its sounding like an affirmation. It says it is my hope that God's will be done through me or for me. I pray rather than simply being the vessel through which God's will be done, and knowing it. This rather than knowing that the divine will is ever active and nothing can proceed that does not comply to divine wisdom.

The prayer becomes the proof of lack of confidence in my person, self, and God because it assumes the possibility that something could be out of order in a world created by a supreme being. The Supreme Being is a perfect, and thus infallible, entity. Additionally, prayer assumes the person does not have the capability to perform the task. It assumes what is prayed for is in the best interests of the natural order (ultimate good) because the natural order of life is founded on the equilibrium of all things. It assumes that the perceived error must be stated by a person who is fallible before it will be corrected. It assumes the fallibility of God and all that proceeds from God because with the prayer, the person is requesting from the deity something it perceives as necessary that does not currently exist or does not exist to the satisfaction of the mind perceiving its own existence.

I have found those words and the reasoning they represent to be in contradiction to my belief in God. Those words, "God's will," are full of arrogance and selfishness. I have determined, in fact, that any words I would have in the form of a prayer for my god are unnecessary. All that is required is a commitment to do the work necessary to become better in being. My being is the concert of physical, intellectual, and spiritual energies of which I am composed. A sound mind lends a clearer perspective of this life. Having a clearer perspective has allowed me to see there is no *I* on this team—that is, the erroneous idea that damned the Morning Star. There is only God, and all proceeds as God, because of God, and in complement to God.

On the other hand, I alone exist, as it has been from the beginning. It is I that must choose to be in or out of compliance to the divine path (the natural order of life). Because it is my purpose to walk the path and to do so to the best of my ability, I have since refrained from saying any prayer. I have since used that energy to discipline my person and self to be more a reflection of the divine spirit that created and guided me. I have since come to a better understanding of the relationship of God and me.

I have heard prayers asking for a great many things. Some seemed blatantly selfish. Then there were those that did not seem selfish, but ultimately were. Is there a person wishing for world peace who does not wish to experience world peace?

Curiously, whatever is prayed for is a thing what's proof is determined by the person praying. It appears to me that all proceeds from the person. It is inherent of us from God that we are capable of creating whatever reality we desire. A prayer is not necessary, but a clear and focused mind, which is disciplined by divine wisdom and giving right attention to the example that the natural order of life our source parent (earth) has always provided, is essential.

The natural order of all life on this planet is the only word of God. The natural order of life is the only universally irrefutable truth that the conscious minds on this planet are subject. It is the divine word manifest. We are the divine word manifest. We are at a stage of development, though, and whatever advances of mind and body may be realized from this point will not be achieved because of a prayer. Our most positive evolution will be the result of a complete connection of our being to the divine consciousness.

I think what progress is made from this point will be because of a greater recognition and understanding of the science of the natural order of life. The world will eventually realize peace. The individual must first realize the potency of "I." Peace will occur when more individuals begin to realize personal peace through the discipline of their selves. When a person's being is at peace, they have done everything possible to assure the realization of what beautiful dreams may come because they have not contributed to the forces that are in contradiction to being.

To pray is an imposition on the potential of the person and the person's relationship with God. That common prayer retards, if not destroys, the person's belief in their inherit ability to will their own reality. That reality begins and ends with self-perception. When a person's self-perception becomes the catalyst for their personal inner peace, then there are no

285

external or other internal circumstances that need to be altered in order to be at peace. The person understands the perfection of every moment. Prayer of that selfish form only verifies that there is doubt within the person that the facts created by their self in the world are a perfect reflection of the perfection that created all—even the pain.

What of self-perspective? It is a simple answer. If you do not feel you are complete without all of the excesses of living, then you will not be complete living in excess. The person whose perspective allows them to be at peace with nothing more than their self and the natural order of God's divine wisdom will be at peace under any conditions. That person only desires what is, and what is has always been and will always be God's will.

When a prayer is cast from the mind or lips of a person, there is an expectation that precedes and follows those words. It is the same expectation that those practitioners of sacrifice have when they offer anything to a form of deity. The expectation is that desire will be satisfied as a result of the offering. If the intent was to bring rain, then they expect rain. Whatever the intent, though, it is plagued by self-gain.

Do farmers suffering a year-long drought in their county wish for rain in the neighboring county because they have suffered for two years? Farmers wish for rain so that their crops will grow. Once the crops grow, they will collect them and sell them at fair market price. Profit is the motivation. There is as much lack of concern for the greater good in a farmer as there is in a nonfarmer when the desire for something motivates their reasoning.

The person has trained itself to accept the lack of rainfall as an opportunity to cater to those fears created and maintained by society. Those fears are supported by superstitions and rituals that have been established and nurtured for generations by a people. The fear attached requires your perceptions of self and environment revolve around its dynamic rather than that which would allow the person to view the drought as an opportunity for ritualistic personal growth. Lack of rain could motivate a person to no end of abuse of self and others as the sense of loss and desperation begins to grow; or the lack of rain could cause a person to find a positive alternate means of acquiring the needed replenishment.

One who relies on the power of religious ritual to satisfy a situation is as fully invested in those ideas surrounding their belief as one who is not. One who accepts their life and those circumstances promoting it as within divine compliance, and therefore above the need for prayer, is as correct as that person who believes their life and circumstances need prayer. It is all a matter of subjective perspective.

The problem may be that practitioners of the various belief systems have gotten so arrogant in their particular version of truth that they believe they are entitled to discount those perspectives that are not compatible with their own. If this is true, then I can see why so many feel the need to pray; it is some unconscious psychological reflection.

I have had many conversations with the practitioners of Islam, Catholicism, Judaism, and Christianity. I have experienced many a shocking and often insulting statements from people in every one of these groups. One such statement went something like this, "I am not going to hell because I am a Christian showing bigotry toward another because they are not. You will go to hell because you are not a Christian." I gave that statement some thought, and after a review, it sounded like this, "I am not in error because my reality within this world is distasteful or unsatisfactory to me, God is in error because I was created full of the contradiction to the word [sin] that has disgraced me."

At end, I think the best replacement for the need to pray is the desire to live in right alignment with the divine consciousness. I think people who are in right alignment with the divine will not have an occasion where they feel pressed to pray. They will be an active reflection of the divine word (life), and there could not possibly be anything wrong with that perspective.

Fear

The second topic of discussion is my primary reason for the level of contempt I feel toward the various organized religious systems.

Catholicism, Judaism, Islam, and Christianity were all created by a people who maintained high levels of fear of their environment (internal/external). In my lifetime, I have observed people making what seemed poor choices in regard to the difference between what it is they claim to represent and what they come to represent through thought and action. I am one of those people. That intellectual and physical energy can only take one of two paths, that in compliance with the established directives of their God or that in contradiction to those same directives. The difference can mean the achieving of personal grace or disgrace.

When an entire people subscribe to a body of ideas, thoughts, and actions, those can fairly be said to represent the core ideology of their common belief system. The group, like the individual, can achieve grace or disgrace through how it chooses to represent itself through those intellectual and physical energies.

The individual is a singular person. The group is composed of individuals. An individual guides its life by a set of internalized ideals. The group (people) guides itself by a similar or same set of ideals. Both the individual and group inherited their perspectives on life and living from the institutions that are at the center of the various social spheres, such as government and religion. It is the perspectives contained within those philosophies and theories, thoughts and actions of these institutions that shape the body and mind of a people.

Fear is a thing that I view as uncomplimentary to any version of a positive and well-meaning deity. The deity does not speak for itself in any case. The work of defining the qualities and attributes of a god is accomplished by a person. The person imbues that God with those ideas of being that are most comfortable to that person's self-image. A god, therefore, as described by people, can only be a reflection of that person or those persons who penned that legend. Despite what a deity might actually be, a deity, as described by a people, can only aspire to be as good or bad as the self-image of the people whose consensus on being created the legend of that god. That god then becomes that people's self-identity or part of that people's self-identity.

Fear is the product of an undisciplined mind. Fear is what a child has in the dark of a room. The child fears because it has not yet realized that there is nothing in that room with the lights off that was not there with the lights on. The adult realizes that the only difference between dark and light is perspective. What is in any environment is only what we conscious minds have brought with us. There are those who are plagued by the demons they carry with them. It would not matter how dark or light the environment. They are haunted by fear.

It is within the influence of fear that the world's top belief systems were created. Catholicism, Christianity, Islam, and Judaism all have at least that fact in common. They all had their genesis within dark times. They all grew from their pagan roots under the shadow of some dominating system whose means of communication were through corruption, oppression, and war. They all assimilated a great deal from those older systems that became their chrysalis to a rebirth and eventual power. Finally, they all kept at the core of their ideals the motivation of fear through which their predecessors had become notoriously famous and powerful. They utilized fear not only as a motivation for the devout to remain so for fear of sanction, but also as a means of dominating and oppressing any of those others whose perspective was different.

These new belief systems became like the children who grew up in homes full of parental abuse. Despite how criminal the abuses or the abusers, those children had a choice to make. They could become like or unlike the example being given. They could subscribe to and assimilate into their lives the ideals, philosophies, and practices that caused them so much pain and grief in their childhood, or they could purge them from mind. If they accepted them, those children were then en route to becoming as proficient of abusers as those parents whose behavior they despised. If they purged them, those children were en route to discovering some personal truth.

Those infant belief systems did not purge the toxins created within them because of the circumstances of their origins. Each one of them became a mirror image of the abusive parent. On the surface, they seemed motivated by a slightly different agenda than the parent, the promotion of a single deity rather than a pantheon of deities. However, the core motive did not change—the domination of people through fear for the purpose of acquiring and abusing wealth and power.

No matter how clever, eloquent, or flattering the language used to describe an entity's behavior toward another, the motive cannot be disguised. The penchant for abuse will show. As long as there is an external outlet for that mean energy, they will continue to channel their barbarism upon others. Once there are no others, they will turn their hatred upon themselves until what they have created has crumbled. That is the legacy those things built on a foundation of fear have to look foreword. Those infant systems of belief would enjoy the same fate as their parents. They will all eventually be nothing more than some eloquent words on a page—words that will describe a pathetic tale of some possibly well-intentioned, but misguided, system of people who became infamous for choosing to continue in contradiction to the natural order of life. There is no amount of barbarism that can change that. Neither will there ever be enough ink or influence to disguise the products of such barbarism

Fear is a product of self-misconception. If left uncorrected, it will fester until it retards the person's self-image, and they will forget they are of God. They begin to believe they are separate from God and everything that is God, especially you and I. That person no longer feels the unity of all things. With lack of unity comes a lack of remorse for any barbaric action taken toward a thing. They are the abuser because they choose to be in contradiction to the natural order of all life.

Fear is a tool of an oppressor. It is used to destabilize the positive self-image of a person or people. Without a positive self-image, an entity will commit its person and self to no end of abusive endeavors.

Fear is used to remove or damage a person's will. Without a will or a positively functioning will, a person is no more than a slave. A slave is a thing that has no choice. If the Divine so loved people that we were given the power of will so that we may choose to comply or not to the divine wisdom found in the natural order of life, then that same divine entity would not require a person to maintain an element of fear within their perspective that eliminates the power to choose.

Fear is not divine, it is diabolical. It is the vessel for ignorance, misunderstanding, and destruction. It has no place among a divine entity (God) and its divine creation (life). Sadly, the King James Version Bible is full of fear, as are most of the other books containing legend of God. For me, the words found in those collections and the intent of those words do not reflect the direction of an amiable supreme being. They rather reflect the accounts of a frightened and abused people who have every intention of following the poor example of intra/interpersonal conduct they inherited from an abusive authority/parent figure.

The followers of those various belief systems did in fact create their versions of truth and continued to infect the world with it. They spread the doctrines of their beliefs by force because force is usually necessary when attempting to gain the compliance of a people to concepts and ideas that are contradictory to their self-image. The world is still plagued by the wanton impulse to violence and destruction created and maintained by those entities who still cannot will a seed-sized portion of peace within themselves. They still refer to themselves as authorities or guardians of an ideal such as spiritual or social morality, or as leaders of people or the world.

Can an elected official whose integrity is at or beneath the common persons really be considered a trusted authority figure? Can a practitioner of any belief system who is not on a disciplined path to enlightenment and has in fact not achieved any more enlightenment than the common person really be considered a proper guide for those seeking spiritual direction?

Fear can cause the normally astute person to miss the grossly obvious when it is before them. Fear has no place between people except as a means of control. Fear has no place between people and God except as a means of control. The many books of the many beliefs I have mentioned still embrace fear and all of its products as a tool for intra/interpersonal interactions and for those interactions between deity and people. The continued use of fear by any entity, but especially by religious entities, as motivation for compliance not only stands as proof of their role as abuser, but also shows without doubt that they have a complete misunderstanding of the Divine. Their business sense, though, is working just fine.

The Crucifix

I have heard it referred to as the symbol of Jesus sacrifice for people. I am certain there are many other reasons for its existence. I will try to be brief.

I have heard Jesus referred to as the dove of peace, the sheppard, the bright morning star, which for me is curiously similar to Lucifer's reputed title when he sat at God's right hand, and the fisher of men to name a few. I found myself asking why a belief that claimed the highest ideals of their God's character as the goal of their system would not create a symbol that reflected that noble aim.

A lone dove perched or in flight whether holding an olive branch or not in its mouth would have been a peaceful symbol. A shepards crook would not be as powerful as the dove, but still it makes the point of a passive but ultimate authority. The fisher of men would be a hard sell. Coming up with a powerful image to represent it may be like trying to rhyme with orange. The bright morning star (Morning Star), though, is an extremely powerful image. It is an image so full of potency that I believe it would have well represented the goals of a well meaning belief system to spread peace and love through the positive effecting of community through unity.

The Crucifix was the choice, though, and I find I must ask myself why. First, the Crucifix is the antithesis of the Ankh. Where in an interpretation the Ankh represents eternal life on Earth through the power of woman and man, the Crucifix represents the destruction of life on Earth, or simply death. I am not going to attempt to prove it, but with the early Roman Empires knowledge of northern and eastern Kemet (Africa) I am certain they had been exposed to the Kemetian Initiation System and had become familiar with one of its greater symbols, the Ankh. Second, that perversion of the Ankh, the Crucifix, was from its inception a tool of war. Its purpose was to instill fear within those domestic and foreign enemies.

That Christian Crucifix, though, is no mere image of some intersecting beams. Those beams support a blond haired, blue eyed, and pale-skinned male. That male had been beaten and tortured and was hung in as inhumane and humiliating a fashion as possible. I am certain the loin cloth was later added to the image for a measure of political correctness. I cannot imagine the Roman Empire giving even a measure of dignity to an enemy of the state.

As accounts written much, much later would have it, this was no mere person. This person some called the messenger, others called him the son of God, and still others called him God in the flesh. Assuming any or all of these are true, what does that image of the present day Crucifix say to the conscious and unconscious mind?

The messenger of the word of God silenced and hanging dead on a Crucifix; or, the son of God humiliated and hanging dead on the Crucifix; or, God defeated and hanging dead on the Crucifix.

It seems to me that image speaks more for the state, the then Roman Empire, and the arrogant belief in its ability to suppress opposition as simple as a rabble rouser to that of a God. I am at a loss to see how that gruesome imagery depicts any kind of positive sacrifice of person or God for the good of people. I am likewise at a loss to see how the depiction of any person suffering on an ancient torture device was chosen as the icon for a system of belief that claims its goals are peaceful.

And how do you represent the ideals of a God who was destroyed by its own creation? Perhaps that symbol does not represent a peaceful, loving, and munificent God at all. Perhaps that symbol represents Seti's (Satan's) defeat of God on Earth, and as such, it better represents Satan's dominance over Earth.

Satan

I will begin by stating I do not believe in Satan as an entity. I believe people can be satanic in thought and action, but that is a result of being in extreme contradiction to the natural order of life which is the divine will working. Whether a person is divine or satanic in thought and action is ultimately that person's choice. Our power is in choosing our path and how we manage our journey.

The question is, how can a supreme being with all-knowing, all-present, and all-capable attributes have an antagonist? And then an antagonist who is the creation of that supreme being, and who does not possess the attributes of all-knowing, all-present, and all-capable? I find it ridiculous that a supreme being has opposition who is in fact not a supreme being.

If what is said in the King James Version Bible of Lucifer before, during, and after the fall is true, then I am all the more unconvinced of the validity of the character and the story. Lucifer was the most trusted, the most beautiful, the Morning Star. This means that Lucifer knew God better than all others. Either Lucifer was a great moron in challenging an opponent who knows the beginning and end of all things when Lucifer did not, or Lucifer knew something about The Supreme Being that no other knew.

There is another possibility. Supposing that legend and lore were true, what if it were all a test? What if Lucifer has been following orders, and being God, who would you choose to play the role of your antithesis more than your most trusted creation? The test itself might be for people. What path would people choose if they were given a choice, and then even if that choice meant certain failure, disgrace, and death?

Satan makes no sense to me except as an agent of God to test people or as a tool of people to frighten other people. Why bother to bind Satan who had become the source of great sorrow for the world, and then for only a thousand years at the end of which he would be released? Why would Satan make a bet with God knowing God knows the outcome of the bet? Would you pick a fight with an entity that could undue your being with a thought? Is it true that Satan's only power is in making suggestions, and that at times those can appeal to a persons fears which tend to lead to some vile actions? But then, a person must still choose the thought and the action. So, is it really Satan that is the problem, or is it we people using Satan as a crutch for our spiritual weakness that is the problem?

So at end, I do not believe in the character Satan. His circumstances do not support his actions and his ability does not support his infamous position.

The Foothills of Mt. Sinai

Exodus 32. I shall summarize and hope I do not damage the intent of the chapter.

Moses went upon the mountain to commune with God. While he was away the people, and I assume that means everyone, convinced Aaron to construct them Gods. Aaron, who is Moses's brother, instructed the people to collect what gold they could and he did construct them a golden calf to worship and built an alter before it for use of burnt offering that next morning.

Meanwhile God and Moses were conversing on the Mountain. God informs Moses of the ill actions of his people and informs Moses that he, God, is going to kill them all because of their having corrupted themselves.

Moses then replies to God that such an action should not be taken against the people. He assures God that to bring those people out of bondage in Egypt only to slay them in the mountains would be foolish. Moses then tells God to turn away from such an evil idea.

Moses then reminds God of a promise made to Abraham, Isaac, and Israel to multiply their seed as the stars in heaven and give them land.

God repents of the evil.

Moses descends the mountain and chastises the people. Moses breaks the tablets that hold the commandments. He then gathers some men who are the sons of Levi, and they go throughout the camp killing men and their companions and their neighbors.

Moses then told the people they had committed a great sin and sought God for a means of atonement. God told Moses those who had sinned would be blotted out of his book. God then told Moses to lead the people to the place spoken of.

What bothers me about this scene is simple. Moses had to shame God out of committing an act of evil by appealing to God's vanity. Vanity. He told God how foolish he would look to the Egyptians if he went through with the action. Moses then commits to that very same evil action, murdering thousands, and with the help of accomplices.

Moses had to remind God of a promise? If all of the people petitioned to Aaron to create a God, then why were not the sons of Levi likewise so severely punished? And why was not Aaron killed with the rest of the transgressors?

Obviously the most disturbing moment is God being portrayed as being susceptible to the same emotions and weaknesses that people are plagued by. God is prepared to kill over a perceived disrespect of that high position of God, and in fact sanctions murder to satisfy that anger.

There are other points I found in this book and in other books of the bible, like the constant reference to precious metals and stones for use in decorating alters, dress, and other ceremonial objects. I cannot figure out why a God would be so concerned about material that would be valueless to a God. I can figure, though, why these things would be of great value to a people.

Then there is that passage where the Israelites rob and steal (borrow) from the Egyptians jewels of silver and gold.

Jesus

Whether Jesus was a messenger of God, son of God, or God in the flesh is of no importance. What is important is how the character impresses upon those who may hear tale of his life the desire to live a higher quality of life through compliance to God.

The role of the savior is a very delicate position. The savior has to possess qualities and attributes that would allow them to perform the seemingly impossible, yet be undeniably believable as a person. The savior is the common person who has managed to develop the necessary discipline responsible for transforming them into the uncommon person. Thus, the savior becomes the living example of whatever theoretical ideas a person or group may have of the higher potential of people.

The problem with Jesus as a savior is that he is an unsuccessful example to people of how to achieve such divine refinement of body, mind, and spirit as to be at one with the all creator through the natural order of life.

Jesus was born into humble circumstances. He grew into a pre-adult then disappeared for over a decade and returned as an adult. No record of that period is contained within the book believed to be God's word by the practitioners of this belief. Upon his arrival he is already the icon of spiritual discipline held by these same practitioners to be the pinnacle of achievement for a person.

The practitioners of this faith, though, do not know how Jesus achieved such development, except by being god in the flesh, and neither do they believe they can achieve in their lifetime what their lord and savior was able to achieve in his lifetime. They disbelieve so much in fact, in their ability to mirror the efforts of Jesus that they settle for being less. This is part of the reason why Jesus is unsuccessful as a savior. Practitioners of that belief do not believe they can follow in the footsteps of their lord and savior. They observe those footsteps from a distance and most times a great distance. They live their lives in great separation from the letter and intent of the doctrines that the character Jesus professed and which he used to guide his life.

But then, all we people today have for any example of these instructions is Jesus word through others. People did not then and do not now have the benefit of reading that character develop from a carpenters son into an amazing man who was completely connected to God. That transitional period from boy to man and then from common man to a super man would have been a much more powerful story.

That transition in fact, would certainly have been a much more inspirational story. We would read his mortality. We would have read how that character developed as a child in his parent's home and within their specific social circumstances. We would read how that character learned and progressed at his craft which was passed to him by his father. We would read his life into adulthood and marriage with the woman he loved or to whomever a marriage was arranged. We would read about him as a father. We would read him through the variety of life events people must endure, and then until his death as an old man. It does not add to his resume having been murdered at an early age. Through those words the reader would recognize something of themselves and their life in that character Jesus, and know the truth of his life because the reader would know the truth of their own life. We should know the truth of our life. Finally, we would read how others responded to that character in and out of their life. We would read the opinions of his contemporaries. Those would state that person's life was an example to all of how to transcend such intellectual perspectives that would limit ones spiritual growth. The life of that character would reflect the potential within us all, and we would know that any of us could repeat that effort within our lifetime given the same effort at representing a peaceful God. That would have been a much more effective character.

At end, that character does not impress upon the reader the joy of enlightenment found on the path of the traveler. That character and the accounts of his life until the end do not support the power of the individual through God, but dams the individual because of their godly pursuits. This is greatly emphasized by the church sanctioned state execution of the peacemaker.

Miscellaneous

The one thing that all practitioners of any belief have in common is complete confidence in the legitimacy of whatever system to which they have subscribed. They all believe that those words in those books that support those philosophies and practices attached to those beliefs are without doubt the words of their respective gods. They believe that as the word of God, even those who do not subscribe to them are still ultimately subject to them.

I believe that the word of God certainly is universal in its effect. I believe that the word of God is constantly in effect as life, and therefore, all life is subject to its laws. Transgression of the word of God certainly should draw some correction from whatever source is qualified. I believe the only qualified source is the source of wisdom that created the laws to which most life abides.

People, though, have a need to define the parameters of their societies through some deity or another. Transgression of the established law meant severe punishment up to death. Paupers, kings, and civilizations have been crushed by the movement of an entities desire to maintain the integrity of the established law concerning its God.

That being said, what correction do the various religious organizations deserve for their disregard of the words of their Gods?

I will repeat that I was raised Christian. It is what I know best so that is what I will concentrate on although what I have had to say, I apply to all the world's major belief systems. Therefore, the first commandment, "Thou shalt have no other gods before me." Certainly the hosts of saints and saviors have been so widely promoted and accepted that they have been first on the lips of believers. Their God has been pushed behind the saints and saviors.

I find it disturbing that anyone should believe I should attach myself to a system that has either completely excluded me or my ancestors, or has left us among the most disfranchised of people to occupy the lowest ranks of being within the world they describe.

Why is the natural and godly state of nakedness such a vile and shameful thing to these authors (Rev 16:15, Gen 3:7, 9:22-27)?

If Jesus was in fact God in the flesh, then is not the act of sacrificing that body for the good of people a hollow gesture from an entity that cannot die?

In John 1:3, why did John refer to Jesus as the son of God rather than his lord God?

Why does it appear to me that the most damned and persecuted peoples in this entire book are Kemetians (Africans), their descendants, and their colonies?

What kind of merciful and forgiving deity would allow the existence of a hell? And then allow those who have made mistakes to burn in it for all eternity?

What kind of deity is merciful and forgiving, yet vengeful? And even more, of what utility is shock, anger, and vengeance to an entity possessing the all-knowing attribute?

What is the motivation for the use of color as a reference to alignment, and how did the darker shades come to represent evil?

What kind of God exhibits the same animalistic and emotional qualities as a person?

What does Amen mean, and what is it a reference to?

Why the fixation on death and the horrific destruction of life?

Why do none of the images I have seen of the Son of man (Jesus) reflect the description given as God's word in Revelations 1:13-15?

What point is being made when a multi-million dollar church facility with its rules and conditions of membership are beyond the financial capabilities of the common person to attend or join?

Is absolution still for sale?

Whatever happened to the mission of helping people?

Why was a messenger like Jesus able to help an impressive number of mostly encumbered peoples to find joy in their selves, and without a dime in his pocket? And, can those who now refer to themselves as Christians (followers of the ways of Christ) truly be so while abandoning those very same types of encumbered peoples?

I will stop now, but I hope I have made the point. If from the highest levels of a belief system to the lowest, the words of that God are being transgressed, ignored, or ritually abused, then what is your belief system? And then, if those transgressors not only go without sanction but also prosper, then what is your God?

When an entity presents itself as in possession of the ultimate answer for some dynamic of being like a people's beliefs, it must earn that position. It must show that it maintains the highest levels of morality and integrity. It must show that it knows and can demonstrate the path of discipline that must show beyond a shadow of doubt that the ultimate goal, divine ascension, is a real and attainable state of being, and it must show that through the proficiency of its leaders to spread peace. Peace is the state of being where a person is successfully connected with the divine.

Nothing should be in a position of authority because it was more aggressive, aesthetically pleasing, or had more financial means than an equally unqualified opponent.

In these modern times plagued by big business interests that run governments and religions, there is no peace. It is not profitable. The four corners of the world are dominated by belief systems who claim to have the exclusive truth of God. There is only mounting pain and suffering, blood, bones, and misery.

It would seem to me those concerns do not have the answers they claim. It would seem they do not represent the highest ideals of being, and they certainly do not represent a deity whose chief quality is peace.

They all do seem very proficient at taking advantage of the naivety, complacency, and fear of a people. This would all be consistent with a belief in a god of war. Curiously, the same types of gods of war made popular by their fore-bearers.

It is definitely not that any of these institutions exist that have made them a target for thought and comment. It is the fact that they exist and have taken an undeserved leadership position. It is the fact that while in those leaders positions, millions worldwide have been murdered in the names of those respective systems or because of them. Life has become incidental to the business pursuits of these institutions. I think that would disqualify them from any kind of representation of a peaceful deity, or a responsible and adult society.

Belief is a beautiful thing. The most beautiful thing about it is the effect a single belief can have on an individual. Belief can turn a person who is full of self-hate and fear into one who is free of those poisons; or belief can turn the free person into a slave. This brings me to my final point about why Jesus and like characters within other belief systems are unsuccessful. They each have been so intimately and specifically designed and interwoven into their respective belief systems with all of their respective poisons that the most important idea, that of the peaceful unity of all life, has been lost to the politics created by the pursuit of power. In this way, Jesus, Muhammad, saints, and whomever else all represent yet another wedge used to separate people from the godly pursuit of unity through peace.

If I am doomed to hell, and I do not believe in hell either, then I will suffer that because I was wrong in my determination of my self and the world. I refuse to suffer because I was following the lead of some other fool who has never bothered to give their own existence or that of a system of belief to which they have subscribed more than a casual thought. I will not die as a follower who is blissful in my ignorance. If I find there is ultimate truth in any of these systems, I will hurry up and contribute to their efforts at advancement. Neither will I die a coward too afraid to stand up for what I believe is right. If I find the only ultimate truth is in me, then I am compelled to contribute to my efforts at becoming better. However, I refuse to follow the example of an entity that has not only not been the epitome of spiritual virtue, but also whose history in total is in complete contradiction to a selfless and peaceful goal.

Believe what you must believe, but do so with every fiber of your being. Live your belief. Be that person who has dedicated their life to the service of the aims of your god. Become the shining example of the power of your god through your works. Hopefully, your works are peaceful, and thus in compliance to the natural order of divine life.

However the final chapter of this life plays out, it will be because I chose that path. I choose God and the divine path contained within the natural order of life as I comprehend it to be. I may be correct or not in this determination, but I can guarantee I am willing to find out.

In Conclusion
(that's all for now)

I believe my son is one of several sources that has helped me to discover joy. He is discovering himself. He is realizing his dependence and his independence. He is a child so he perceives things as a child, and I had forgotten how to appreciate that. Many of my sources are as external to me as he, and they therefore are not as important as that divine inspiration that manifests through me and as me. All of those sources however, are reflections of that same divine inspiration and therefore serve as reminders to me of what life is, what life is about, and what my responsibility is as a caretaker of life through my divine being.

My son is beautiful not only because he reminds me of the potential to be and do anything, but especially because he reminds me of the fragile nature of life as it expects to evolve from infancy to adulthood and beyond; and most additionally, the importance of the mind-set of the nurturing parent figure.

My wife is one of many sources that has helped me to discover discipline. We are all married. We all live in some version of a community where we are asked or expected to compromise, share, confide, encourage, support, forgive, correct, respect, guide, instruct, and communicate with some other party. I believe it is important that people learn to live with people. However, before a person can achieve such a socially necessary goal as being a good neighbor or spouse, a person must first learn to live with themselves. A person must first learn to be among other things, confident, supportive, forgiving and respectful of themselves. When a person looks into the mirror in their mind, the face of society, or the one hanging on the wall, they must be at peace with that reflection; it is the truth.

There is no question that we need each other. Each person is a reflection of the society they inhabit, and each person is a reflection of the mate they choose. The question is, which individuals will sooner rather than later realize the discipline necessary to be at peace with themselves so they can successfully and peacefully manage the marriage of seemingly separate bodies and minds that is social living?

My wife is my mirror and I am hers. What she has reflected of me has often been so disturbing that emotions ran wild and dominated whatever discipline was present. It has not been a smooth road, but I am growing stronger. Marriage, it is the toughest job I have ever loved.

My wife is beautiful because she shows me my weaknesses' so that I may improve my focus on what discipline is required to become stronger. I think the strength of discipline I require is that which would allow me to be man, the complement of woman.

My father has been a key source in my growth. His life has been proof of why a person should maintain their integrity, and then even against the most oppressive of opposition. My father was born in Kosciusco, Mississippi, in 1932. He was the son of a farmer and sixth out of ten children. He had a very short and troubled childhood full of lost dreams and pain. He wanted to be a teacher. He left home, though, at the age of sixteen to pursue work to help support his family which had been displaced by the Ku Klux Klan. Though his pursuits took him all over the country, he never stopped moving forward. He never stopped moving.

My father is beautiful because his life is an example of how in life a person may not get what they believed they wanted, but through perseverance they may achieve far more than they expected.

My mother has been a key source in my growth. She was born in nineteen forty two. She was an unwed mother at the age of twenty and a high school dropout. She achieved her GED at the age of 40 plus. She was working toward her associate's degree from the College of Staten Island. She wanted to work as a psychologist. She suffered years of complications with her kidneys until they finally failed. She spent the next many years with dialysis. She died at the age of fifty-four due to complications after a kidney transplant.

I will not detail her life, but let it suffice to say that she could have easily allowed her life circumstances to crush her spirit and mind along with her body. She chose to triumph over her circumstances. She laughed and she fought. She mostly fought.

I remember when I was about six years old, my mother, younger sister, and I went to the grocery store. It was the A&P in Rosebank on Staten Island. The moment we entered the store, a group of three white males who appeared to be older than my mother began harassing us. I remember hearing the phrase "nigger bitch" a lot, and I remember the faces of the many people who were standing around. Their eyes were either blank or spiteful. Their countenances were either a smug grin or unconcerned. None of those faces, though, moved from whatever they were doing to come to the aid of an African American female and her two children. Not until the shock of the initial assault wore off and my mother had one of the males by the collar and had pushed another away. At that point, all of those law-abiding, and more than likely, God-fearing Christians/ Catholics stepped in to tell my mother to leave the store before they call the police. My mother fought.

I think one of the reasons she and my father had such an occasionally turbulent relationship was because she was a not a weak female. My mother was beautiful not only because she knew how to dream and how to achieve her dreams, but also because she was willing to fight for her dreams. Her children were her dreams. She could no more allow us to be oppressed by the tyranny and cowardice of others than she could allow us to accept an education on how to oppress ourselves through maintaining fear as it ultimately leads to personal disgrace.

You are the most important source in my world. I thank God that I had all of you to keep me company through this bit of time that is life. I thank God for your bigotries and understanding. I thank God for your compassion and prejudice. I thank God for my being the sum of all of your fears and love; indeed, through the senses of any who have experienced my person, I have been a great variety of things.

You have all been my instructors. You have demonstrated to me the best and the worst of all things a person is capable of. The examples were not limited to this lifetime, but extend through recorded history. I now know what I expect and do not expect from myself. I now know who I am and who I am not. I have experienced your greed, anger, and cowardice—all guided by moments of fear and expressed through childish barbarism; additionally, I have experienced your selflessness, compassion, and integrity—all guided by moments of love and expressed ironically through childish barbarism. And you have experienced mine.

You are beautiful because in your strength and weakness, I observed the slave and the master. Slaves, like masters, are people who are so dedicated to a way of being that they become numb to other possibilities. All that exists is measured against what they have been taught. The great majority of their education, though, was in error. The slave and master are opposing hemispheres of the same side of a coin. The other side of that coin is freedom. They are codependents who enable each other to continue as victims. That some of you exist serves as a constant reminder to me of why I choose to be free.

Now, though, that I have such a comprehension of my self and the world, it is time for me to be what I am. I will no longer be the figure of those base and undisciplined thoughts you needed or wanted me to be for your validation. What you actually desired from those mean thoughts and subsequent acts was freedom from your fears, so you made me the icon of them all in a typically childish attempt to control them through me. Saviors and I have something in common there.

Neither will I be what I thought I should be or in fact attempted to be for my validation, and curiously for the same reason. I was trying to take control of a thing that was an illusion. Illusion is the judgment of others. Illusion is a self-image created by a childish and undisciplined spirit. I spent a long time grasping at the illusions used by corrupt people, and my weakness.

I have been a nigger (mob member), and I have been a prince. I have been the spiritual guidance for a person who needed spiritual guidance, and I have been a hard dick for the exclusive physical pleasures of women. Now, though, it is time I be me. I am a reflection of God. I am divine perfection made manifest with a word.

I was born with chronic asthma. My childhood is full of memories of emergency rooms and medication. I was told that when I was very young, I suffered an especially severe asthma attack. That attack brought on heightened respiratory distress, which resulted in cardiac arrest. By the time I reached the emergency room, my heart had been still for some time. I was told I was given an Adrenalin shot and CPR, and apparently it worked. From that point, my experiences were dominated by moments where I was trying to keep up with other kids my age, but from a diminished position. I was teased. I was left out of events. And I cried, but I did not stop fighting. Eventually, I grew out of the ailment, and if you do not mind my being brief, I wrote down some of my thoughts and experiences for others to read. I am beautiful because the fact that I am here is a testament to the power of will over circumstances.

I had a few circles of associates during those adolescent and preadult years. I only had one circle of friends. They were John N. Wells, David N. Wells, and David J. Owens. There was a game we were obsessed with for a number of years. The game was called Dungeons and Dragons. I feel it necessary to mention it was the version that required books, dice, and active imaginations. The first character I assumed as a player in this game was a cleric. A cleric is a man of god. The second character I assumed was the only son of that cleric, and he was a paladin. A paladin is a knight who is lawfully aligned and almost always works in the service of some divine pursuit or just cause.

I think there was a message in that. I think if people were asked to use their imaginations to create whatever character they would, or in fact, to choose from a list of characters that represent the various pursuits of people, the results would be reflective of how each person considers themselves. I am a caretaker of the planet because it is my nature to comfort and heal. I am a defender of life because it is my nature to protect. My work now is to become better at being me.

Get Published, Inc!
Thorofare, NJ 08086
11 September 2009
BA2009254